Art and Soul:

Signposts for Christians in the Arts

July 2001

Dear Andrew —

many blessings to
you and your family
as you meld art and
soul in everyday things

Jon
ali

Art and Soul:

Signposts for Christians in the Arts

Hilary Brand and Adrienne Chaplin

solway

Copyright © 1999 Hilary Brand and Adrienne Chaplin

First published in 1999 by Solway

04 03 02 01 00 99   7 6 5 4 3 2 1

Solway is an imprint of Paternoster Publishing,
PO Box 300, Carlisle, Cumbria, CA3 0QS, UK
http://www.paternoster-publishing.com

British Library Cataloguing in Publication Data
A catalogue record for this book is available from the British Library

ISBN 1-900507-82-X

Cover Design by Mainstream, Lancaster
Typeset by WestKey Ltd, Falmouth, Cornwall
Printed in Great Britain by Bell & Bain Ltd, Glasgow

Contents

Preface

Why this book?

Until the last couple of decades, the Mrs Worthingtons of the Protestant world were as reluctant to put their sons into art college as their daughters on the stage. Now the climate is very different and more Christians than ever before are pursuing the arts. The resources to help them integrate their faith and their art, however, have not kept up. This book is an attempt to redress the balance.

More people now work in the arts than the steel, coal and car industries combined.
Melvyn Bragg[1]

It deals with many of the complex issues facing those studying or working in the arts. It is for interested observers as well as enthusiastic practitioners, but perhaps most especially for those seeking to make the arts their life's work.

For many young Christians, entering a course of study on the arts can be an acute shock. Some cope by separating faith and work into watertight compartments, others abandon one or the other – more often the faith.

It need not be so.

It *is* possible to work as an artist in a way that is both thoroughly Christian and thoroughly contemporary. Indeed, it is not only possible, it is urgently necessary.

Such an integration is not easy. It demands sacrifice and prayer, support from the church at large, and a firm intellectual base, rooted in a Christian worldview.

Who has influenced it?

That the arts are corrupt does not mean that Christians can abandon them. On the contrary, the corruption of the arts means that Christians dare not abandon them any longer.
Gene Veith[2]

For a previous generation of evangelical Christians, that intellectual base was the teaching of Francis Schaeffer and Hans Rookmaaker. Here at last, in the sixties and seventies, were people with a deep understanding and appreciation of the arts, grappling with the issues from a biblical standpoint. The world they addressed had yet to hear of the term 'postmodern', but much of their teaching is still valid and needing to be re-applied to today's generation. After them have come writers such as

Calvin Seerveld, Leland Ryken, Gene Veith, Nicholas Wolterstorff and Jeremy Begbie, each in their own way bringing new and profound insights. Each of these has worked from a deep commitment to biblical truth, and it is in that same tradition that this book now stands.

We are not alone in our quest to shed Christian light on the arts at the turn of the millennium. There are many others, well and little-known, in Britain and beyond, to whom we are indebted, and their names will crop up in our various quotes. This book attempts to digest and bring together central insights from Christian writers on the arts and from many other sources. Plus, of course, adding a few ideas of our own.

Art and Soul began life in a very different form, as a study guide written by Adrienne. Hilary then developed the material into book form, adapting it for a wider audience and adding illustrations and historical information. We are greatly indebted to the Greenbelt Festival for their funding contribution.

As authors we come with very different approaches: Adrienne with an academic background provides the philosophical input, whilst Hilary as a jobbing writer is more inclined toward the practical hands-on issues. Our discussions have been lively, and we hope we have produced a richer book as a result.

We have consulted with a range of practising artists – many of whom, like us, are members of the Arts Centre Group, an organisation for Christians working professionally in arts and media (see 'Recommended Resources') – and have tried to incorporate their thoughts and concerns from the rock-face of artistic endeavour.

Art is a battlefield and a playground, a bona fide calling for Christian activity.
Calvin Seerveld[3]

Foreword

Everything about this book by Hilary Brand and Adrienne Chaplin rings true. It is written with verve, sparkles with inside artistic knowledge, and simultaneously breathes a generous love for the reader. These authors know the contemporary artworld intimately and have respect for artistry well done. They also have a no-nonsense way of giving Christians at large help in understanding a God-ordained task for artistry, and make clear also why art has often been a thorn in the flesh of the (Protestant) church.

The text is rich with careful insight and reflection put in concrete language. 'The Christian message is that grace is free, but it is not cheap' (65). '. . . as art museums become more like churches, so churches in their turn become more like museums' (84). '. . . still we believe there are certain constants in reality for humans to discover' (112). All the while, art is explored, given context, and interpreted. Some 50 black-white illustrations with boxed comments keep the reader visually in touch with what is going on, whether it be Lorenzo Ghiberti's bronze Baptistry door or *Babette's Feast*.

There are bountiful quotations in the margins, from Jesus to Picasso, the Schaeffers to Nick Park, Tolstoy to Dorothy Sayers and Nick Wolterstorff, which hint at the range of research teeming in the authors' consciousness that has been distilled in *Art and Soul*. You get a sense that this book articulates the biblical tradition of a Christian community of reflection which can be wise and simply stated because the many strands of thought have been assimilated and reached maturity. For example, 'As writers, our task may be to speak obliquely through creative imagery, or where necessary replace a worn-out word with a new one. We may need to call a spade a shovel. . . . Our society may be resisting the Christian "grand story", but it is still looking for answers' (57).

An admirable achievement of this book with its *Signposts for Christians in the Arts* is its readable, well-paced flow. The writing is free of jargon. The authors level with you as reader in simple sentences. And the pages are full of excitement: a brilliant paragraph on the Romantic Byron (19), talk about the poison of sin, an intriguing analysis of Jesus' story-telling and postmodern irony (182). Adrienne Caplin and Hilary Brand exemplify the responsible, informed integrity they plead for on the part of Christian artists and audience. *Art and Soul* has the makings of being a primer for anybody who wants to know which are the correct questions to ask about the place of artistry in God's world.

And the authors couch their endeavour within the scandalous suggestions (15, 188) that Christian artists together may be the ones with the wherewithal to help set the agenda for leading artistry into the way of truthfulness in the coming millenium. That is a calling full of sterling hope and solid encouragement for the people of God and their neighbours in God's battered world. Take up this book too and read it with great expectations.

Calvin Seerveld
Toronto
March 1999

Foreword

I sat at a computer screen to write this foreword. Catching my eye as I sat were the cover of a Blur CD, a Celtic cross painted on slate, a photograph of a philosopher on the cover of a book, a poster for a concert celebrating Nelson Mandela, and a pocket triptych – an icon given by a visiting Russion Orthodox bishop. I sat down to write words but could not escape images.

I have a series of books dating from the later 1960s which tells of the evangelical tradition's re-engagement and struggle with the arts. Among the authors are Francis Schaeffer, Hans Rookmaaker, Calvin Seerfeld, Nicholas Wolterstorff, Ruth Etchells, John Wilson, Murray Watts, and my colleague Jeremy Begbie. This book by Hilary Brand and Adrienne Chaplin is a worthy addition to the list. It is important for three reasons.

The first is about a cultural and social transition. Western culture is in transition from a modern to a postmodern era. The arts are experiencing the death of modernism without any clarity as to their future and self understanding in a postmodern world. Sociologically the shift is from modernity to postmodernity: from an era which found its focus in industry and production, to one which has consumerism as its core ideology, and is most clearly expressed in electronic imagery and information. At modernity's height a naturalistic view of science seemed to swallow up all other forms of knowledge. What could not be proved could not be trusted – and the arts were marginal and treated as an object of suspicion. In postmodernity, aesthetics and literary theory threaten to swallow up everything else. This is creating an intellectual world which has lost any sense of (capital 'T') Truth and replaced it with endless interpretations; games played with the meaning of texts. It also creates a society full of images which seem to refer only to other images. In postmodern society imagery is chiefly put to the service of consumerism, and the allusiveness of art is overwhelmingly used for commercial purposes. The gift given for awakening the imagination is used to numb the imagination while seemingly stimulating it. The age of the arts has arrived, but at what cost to the arts?

The second reason for the importance of this book concerns the Church. As the authors point out, the evangelical tradition in particular, sits uneasily with the arts and has little understanding of their nature or how they function. The challenge to a Christian engagement with the arts, which combines respect for the integrity of each artistic medium and for the truth claims of God in Jesus Christ, needs to be 'proclaimed afresh in each generation.' The battle to understand the place of thearts in God's creative and redemptive purposes is not yet won.

Thirdly, as these authors recognise, more and more young Christians are going to college to study for a wide range of arts and media courses. They have the possiblity of being bearers of the Christian vision in a culture which is still taking shape. To do so successfully they need a map which relates together Biblical faith, the nature of art and the emerging contours of a social era.

Hilary Brand and Adrienne Chaplin have done us all a service. This insightful book will help anyone with an interest in the arts. For some it will explain what they have not properly understood before, and so will free some Christians from their inherent suspicion of the arts. For others it will confirm a calling, a vocation to life in the arts and media.

Art and Soul provides a much needed map for an understanding of the role of art and the calling of artists in the postmodern world. It explains the nature and integrity of the arts and how they work. As such it is of service not only to artists and to those who consciously enjoy the arts, but to all who live in a society dominated by images, but starved of meaning.

Art and Soul also opens up one further possibility. There have been several decade of thoughtful evangelical engagement with the arts – through the authors mentioned above, through the Arts Centre Group, the Greenbelt Festival, the L'Abri Fellowship, Third Way Magazine and many more. Could it now be time to open a new stage of biblically centred engagement in and with the arts. One in which engagement with different art forms opens up new understandings and new depths of insight about the biblical faith. Could we at last recognise that the Scripture through which our faith is revealed is rich in narrative, imagery, drama and poetry. Its depths cannot be plumbed by analytical words alone. We need to learn Christianity through the arts as much as to express Christianity through the arts. We need a Christian faith enriched through the arts as much as the arts enriched by the Christian faith. Only images and works of art that are the fruit of this depth of dialogue, of hard work, theological as well as artistic and imaginative, can restore the possibility of trandscendence to our increasingly one dimensional image culture.

Could it be that the time has come for artists in Christ?

Graham Clay
Ridley Hall Cambridge
March 1999

Introduction

What is this book about?

We must begin with a series of definitions, the first of which ought to be 'What is art?' But this is a big question and we must save it for later in this book. For now, just an explanation that when we talk of Christian artists, we do so in the broadest sense possible – those who make TV documentaries, installations, pots, poems, rock music, classical music, dance, film, theatre, interactive video, magazines, interior design and a hundred other things beside.

But then, we have used the term 'Christian artists'. Does that mean there is such a thing as 'Christian art'? Well, yes and no. We hope that by the end of this book you will have a clearer idea of the 'yes', but let us first say here what we do *not* mean. We do not mean simply those art forms utilised for church purposes: worship or evangelism. They may well be Christian – they may or may not be art! Nor do we only mean art which incorporates Christian imagery or Christian themes. These can be employed by believers and non-believers alike and of themselves do not make a work 'Christian'. And we certainly do not mean that any and all art that happens to be made by a Christian automatically deserves a 'Born-Again' label tagged to it. Christian art, in our view, is art which is produced from a thoroughly Christian worldview – and for what that entails, read on.

But that leads to another definition: what do we mean by 'worldview'? A worldview can be defined as the spectacles through which we view the world. It is the set of assumptions that colour everything we do, from who changes the baby's nappy to how we design our public buildings.

For one example of different worldviews, contrast the Victorians' view of the Great Exhibition of 1851 – pride, optimism and almost religious awe – with the initial media reaction to proposals for London's Millennium Dome – scepticism, pessimism and almost universal cynicism. For another, look at Arthur Miller's play *The Crucible*. The psychologically aware twentieth century puts a completely different interpretation on the events of the real-life Salem witch trials from the one held by a society that believed implicitly in demons.

A worldview, however, is not necessarily the same as a coherent philosophy or a set of religious beliefs. As Leland Ryken comments:

> Given their theological bent, Christians have often operated on the premise that the only truth that matters is abstract or philosophical truth. They have assumed that a person's worldview, including their own, consists only of ideas. This is a dangerous fallacy . . .
>
> We are influenced by images at least as much as ideas. We may assent to the proposition that the true end of life is not to make money and accumulate possessions, but if our minds are filled with images of big houses and fancy clothes, our actual behaviour will run in the direction of materialism.[3]

This is why artists, society's purveyors of images, are so important, and why they need first to examine their own worldview spectacles before they set to work.

The thing about spectacles, of course, is that all the time they are doing their job properly you never notice that they are there. It is only when you start seeing double, or things go out of focus, that you begin to think about changing them. It is the same with assumptions. It is only when one set of presuppositions collides with another, or something happens to rock the belief system of a whole society, that people start to question what those assumptions are and which of them are still valid in a changing world. It is in such a time of shaking and collision that we now live.

How is it put together?

This is why we have begun this book with a section on some of the conflicting influences which Christians entering the arts might encounter. We have not attempted a comprehensive history of art or of the church, but have focused on three different worldviews and tried to sketch in a little of their origins.

From there, we have returned to our Christian source material, the Bible, relating its basic themes to the activity of art. The third section then goes on to apply those biblical principles to the worldviews with which we began. Part 4 takes another step back to examine more precisely how we can define, evaluate and appreciate art; while Part 5 moves us on to look at some more practical ways of serving God as artists in the twenty-first century.

A note on illustrations

The arts speak most often without words and any book on the subject must try to do the same. For this reason we have tried to include as many examples of specific art works as possible. All are chosen to illustrate a particular argument or idea. Some are well-known; others are by Christian artists who deserve to be known better.

Of course, selection immediately invites criticism. Matters of taste are notoriously subjective, and not everyone will agree with our choices, which are, in any case, tailored to fit the subject-matter of the text and the constraints of black-and-white reproduction. Some might justifiably take us to task because their arts discipline is sparsely represented, or perhaps omitted altogether. In defence, we must point out that some art forms (i.e. visual ones) are easier to use as illustrations than others.

However, we must admit to a strange inexorable tendency, observable in other books beside our own, towards so-called 'fine art'. Why ever this is (and we must admit we are not quite sure), it is emphatically *not* because we believe it more valuable than any other form. Our hope is that our readers will be able to apply ideas expressed in terms of fine art to whatever their favoured arts discipline happens to be.

A word or two about gender
For simplicity, we have chosen to retain the traditional 'he' when describing God. This has more to do with the limitations of the English language than our theology. We affirm that God can be experienced as both male and female, and is far bigger than our finite definitions.

When referring to artists we have tried to avoid specifying gender as much as possible. Obviously when quoting from other writers, we have retained their original form of words, which may well be more male-dominant than we would choose!

Where are we now and where are we going?

This book was written in the year of the 'Sensation' exibition at the Royal Academy, a year when aggressive young Brit-art finally penetrated the last bastion of establishment. It was written while the shockwaves from Princess Diana's death were still reverberating and posing some hard questions about the media and its icons; in the year that *Teletubbies* became cult viewing and Oasis partied at 10 Downing Street; when *Kiss* brought necrophilia to the silver screen, *Crash* gave auto-eroticism a new meaning, and the surprise success film was about some unlikely male strippers in a run-down northern town.

In addition, as you can see from the above examples, it was written in a British context. Any view of the arts will reveal the author's own time and place. A book that tries to look specifically at contemporary issues is likely to reflect that even more. For that limited vision we apologise. Our hope is that the principles behind our rather localised view can nevertheless be applied to other contexts.

How good is this art? How does it measure up against the art of previous centuries? On this evidence I would answer: spectacularly well. An excitement runs through the art of our times, a need to do things differently, which no other century can match.

Waldemar
Januszczak[4]

There is no doubt that we are writing at a time of both cultural and technological transition, and where that transition will take us is far from clear. The future, both on-line and in studio, is up for grabs. Some would say that we live in an age of unprecedented decadence. Unquestionably, it is a time of moral confusion. Certainly, the taboos of previous generations are steadily being broken. But it is also an age of searing honesty, a time of renewed searching, both for spiritual meaning and new expressions of art. It is, as Waldemar Januszczak said, reviewing an exhibition of twentieth-century art, an exciting time to be around. We believe the twenty-first century could be even more exciting – especially if Christian artists take an active role in shaping the way the next millennium unfolds.

Part 1

Deconstructed, Disillusioned and Distrusted: Conflicting influences on the Christian artist

1

Art in a Post-Modern Age

Pictures at an exhibition

In order to understand where the arts have arrived at the turn of the millennium, let us make a couple of visits. The first is to an exhibition of contemporary art. It could be one of many: for the record it happens to be East International, held in Norwich in August 1997. The first thing you will notice is how few of the exhibits are paintings. There are installations, video, film; the works include a metal shed, spiders' webs, tartan squares, even a board-game. The items are often accompanied by an 'artist's statement', sometimes by a title almost as long. Thus a couple of closed-circuit TV screens showing nothing more exciting than the viewers' backs are entitled: *Historical Engineering, The Lost Object (desire/representation) THE END.*[1]

What are your reactions as you leave the gallery? Fascination, infuriation, a feeling that you may have just been viewing the emperor's new clothes, an awareness that you are now seeing the world around you in a new light? All of these, probably. When art becomes art because 'It's in an art gallery, init?',[2] even the coolest right-on experts are a little dazed and confused.

Room with a view

Our second visit is to a much smaller museum of contemporary art. Here also paintings are in the minority. There are one or two – some brightly coloured abstracts, a watercolour of a cathedral city. Photography is in evidence – a bank of informal portraits collaged together, a study in misty greens and greys which on close inspection turns out to be a mountain view. The textile exhibits are of a high standard, exquisite colours and textures, carefully chosen to stand in juxtaposition to each other. A few ceramic artefacts are on display, with the lighting showing them off to full advantage. A section of the museum is devoted to the library – small by some standards, but an eclectic range of the best in contemporary literature. There is also a section for quality journals.

In truth this is more of an arts centre than a museum. Just along from the library is the concert hall: brilliant acoustics and a programme ranging from baroque orchestral, through modern jazz to all the big name rock bands, with even some Peruvians playing Pan-pipes and monks singing plainsong thrown in.

But here, as in East International, it is the illuminated screens that form the focus of the whole museum – an endless succession of vivid flickering images dominating the gallery space around the clock. This centre has everything – theatre, light entertainment, illustrated lectures, a vast resources room, even cookery classes.

What are your reactions as you enter this arts centre and survey the choices on offer? Bewilderment, excitement, astonishment that such a vast array is on offer in such a small provincial town? None of these probably, as this (or something quite like it) is your own living room.

Zapping our way to Cyberia

The media have substituted themselves for the older world.
  Marshall McLuhan[3]

The end of the second millennium has witnessed a seismic change in the world of the arts, a change symbolised in our generation by an insignificant black plastic gadget – the zapper, or remote control. Without leaving the armchair we can flick back and forth between game shows or genocide, soaps or sports, politics or passion. The minute we are bored, on we go to the next channel. Really bored? There's always the video or the CD, all there at the touch of a finger.

The symbol of the next generation is similarly small and plastic – the mouse, our rodent guide to the mysterious virtual world of Cyberia. You don't just watch this world, you can talk to it as well. You can shop, book airline tickets, chat to strangers, tell the whole world your latest theories, visit Gracelands, the C.S. Lewis Foundation or the porn store with equal ease. You can pilot your way through galaxies, indulge in some cybersex or become the hero of your own adventure, mowing down your enemies with aplomb (zapping again). There are no national boundaries in this world – and no commitments either.

Past the post

Does the technology precede the philosophy or travel hand-in-hand? Whatever the timing, there is no question that the two are indissolubly linked, and no doubt that alongside the technological revolution has come an equally revolutionary change in ideas. We have reached the post-modern era.

In order to assess an era that is 'post' something, we need at least to define what it is 'post' to. To call something 'modern' often simply means 'latest' – this year's fashion or 'state of the art' technology. What is meant here is modernism – a certain worldview that has shaped Western culture for around three hundred years, before finally petering out somewhere around the 1980s.

Trying to pin dates on worldviews is of course invidious. We don't wake up one day and say, 'Ah, the new era has arrived.' Not only is the transition gradual, it is also ragged, with some aspects changing while others stay the same. Two possible dates for the demise of modernism have been claimed, both, strangely, focusing on a demolition. Architecture cites a precise time and place: 3.32 p.m. on 15 July 1972 in St Louis, Missouri, where a prize-winning apartment block in the 'machine for living in' style was dynamited, its occupants having declared it uninhabitable. Others pin the transition to November 1989 when the destruction of the Berlin wall signalled the end of communism. Both events illustrate the collapse of the dominant theme of modernism outlined below, and the bursting out of the minor theme that had for a long time been welling up beneath it.

Books aplenty have been written on the art and theory of the modern era, and our purpose is not to repeat them here. We will return at various points to those streams that still feed into our current situation, but before diving into the fluid and somewhat bewildering concepts of post-modernity, let us take a quick look back.

The death of optimism

Flowing out of the eighteenth-century age of reason, modernism can be defined as man's (the word is used advisedly) faith in his own capacity to understand and control the world and in the inevitability of progress. No part of the globe could not be tamed, no problem was beyond the reach of scientific solutions, God was no longer needed. Better education, the relentless advance of the machine age, the abolition of class differences – it was only a matter of time before war and poverty were eradicated for ever. Optimism reigned.

It was an era of 'isms' – rationalism, empiricism, idealism, and, perhaps the most dramatic manifestation, communism. Art too had its 'isms' – impressionism, expressionism, futurism – each with its own philosophy, and all tellingly linked together under a military term, *avant-garde*: at the forefront of the advance.

But beneath modernism's dominant theme of optimism grew a dissenting and potentially subversive opposite, a minor theme of pessimism and cynicism. Two world wars demonstrated what 'modern' technology could do. A society with unprecedented comfort and leisure discovered that contentment was just as elusive as ever. This strand could be seen in the nihilism of Nietzsche and in the existentialism of Jean-Paul Sartre. It

Having created a society of unprecedented sophistication, convenience and prosperity, nobody can remember what it was supposed to be for.

Clifford Longley[4]

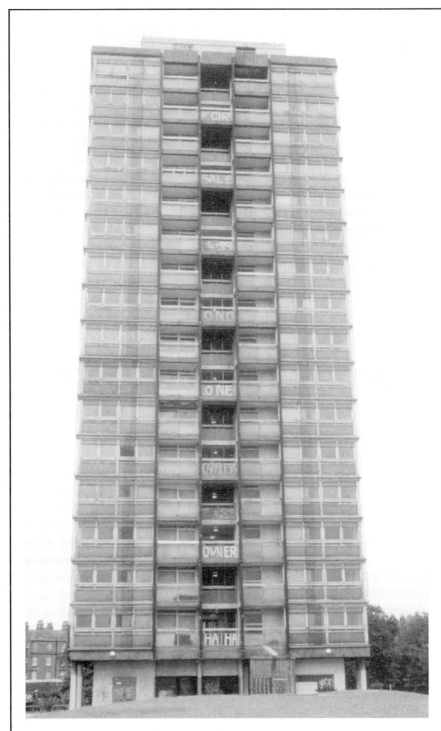

1. *The death of the modernist dream?* Condemned apartment block in Stepney, East London (1998) (photo: Hilary Brand)

was seen too in the growing art of the absurd, from dadaism to Samuel Beckett's *Waiting for Godot*.

The old certainties were being eroded. The only thing we could turn to was our own experience and that made little sense. Modern optimism finally went up in a mushroom cloud of smoke.

Don't believe a word of it

The claim that there are no absolutes once shocked people; now it is the accepted wisdom. Planes, trains and automobiles – the world has shrunk. Colonialism, the melting-pot of the New World and immigration into the Old – we now live in a pluralist society whether we like it or not. Even if we attempt to pull up the drawbridge and ignore it, the multiplicity of voices coming over the media will ensure that we cannot. Faced with so many conflicting truth claims, the easiest response is to trust none of them. The French philosopher Jean-François Lyotard summed it up in this statement: 'Simplifying to the extreme, I define post-modernism as incredulity towards meta-narratives.'[5]

Capital T truth is dead.
Don Cupitt[6]

Lyotard's 'extreme simplicity' may sound a little complicated to the rest of us, but what he is getting at is this: we can no longer believe in any truth claims that declare themselves to be the key to understanding the whole of life. Whether they are the meta-narratives (grand stories) of Marx or Freud, militant feminism, Christianity, or the Enlightenment, they are no longer credible. It is acceptable to say, 'This is *my* story,' but not 'This is *the* story.'

The post-modern assumption is that anyone making a truth claim must be in the business of manipulation and abusing power. At its best the melting-pot has led to respect and a willingness to learn; at worst, indifference or mistrust. One of the saddest aspects of our society is that distrust of truth claims leads inevitably to distrust of commitment, something which manifests itself not just in intellectual scepticism but at the heart of human relationships.

Post-modernism knows no commitments.
Peter Fuller[7]

Undergirding this relativism and scepticism is another post-modern strand concerning the use of language. In 1967 Roland Barthes proclaimed the 'death of the author'. He meant that readers create their own meanings regardless of the author's intention. Any text (and by implication any idea, because ideas can only be conveyed in language) is therefore ever shifting, unstable and open to question.

Jacques Derrida, too, showed that words never possess fixed meanings and that any attempt to interpret and explain words can only be accomplished by means of yet more words and texts. For some, although not for Derrida himself, this was enough to conclude that there was therefore nothing outside of the text.

Here, of course, we really *are* 'simplifying in the extreme' and more detailed explanation is outside the scope of this book. (Exploring contemporary philosophies may leave some feeling like *Guardian* journalist Sally Hill: 'What the post-modernist does is to accept the unintelligibility of the world and then strive to make it just that little bit more unintelligible'![8]) However, for anyone bold enough to dig deeper, the recommended resources at the end of this book include further material at various levels of accessibility. For the moment, let us confine ourselves to charting some other features of our culture that define it as post-modern.

> The locks are changed
> new borders everywhere
> maps fall apart
> the centre is missing
> all surface, all edge
> no fixed exchange rates
> things become what they seem
> languages no longer translate
> structures built only of confidences
> life and t.v. blur
> new hybrids everywhere
> joyful mass amnesia
> brilliant uncertainty
> self forgetting and self reinventing
> opposites merge
> slang evolves and mutates
> languages no longer translate
> conquest gives way to surrender
> the locks are changed
> throw away the key
>
> Brian Eno[9]

Shop till you drop

'Back in modernity,' explains Graham Cray, 'the basic value was progress. Therefore people would make sacrifices for a better future they believed they were heading towards. Now we are not producers making things for a better world, our great belief is not progress, but choice.'[11]

It can be seen in how we spend our leisure time. Taking the family to the shopping mall, superstore or garden centre has far superseded church as a chosen Sunday activity. It is not just products that we shop for, but ideas, images and people. The whole world and its history is

If the symbol of modernity was the savings book, the symbol of post-modernity is the credit card.
   Zygmunt Bauman[10]

seen as a vast supermarket from which to pick information and theory according to taste. Even religion has become pick and mix. In this respect the New Age movement is typically post-modern, offering bits and pieces from all religions and from none, to assemble as your own.

The church is not exempt. Denominational boundaries have all but fallen for the average Christian, who will find a church that suits them and move on if it does not.

And then of course there's the zapper, allowing us to watch what we fancy from potentially hundreds of TV channels. Shopping has become the ultimate metaphor of post-modern culture, and selling has become an art form, within the arts and without.

'British art is high on its own vulgarity,' read a headline in the *Guardian*. 'And it's all Margaret Thatcher's fault.' The article went on to chronicle how consumerism has become a driving force in the arts, citing Damien Hirst and others such as the Chapman brothers and writer Irvine Welsh as creating 'savvy pieces of easily marketed artworks'.[12]

Hardly surprising when the difference between earning a small fortune and earning nothing at all can be no more than good publicity, and nothing brings better publicity than a good shock. There are other reasons to stun and surprise, of course, and not necessarily invalid ones – a quick read of the gospels will show that Jesus was not averse to shock tactics where necessary.

The classic Brit-art exponent of 'in-yer-face' tactics is Damien Hirst and any straw poll of opinions on his work brings wide variations: 'One-look art', 'His images are arresting', 'He's got nothing to say and he says it', 'His work is reasoned and worked through.' Perhaps only time will tell whether he is a genius or a charlatan, but most commentators are agreed on one thing: 'He knows what he's doing', 'He knows the art market and he knows how to attract media attention', 'He knows how to sell.'

Who will you be today?

If you can shop around for products and ideas, you can also shop around for your own image. Madonna has often been described as a post-modern icon. She not only strictly controls her own image, she also obsessively controls those who are communicating that image to the wider world. Novelist Martin Amis calls her 'a masterpiece of controlled illusion'.[13] She can turn herself into Marilyn Monroe, Eva Perón, or a sadomasochistic porn object. But is she in the end simply a style victim? As Jock McGregor of L'Abri put it, 'She lives totally within the artificially constructed reality of the image. This is why I am not interested in the real Madonna behind the myth, because I do not think there is one. I think she has so lost herself in the image that the difference is immaterial.'[14]

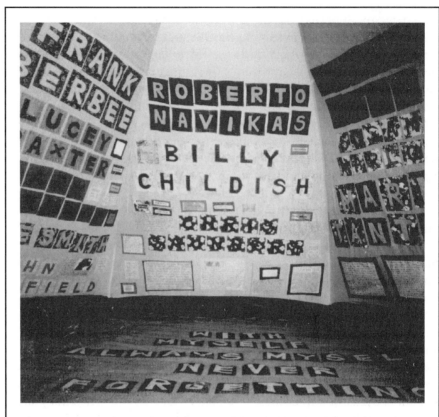

2.   Tracey Emin, *Everyone I've Ever Slept With* (1995), appliqued tent, mattress and light, 122 × 245 × 215 cm (detail) (photo: Stephen White)

In a world where you can trust nothing but your own experience, it is no wonder that one stream of contemporary art is fixated on exploring the self. For Tracey Emin, the turbulent history of her life – her Turkish-Cypriot father, suicide attempts, sexual encounters, rape, abortions – has become the material for her art. Bill Viola's video installation *Nantes Triptych* features the death of his own mother and the birth of his child. For many other artists the human body, and in particular its secretions, emissions and evacuations, have become the stuff of art. Helen Chadwick's *Piss Flowers*, Andrés Serrano's blurred photographs of his own semen, Mona Hatoum's journey through her own body with the help of a miniature camera, French 'carnal artist' Orlan's surgical transformation of her own features – the examples are many and bordering on the tedious. While shock may be part of the agenda here as elsewhere, it also poses some intriguing post-modern questions: Who am I? Where does my body begin and end? Am I no more than a mass of fluids? What else is there?

    Incidentally, it is curious to note the title, no doubt ironic, of one of Tracey Emin's exhibitions: *I need art like I need God*.

We may not all be playing the identity game as deliberately as the material girl, but in a society as self-aware and image-conscious as our own, the question shifts easily from 'Who am I?' to 'What image shall I adopt today?' Instead of maturing unselfconsciously, rooted in a family and community that knows and accepts us as we are, we have unprecedented freedom to choose how we would like to be seen – freedom that can also be a burden. We have to keep up the image, to play out the role we've set ourselves, to work at it at all costs. And even though we may convince others, the problem is that we may not convince ourselves. We are in danger, not of creating an identity, but losing one.

Each of us knows that our self does not amount to much.
Jean-François Lyotard[15]

What you see is what you get?

It is for the media, of course, and its insatiable demands, that celebrities such as Madonna and Michael Jackson continually re-invent themselves. It is the media that has led to another major feature of post-modernism – the reversal of reality and image. Some years ago the Yellow Pages business phone book had a very successful ad. It portrayed a sweet old gentleman phoning secondhand bookshops in search of a manual on fly-fishing by J.R. Hartley. 'My name? Oh, J.R. Hartley.' The author and book were, of course, invented, but someone had the bright idea of creating a book under the same name and title. It sold 80,000 copies in the first year.

This example may be mildly amusing but far more serious is the replacement of image for reality in the arena of politics and world events. Elections are won or lost on five-o'clock shadow or the sincerity of a smile. The Royal soap opera playing in the tabloids is discussed at coffee breaks in exactly the same way as *Eastenders* or *Friends*, and it takes a tragedy to remind us that these are real people's lives. The Gulf War was the first war played out moment by moment in front of the TV cameras – or was it *for* the TV cameras? News broadcasts were accompanied by film music, images were selected to make it appear a high-tech 'clean' war, civilians caught in the bombing were not dead people but 'collateral damage'. Another prophet of post-modernism, sociologist Jean Baudrillard argued that it had not occurred at all.[16] It was only a hyperreal representation on our TV screens.

Perhaps more important than the images that do appear on our screens are those that don't. If you have to choose between reporting a clash of half a dozen demonstrators against police or ten thousand dying of famine in Somalia, which will you choose? If the report of the demonstration includes footage of angry faces, police with batons, and a car in flames, and the report of the famine has only maps and library footage – no contest. Even where filmed material is readily available – as in the war in the former Yugoslavia – the item may disappear from the agenda. We've seen it all too often before, the warring factions are just too

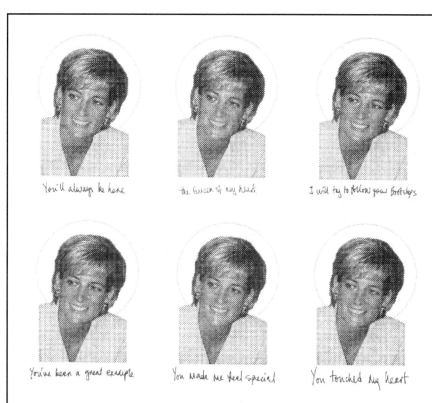

You'll always be here

the Queen of my heart

I will try to follow your footsteps

You've been a great example

You made me feel special

You touched my heart

3.   Mike Gough, *The Queen of My Heart* (1998), screen prints on paper

What did we mourn – the image or the reality?

How was it that a whole nation could be thrown into genuine shock and grief over someone it had never actually met? 'We felt we knew her,' people said, yet how much did any of us really understand of the complex woman behind the glowing smile? Did she really give herself to charity more than any other Royal? Probably not, but every time Diana did it, it hit the headlines. Was it really so glamorous wearing all those designer gowns? Undoubtedly not, but it looked it.

The irony, of course, is that the image completely consumed the reality. The nineteen-year-old nanny with the backlit skirt soon wised up. She learnt to play the media at its own game. 'Shy Di' entered a love/hate relationship with her pursuers and became the 'Queen of Hearts'. The media did not simply portray Diana's life: it shaped it, formed it and hunted it to destruction.

Did Diana's death shock so much because suddenly we were left with nothing but images, 'as if,' in Judith Williamson's phrase, 'paper money was suddenly revealed as just paper'? Was the drive to go to London and lay flowers, as she put it, 'an attempt to grasp something more solid – a run on the bank of the Real'?[17]

Or were we crying with guilt at our own complicity?

complicated to explain in one minute twenty. Which events are perceived as important in our world are decided on image alone.

Beg, steal or borrow

If it is easy to define some of the characteristics of a post-modern culture, it becomes a slightly harder task to define post-modern art. The very fact that it is post-modern means that anything goes. It takes incongruities and complexities as its very subject-matter. It thrives on paradox, fragmentation and impossible juxtapositions of styles, techniques and imagery. Just as deconstructionism has peeled away the layers to understand what language is, so art has been peeling away its own definitions until none remain. Art can be anything you say it is – inside the gallery or outside, permanent or fleeting. It can be a bouncy castle or your own faeces, a dead cow or a sleeping actress.

The issue of what, if anything, defines art, is explored further in Part 4, but for now let us look at the exciting possibilities that post-modern art presents. One aspect is that the boundaries between so-called 'high' and 'low' art are increasingly blurred. Exhibit at the Serpentine this month, make a rock video the next. Play the concert hall Saturday and busk in the subway Monday. This week on stage at the National, next week a villain in *Terminator 10* or a voice-over for a car ad. Why not? When Pavarotti and Bono start duetting, you know a shift has occurred.

The boundaries are blurred too between styles that would have previously seemed unreconcilable. Who would have thought a jazz saxophone would flow so beautifully together with early Renaissance church music? Jan Garbarek tried it with the Hilliard Ensemble and the haunting music of *Officium* became a hit.

In architecture too, the clean lines (or carbuncles, depending on your view) of modernism have given way to a more eclectic style – a hint of gothic here, a classical pediment there. In talking about the architect Le Corbusier, art critic Brian Sewell hit on one of the driving forces of post-modernism:

> He failed to recognise the Betjeman in us all – that deep down in the cultivated man there lurks not only the instinctive demand for perfect logic, harmony and proportion, but the monster Sentiment, and that it takes more than the perfect chicken coop to eradicate the heart-felt nostalgia for fire-place, door-chimes, oak beams, leaded lights and the Georgian porch.[18]

In a world where faith in the future is a thing of the past, nostalgia is a growth industry, as a plethora of Jane Austen revivals has testified.

History is there to be plundered. Pick and mix is the order of the day in art as elsewhere. Whilst the modernists strove to create a new language of

We're the TV generation. Low culture and high culture are looked at equally. For us, a still life could be the couch and the telly.
Gary Hume[19]

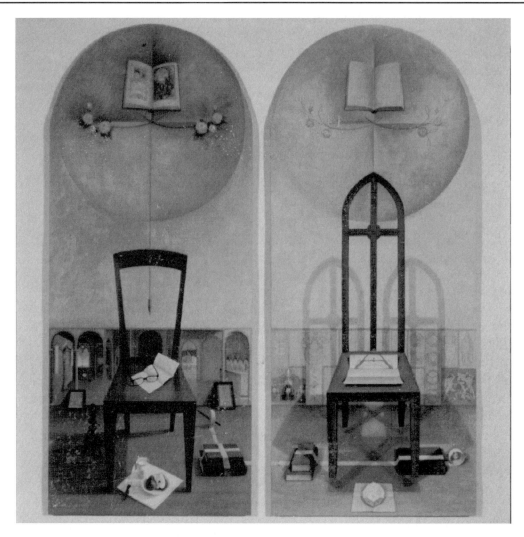

4. Laura Lasworth, *St Thomas and Mr Eco* (1994), oil on panels, 198 × 84 cm each panel (courtesy of the collection of Ronald Steen)

How does the worldview of a medieval monk relate to that of a twentieth-century professor of semiotics? This is what Laura Lasworth, a Californian Catholic who has been dubbed a 'post-modern mystic', set out to explore in this ambitious diptych. She believes that the ideas of the past and the present are not only reconcilable, but must be in relationship, a belief encapsulated in details such as the book illustration in the right-hand panel where Umberto Eco is shown being baptised by Thomas Aquinas, and the copy of an ancient Greek mosaic, bottom left, denoting Aquinas' debt to the earlier wisdom of Aristotle. She also raided the techniques of the Italian Renaissance in her painting style and use of perspective and 'sacred geometry'.

Lasworth has been pleasantly surprised by the mounting interest in her work which only a few years ago would have seemed hopelessly anachronistic. *St Thomas and Mr Eco* has been described by its owner, art historian and collector Ronald Steen, as 'the most intelligent work of art made by a female, American, living artist'.[20]

art, the post-moderns cheerfully borrow any one they fancy. Parody, pastiche, sampling, 'quoting' a previous work of art, juxtaposing images, sounds and symbols from wildly difference sources – no wonder Jacques Derrida has defined collage and montage as the post-modern discourse.[21]

If in doubt, smile

Whatever elements make up this cut-and-paste discourse, one thing is essential: a gloss that covers the whole, the all-pervasive sentiment of post-modern culture – irony. Borrow from wherever you feel like, but don't take anything too seriously. Make any statement you like, but make sure your tongue is firmly in your cheek. You can't believe politicians, preachers or even post-modern philosophers, so send them up. Values are *passé*, so are strong emotions. How to deal with them? Umberto Eco has a suggestion:

> I think of the post-modern attitude as that of a man who loves a very culti-vated woman and knows he cannot say to her, 'I love you madly', because he knows that she knows (and that she knows that he knows) that these words have already been written by Barbara Cartland. Still there is a solution. He can say, 'As Barbara Cartland would put it, I love you madly.' At this point, having avoided false innocence, having said clearly that it is no longer possi-ble to speak innocently, he will nevertheless have said what he wants to say to the woman: that he loves her, but he loves her in an age of lost innocence.[22]

Lost in a familiar landscape

All of the above has been by way of describing a familiar landscape, rather than mapping a safe route for Christian artists across dangerous terrain. There is, of course, no such clearly defined path. Rather we need to understand where we have come from and where we are going and how to recognise some of the signposts along the way (subjects to be ad-dressed in later chapters). But for now let us simply point out that in such a barren landscape people are thirsty for meaning and wide open to anything which offers genuine hope.

In an age when bald statements of capital-T Truth are discounted, society turns to its poets and artists for the most truthful accounts of the human condition. 'Grand Stories' may be treated with the utmost suspi-cion, but people will listen to any number of stories on a human scale, especially those that come from the depths of experience.

Graham Cray comments that a generation which calls itself 'post' something, probably doesn't yet know what it is.[23] The values and ideas that will shape the third millennium are not yet in place. As we go into that millennium, Christian artists have an unparalleled opportunity to help set the agenda.

But you see, God doesn't rule over men as he used to, and for a long time people haven't been able to feel that life was firmly attached at both ends so that they could confidently stand in the middle. That kind of faith is missing, and for many years poets have tried to supply a substitute.

Saul Bellow[24]

2

Art and the Quest for the Spiritual

One of the pendulum swings of the post-modern era is that spirituality is in fashion again. Not the Christian sort necessarily, although charismatic evangelicals are enjoying a resurgence. The search for enlightenment is just as likely to lead to the ancient faiths of the East or the latest New Age cult from California. For it is a search with a difference. The question is no longer 'Is it true?' but 'Does it work?'

One of the things that seem to work is art. In reply to an article on religion in the *Independent*, one correspondent refuted the idea that faith was a refining and calming influence and spoke for many by explaining: 'In my life, it is poetry, music and art that perform that function.'[2] It is a claim with which we can identify. Glory does seep out of a Rembrandt, mystery from a Rothko. Mozart or Tavener do calm us and lift us for a while above the petty concerns of life. We leave the theatre exalted after a performance of *Les Misérables* and re-examining our integrity after a play by David Hare.

In a room of
*   Rembrandts*
Liquid light shines
From nothing but
*   brush strokes.*
A spirit mixed on a
*   palette*
Illuminates us.
From something flat
*   and framed*
Truth glistens.
*   Stewart Henderson*[1]

But before we decide that art is an automatic doorway to the transcendent, we would do well to examine the idea more thoroughly. The linking of art and spirituality is not a new idea. It is present throughout history, one of the earliest links being in the second book of the Old Testament[3] where Bezalel, the craftsman responsible for the rich decor of the tabernacle, is the first person referred to as being full of the Holy Spirit.

In the Middle Ages, art, music and architecture were considered 'spiritual' because their most frequent purpose was the service of the church. They were tools in the worship of God and, in an age without books, in the telling of the gospel story. In a society where most people lived in wattle and daub huts, the soaring magnificence of a cathedral could not but tell of God. And if it took eighty million man-hours to build (the length of time, incidentally, that the British now spend per week watching soap operas),[4] then no matter that poverty and disease were spreading in the town at its feet – it was time well spent.

By the eighteenth and nineteenth centuries art and spirituality had a completely different link. Art had long since spread beyond the sheltering confines of the church. In fact, many sections of the church were

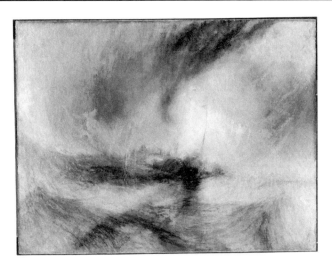

5.   J.M.W. Turner, *Steamboat in a Snowstorm* (1842), oil on canvas, 91 × 122 cm (London, Tate Gallery)

Romanticism – Nature with a capital N

The Romantic era reacted against the rationality of the Enlightenment and the industrial revolution with its move to the great cities. In painting, it was epitomised in France by Géricault and Delacroix, with canvases full of writhing figures and rich colour, and in Germany by Friedrich with dark, ominous seascapes.

Where the Enlightenment had stressed the order of nature, the Romantics favoured its wildness. And nowhere was there more 'wilderness' to be explored than the New World. Most people were more busy trying to survive it than contemplate it, but there too Romantic artists such as Bingham and Bierstadt were capturing the vast, untouched panoramas of the west.

In Britain the Romantic era culminated in Turner who turned landscape into astonishing near-abstractions of incandescent light and the raw power of nature. It had begun with William Blake, a strange visionary who expressed his mysticism and his hatred of the machine age with its 'dark Satanic mills' in both poetry and paintings.

It was in poetry that Romanticism perhaps reached its fullest flowering. The Romantic poets, Wordsworth, Coleridge, Keats, Shelley and the flamboyant Byron, found in 'Nature' not just an expression of their feelings, but what Wordsworth described as 'a sense sublime of something far more deeply interfused'.[5] Nature became a doorway to the infinite, so much so that they invested in it the power to transform the human spirit.

One impulse from a vernal wood
May teach you more of man,
Of moral evil and of good,
Than all the sages ˙ can.
   William Wordsworth[6]

distancing themselves more and more from what they saw as the decadence of the arts, which could now be used to express any subject from Germanic myths to contemporary brothels. It was the movement known as Romanticism which now began spreading a secular gospel that art was somehow higher, more transcendent and supernatural than the activities of lesser mortals.

Artist with a capital A

The Romantic style has long since gone out of fashion, but one aspect of their worldview remains – a strange but convenient cuckoo in the nest of contemporary art theory. The Romantics, along with their belief in Nature with a capital N, gave us the idea of the Artist with a capital A.

Back in the Middle Ages, the artist was no more than an unknown jobbing craftsman. By the Renaissance things had begun to change. Leonardo da Vinci could well be described as the ultimate Renaissance man, but in his early days he was just one more jobseeker. In a letter requesting a post with the Duke of Milan, the young Leonardo listed his credentials. Catalogued in numerical order, they included being a military engineer able to construct bridges, battering rams, mines, covered chariots, guns and catapults, as well as being an architect and water engineer. Without numbering the item, as a casual throwaway he added, 'I can carry out sculpture in marble, bronze or clay, and also in painting I can do as well as any man.'[8]

Of course, it soon became known that he painted rather better than any man, and that gift became the most famous of his many and remarkable talents. No longer would great art be produced by anonymous artisans, and Leonardo would come to be known as a genius.

Not, however, until some centuries later. It was only towards the end of the eighteenth century that the word 'genius' began to be used of individual artists. Before that, it was much more akin to 'genie': a presiding spirit directing each person's destiny. You did not have to be especially gifted to have your own genius.

The Romantics changed that, using the word of only a few, specially inspired, individuals. For them, it was artists who most displayed this mysterious creativity. Scholars, scientists, saints and soldiers, whilst worthy, were not in the same league.

Of course, if artists were geniuses, driven by the creative urge, they could be excused some very strange behaviour. Were not their lives expected to be different from those of other mortals? At the end of his poem 'Kubla Khan' (itself inspired by an opium-induced dream), Coleridge defined the Romantic view of the artist: long-haired, wild-eyed and seized by mysterious inspiration.

As if to prove his point, the next generation of Romantic poets, Keats,

. . . Beware! Beware!
His flashing eyes, his
floating hair!
Weave a circle round
him thrice,
And close your eyes
with holy dread,
For he on honey-dew
hath fed,
And drunk the milk
of Paradise.
       Samuel Taylor
         Coleridge[7]

Byron and Shelley, began to live lives as dramatic as their art. They all travelled, seeking their inspiration in the then exotic Mediterranean lands, and they all died young – a sure, though rather drastic, way to become a Romantic hero. Shelley was expelled from Oxford University for publishing a politically radical pamphlet and the next year made a runaway marriage with a sixteen-year-old. Three years later he abandoned her and their two children and eloped with Mary, author of *Frankenstein*. With her he left England for Italy, never to return, drowning at the age of thirty with a volume of Keats' poems in his pocket. Byron, perhaps known as the ultimate Romantic rebel, was a handsome young aristocrat with a deformed foot, a disastrous marriage and a penchant for wild affairs. He travelled extensively throughout Europe and the East and died of a fever whilst fighting against the Ottoman empire. His very name became an adjective, describing the passionate libertine pitting himself against the social order.

The artist had become transformed into 'the stylus of God', venerated as a prophet, a higher being. Mozart, for example, has been described by various scholars throughout the centuries as 'only a visitor on this earth', 'not only reaching heaven with his works but also coming from there', 'more than earthly', 'not of this world', 'divine'.[9] However, as painter Peter Smith comments, 'It is interesting to note that as these ideas took hold, so complaints began to emerge about the unreliable behaviour of artists.'[10] This idea of the artist as anti-social, eccentric rebel has continued to our day and with it the notion that he or she is subject to a different set of values than others. If one must wait for inspiration to descend, then an awful lot of sitting around can be in order. If creativity depends on a certain exalted state of mind, then why not induce it chemically? If, like Gauguin, it is necessary to evade all responsibilities and disappear to the South Seas, then so be it: the art justifies the action.

Should we then, as Christian artists, take on this idea of ourselves as the inspired pencil of God? Hans Rookmaaker thought it was a view that was doing the arts no favours:

> Perhaps one of the main problems of art today has been the result of giving art the wrong function. Formerly art was 'an art', just as we speak of arts and crafts. Art as a higher function of mankind, the work of an inspired lofty artist, comparable to that of the poet and prophet, was the outcome of the Renaissance with its neo-platonic way of thinking . . . Art became Art with a capital A, a high, exalted, more humanist than human endeavour. Yet precisely in that pseudo-religious function it became almost superfluous, something aside from reality and life, a luxury – refined but useless.[11]

As believers in a God who communicates with his children, we clearly cannot abandon the concept of inspiration. But we must be cautious, examining it in the light of a biblical understanding rather than a

The music of this opera [Madame Butterfly] *was dictated to me by God. I was merely instrumental in putting it on paper and communicating it to the public.*
Giacomo Puccini[12]

Romantic one. For this reason we will return to it after Part 2. For now, let us continue our sweep through the history of art and spirituality, by seeing how the two have been connected in the last hundred years or so, particularly in the realm of visual art.

Expressing the inexpressible

It is a curious twist that, in an era when God was deemed to have died, the search for the spiritual in art should take on an even greater intensity. The search for the spiritual in landscape continued in the work of Vincent van Gogh, who only turned to painting after his desperate attempts to be a preacher and missionary had ended in failure. He turned to art with religious fervour: 'To try and understand the real significance of what the great artists, the serious masters, tell us in their masterpieces, *that* leads to God.'[14] It was a fervour bordering on madness, a 'terrible lucidity' that gave the world some astonishing masterpieces and van Gogh himself a struggle that ended in suicide.

In Norway, far from the glaring yellow sunlight that van Gogh used as an image of terrible probing truth, Edvard Munch was preparing to bare his soul. 'In van Gogh's work the self is scratching to be let out,' says Robert Hughes. 'But in Edvard Munch's, the self is out.'[15] It is fascinating to consider that although Munch's best-known work *The Scream* was done in 1893, two years before Freud published *Studies in Hysteria*, the two men had never heard of each other. Munch saw the spiritual in terms of human emotions, wanting to picture 'living people who breathe, feel, suffer and love. People shall understand the holy quality about them and bare their heads before them as if in church.'[16]

Munch was one of the earliest exponents of what came to be known as expressionism which, as a movement, was strongest in Germany between about 1905 and the end of the First World War, although as an art style, in one way or another, it still lingers. No more could art hope to touch transcendence simply by portraying the natural world. Theologian Paul Tillich saw expressionism as a style that was 'most able to express the self-transcendence in life', breaking through the surface of finite things to bring to light the ultimate meaning beyond, showing 'Spiritual Presence in symbols of broken finitude'.[17]

We no longer cling to reproduction of nature, but destroy it, so as to reveal the right laws which hold sway behind the beautiful exterior.
Franz Marc[13]

For Kandinsky this breaking through came as a revelation in 1908 when he returned to his studio one day to be confronted by a picture of 'indescribable and incandescent loveliness'. Coming nearer he realised that it was one of his own paintings turned on its side. 'One thing became clear to me: that objectiveness, the depiction of objects, needed no place in my paintings, and was indeed harmful to them.'[18] It was to colour that he turned in his search for this purer objectless art: 'Colour directly influences the soul. Colour is the keyboard, the eyes are the

The legacy of war

The meaningless horrors of the First World War sent art off in two main directions. One was the continued quest to express the spiritual via non-representational art. The other was a journey into the absurd. One strand of this was Dada, not so much an art style as an exploration of playfulness, nonsense and chance.

Another, harsher strand was the neo-realism of Grosz, Beckmann and Dix. Some, like Beckmann, a medical orderly in the Flanders trenches, had seen the horrors first hand. He returned to Germany suffering from hallucinations and depression, but determined to be an unofficial recorder of a Europe gone mad. It was a madness which he prophetically understood to be far from over. 'We must participate in the

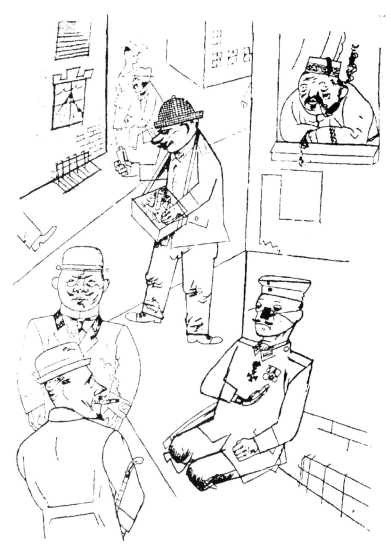

6.   George Grosz, *The Gratitude of the Fatherland is Assured You*. Book illustration from *Das Gesicht der herrschenden Klasse* (The Face of the Ruling Class) (1921)

great misery to come,' he wrote in 1920. 'The sole justification for our existence as artists . . . is to confront people with the image of their destiny.'[19] You did not have to have gone to war to see its legacy. It was there on the German streets, the cripples that Otto Dix and George Grosz incorporated into their work, as they railed against the machine age turned sour.

It was also there in the returning shell-shocked soldiers treated by André Breton in a psychiatric centre in France. As he helped them analyse their dreams, he developed the idea that the dark images of the unconscious spoke a deeper truth than the waking mind. They became a gateway to a new art strand – that of Surrealism.

hammers, the soul is the piano with many strings. The artist is the hand that plays, touching one key or another purposively, to cause vibrations in the soul.'[20]

Kandinsky, along with Brancusi and Mondrian, was a Theosophist, believing that the physical world was a stumbling-block to spiritual enlightenment and that a new day was dawning when matter would be swept away. 'The creative spirit is often concealed within matter,' wrote Kandinsky. 'The veiling of the spirit in the material is often so dense that there are generally few people who can see through to the spirit.'[21]

Probing the void

The more fearful the world becomes, the more art becomes abstract.
Paul Klee[22]

In the years after the First World War painters such as Kandinsky and Mondrian persevered with their exploration of pure colour and pure line, while in sculpture Brancusi found the ultimate unsullied form in the solid curves of an egg. Purity indeed became a popular concept with artists of the twentieth century. The critic Clement Greenberg believed that painting should focus on its supposed true nature, freeing itself not only from any representational suggestion, but from any illusion of perspective or depth on the canvas – a creed which set the scene for a whole generation of two-dimensional 'flat' colour-field painters. Mark Rothko took up the idea of purity in the 1940s: 'The basis of an aesthetic idea is the pure idea. It is only the pure idea that has meaning.'[23] 'Some of us are finding the answer,' added his contemporary, Barnett Newman, 'in completely denying that art has any concern with the problem of beauty . . . We are freeing ourselves of the impediments of memory, association, nostalgia, legend, myth or what have you, that have been the devices of Western European painting.'[24]

It sometimes seems as if the whole of our century has been an exercise in stripping back and back to get to the real essence of art, and in Newman and Rothko we find art stripped down to almost the ultimate simplicity. Both created canvases of almost solid fields of colour, Newman's with his trademark 'zip', a vertical stripe dividing the canvas. A pillar of light, a narrow path, a division of dark from light – Newman never explained it but its intense simplicity undoubtedly spoke of something holy, or as he preferred to call it 'the sublime'. Rothko's powerful rectangles in cloudy monochrome have to many an intense mysticism, although he himself claimed their meaning was essentially emotional. In 1964 he was commissioned to create a cycle of paintings for a chapel in Houston, Texas. To enter the Rothko Chapel with its huge canvases of blacks, plum reds and purples, is to approach the void, a vast emptiness, described by Robert Hughes as 'the last silence of Romanticism'.[25] Only a couple of years after completing the project, Rothko committed suicide.

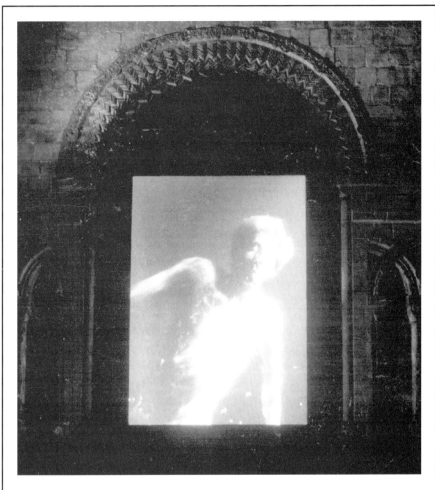

7.   Bill Viola, *The Messenger* (1996), video installation for Durham Cathedral, commissioned by the Chaplaincy to the Arts and Recreation in N.E. England (photo: Edward Woodward)

Somehow the quest for the spiritual can never quite give up. In fact, in the aftermath of modernism, there are signs of its renewed intensity.

Described as the best religious art of the century, Bill Viola's video installation opens with a shimmering form, white against a murky void. The shape becomes a naked man, floating upward through the water toward the light, surfacing and gasping in air before sinking again to the depths to begin the cycle anew.

Is it 'a potent metaphor for spiritual renewal' or a gloomy prognosis that the light remains forever out of reach and we are doomed always to sink again to the depths? For some of the congregational stalwarts at Durham Cathedral, where *The Messenger* was projected on to the West Door, the question was immaterial. The fact that it was a naked man meant that a screen had to be erected to keep it from their sensitive eyes.

Newman and Rothko were not the ultimate in art's process of stripping away. But perhaps they marked a turning-point. Maybe, until the moment when Rothko's chapel became his memorial, it was still possible to believe that the stripping process would eventually arrive at the *essence* of art. Afterwards, there was always the uneasy feeling that essence was in fact *absence*. So Lucio Fontana slit his canvases to show the void beyond and called it *The End of God* and Samuel Beckett wrote *Waiting for Godot* about a world passing the time in the absence of meaning or purpose, a world collapsed in on itself like a black hole.

Oh yes, there was still further for art to go – on and on, always questioning, trying to cut through every last assumption. Why did it need to be in a gallery at all? Why did it need to be permanent? Or even visible, come to that?

In answer to these questions came land and environment art, performance art and, finally conceptual art, where the end result mattered less than the ideas behind it.

And so the process has continued, cutting back and pushing on until the shock of the new has somehow ceased to raise so much as an eyebrow, and as one critic remarked, 'The only way to shock was by being shocking.'

At the end of the century art was going in a very different direction than at the beginning. It had reached a tacit acceptance that it could no longer go deeper; one could still ask spiritual questions, but there was little point in expecting any answers. And if this was so, where was there to go but sideways? The next generation of artists concentrated on pushing back boundaries of taste and definition. Could you really put anything in a gallery and still call it art?

3

Art and a Suspicious Church

When I became a Christian, people suggested I change job and be a nurse.
                                                                Graphic designer

When I go to church I feel like I'm always having to justify what I do.
                                                                        Painter

The negative attitude of the Christian Union towards the media left me wondering if a career in film was worthwhile.
                                                                    Film-maker

My college doesn't understand my faith and my church doesn't understand my art. Where do I fit as a whole person?
                                                                    Art Student

These quotes[1] are not freak examples. They are representative of the experience of many Christians working in arts and media today. If it is not your experience, be grateful, and perhaps skip this chapter.

For some sections of the church the arts have never been a problem issue. For others they are ceasing to be a problem as Christians enthusiastically embrace the arts for the first time in generations (an enthusiasm, however, that can be somewhat superficial and lacking in understanding). But still in some churches suspicion, if not downright opposition, remains. The strange thing about this suspicion is that it is very hard to trace its origins. If there have been any books written in the last hundred years counselling against the arts, or any sermons preached against them, they are very well hidden. In fact, the negative relationship between the church and the arts is barely chronicled at all. Dorothy Sayers seems closest to the truth when she comments that the church really does not know what it thinks about the arts, and isn't too bothered either.

Is it perhaps because the Protestant church (and particularly the evangelical wing), having abandoned the arts some centuries before, no longer has any understanding? Is it now unable to find a point of entry? Is it simply frightened of what it does not know? Officially, the arts seem

The Church as a body has never made up her mind about the Arts, and it is hardly too much to say that she has never tried.
Dorothy Sayers[2]

to have been forgotten rather than frowned on. But unofficially, it can be all too easy for the unfamiliar to become the enemy.

For a long while this divide hardly seemed to matter. Evangelicals withdrew to their own communities and kept well clear of dance halls, concerts and theatres. But when in this century, radio and TV started bringing the arts right into the home, gradually it dawned on many of them that a whole new means of communication was growing up from which they were completely absent. Here was a means of 'reaching the unsaved' that was not only energy-efficient but exciting. But of course, by then they had lost out on the aesthetic understanding that comes simply by being soaked for generations in good literature, good art, good music. So when their attempts to jump on the bandwagon were derided by critics and media professionals, these critics too were seen as the enemy, opposed to the message and persecuting the believers. Unfortunately, all too often the critics were simply pointing out that it was not art but propaganda.

The roots of division

How did this separation between church and art come about? What lessons, if any, does history have for us?

The fledgling New Testament church is of very little help to us here. Singing, of course, is much in evidence, in prison, in homes, in the open air: with gusto and in all circumstances the new believers sang. But of other arts there is a conspicuous absence. 'We search the New Testament in vain for a glimpse of Christians meeting for recreation or artistic activity,' comments biblical scholar Derek Kidner; 'the most we find is an occasional dinner party. Life is too short, and indeed too absorbing, to call for distractions.'[4]

There are many ways in which the New Testament church is a good model for us. Is this then, one of them? Trotsky might come to our aid here, with his observation that 'Art is always in the rearguard of historic advance.'[5] At a time of revolution, everything is in a state of flux, transitory, on the move. Meetings are impromptu – in the open air, in homes, under cover. The newly formed church of the Acts of the Apostles was in just such a state of revolution, albeit a peaceful one. Its lack of art may not signify disapproval, merely the wrong circumstances.

When the first Christians began to get a toe-hold in imperial Rome, at least some art began to feature: a wealth of murals were painted deep in hidden catacombs. Records show, however, that disapproval of other types of art soon kicked in. Theatre, said the Church Fathers, was a 'licentious representation of decadent paganism'.[6] But then theatre, as playwright Murray Watts reminds us, has its roots in religious ritual.[7] And in ancient Rome, by then beginning its decline and fall, theatre was not only rooted in pagan ritual, but degenerate and immoral to boot. There were good reasons for keeping well away.

For as long as the Christians were a persecuted minority, struggling to bring in a completely new world order right under the noses of a huge pagan establishment, the situation was very much the same. But gradually over the centuries, the Christian worldview took hold and spread – around the Mediterranean world and then up through Europe – until at last Christianity itself became the establishment and clasped the arts to its bosom once more.

The flowering of Christendom

As we noted in the last chapter, the medieval age (a period of roughly a thousand years from the fall of Rome to the beginning of the sixteenth century) saw the great flowering of the Western church and its use of the arts. Its most magnificent legacy was a huge church-building boom. In a two-hundred-year period in France eighty cathedrals were built, along with at least five hundred churches of considerable size. The cathedrals were the arts centres of their day – combined places of worship, theatres, art galleries, schools and libraries. Markets were established outside, travellers were welcome to sleep inside and friends met for gossip in the aisles.

All education was in the hands of the church, the eminent thinkers were the monks and clergy and the great universities sprang up from the cathedral schools. Through this period, when books were hand-written in Latin and literacy was the province of religious professionals, it was paintings and sculpture which became the 'books of the layman'. They told their stories around the cathedral walls, using a highly developed system of symbols in which most things had a spiritual as well as a literal meaning. Fire stood for martyrdom, the lily for purity, the owl for Satan, and the lamb for Christ.

Bible stories began to be dramatised, first with the development of liturgy into a form of dialogue and later developing into the mystery plays. Soon they were moving outside the church buildings and into the churchyards and beyond, bringing colour and pageantry to the streets and town squares. The plays were earthy but also profound. They were often funny and not afraid of the occasional dig at those in authority.

Singing, which for about eight hundred years of Christian worship consisted of a single line of melody, developed during this time into polyphony. The development of notation allowed for complex part-singing and new rhythms, shocking to some churchmen who nevertheless could not prevent the rapid spread of the new fashion throughout Europe. Other arts too – storytelling, poetry, dancing, instrumental music – flourished outside the church. In a society where all of life came

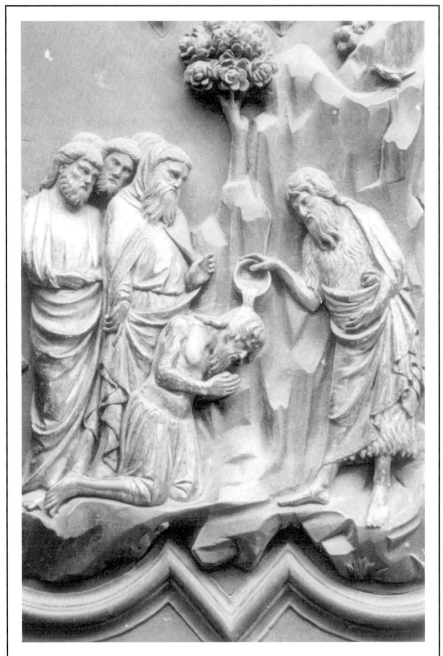

8. Lorenzo Ghiberti, detail from the doors of the Baptistry, Florence (1403–24), bronze (photo: Hilary Brand)

'The picture is to the illiterate what the written word is to the educated,' said Pope Gregory the Great.[8] The people of Florence could stand in their central piazza and 'read' the gospel story (here the baptism of Jesus by John) on the great bronze doors of the Baptistry.

under the auspices of a Christian worldview, there was very little sense that these things were to be shunned.

Cutting away the canker

The medieval age provided a great flowering of Christian artistry, but by the beginning of the sixteenth century the canker had long been in the bud. Something was badly wrong in the Catholic church and, as Machiavelli pointed out, the nearer one got to Rome, the more corruption was to be found.[9]

Unfortunately at least one aspect of the corruption was inextricably linked with the arts. The building boom and particularly the architectural glories of the Italian Renaissance needed finance. And one handy way of funding, developed by the popes (especially the wily Sixtus IV, builder of the Sistine Chapel, and later Julius II, who started the rebuilding of St Peter's), was the sale of indulgences. Medieval people had a real dread of purgatory, the period of punishment they were taught must come before a soul could enter heaven. The purchase of an indulgence could shorten or even wipe out this time of penance: 'a penny in the coffer rings, a soul from purgatory springs'.

On 31 October 1517 an obscure German monk could stand this 'holy trade' no longer and stated his objections in 95 theses nailed to a castle door in Wittenberg. Martin Luther was angry at a church he saw as having buried the gospel under a welter of tradition. Where images and relics had become idolised and detracted from the worship of Christ he condemned them, but he was not opposed to the arts as such. When riots of image-burning and stained-glass window smashing broke out in Wittenberg, he came out of hiding at risk of his life in order to stop the destruction.

Luther also clearly loved music. 'Next to God,' he said, 'music deserves the highest praise . . . Whether you wish to comfort the sad, to subdue frivolity, to encourage the despairing, to humble the proud, to calm the passionate or to appease those full of hate . . . what more effective means than music could you find?'[10] And the quote in the margin would suggest that he rather liked the idea of square dancing as well.

But if Luther wished to preserve that artistry which contributed to worship, there were those of his contemporaries who did not. Whilst he was in prison Andreas Karlstadt took the reform movement in Wittenberg in a more extreme direction, including a blanket condemnation of the arts. 'The Gregorian chant,' pronounced Karlstadt, 'moves the mind still further from God – to say nothing of the mumbling, the shrieking like geese of the choristers and lascivious sound of musical instruments, the wailing of organs.'[11] He produced a tract entitled *Of the putting away of pictures* where he asserted that no one ever learnt

But when natural music is sharpened and polished by art, then one begins to see with amazement the great and perfect wisdom of God in his wonderful work of music, where one voice takes a simple part and around it sing three, four, or five other voices, leaping, springing round about, marvellously gracing the simple part, like a square dance in heaven with friendly bows, embracings and hearty swinging of partners.

Martin Luther[12]

the way to heaven from a picture. 'I tell you that God has not less diligently and truly forbidden pictures than murdering, robbing, adultery and the like,' he insisted,[14] and in the fervent polarising of opinions that the Reformation stirred up, there were plenty to agree with him.

There was, of course, alongside this turmoil of protest another powerful agent of change at work – the printing press. Here we have it again, the same phenomenon we noted in our opening chapter, technological revolution working alongside a revolution in ideas. Soon people were able to read or hear the Bible in their own tongue. From now on paintings in church were no longer needed in the same way, for what could be

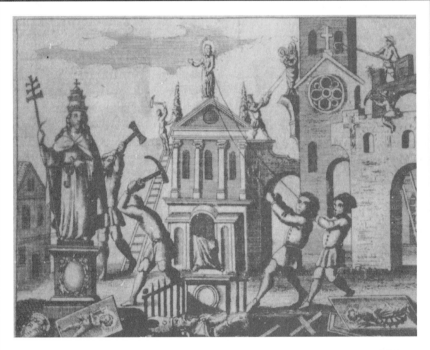

9.　*Destruction of images*, seventeenth-century engraving, unattributed (Mary Evans Picture Library)

Iconoclasm has reared its destructive head many times throughout church history. In Britain it showed itself most clearly in Henry VIII's systematic destruction of the monasteries, and Oliver Cromwell's Parliamentary Ordinance commanding the 'speedy demolishing of all organs, images and all matters of superstitious monuments'. Demolition is not always a negative force, as those anxious to rid our cities of the worst excesses of high-rise architecture and mouldering industrialism would agree. Unfortunately, by its very nature, those who come after are not in a position to judge. It is the tangible that is lost; what is gained is intangible.

better, the Reformers rightly asked, than to get one's teaching straight from the Word?

Luther's actions had opened the floodgates of protest all over Europe. The Catholic hierarchy eventually realised the seriousness of the challenge and tried to reform itself from within. The Council of Trent reaffirmed the value of arts in teaching the illiterate, but laid down that paintings should not conflict with church doctrine or decency. (Following this principle, Pope Pius IV ordered loincloths to be painted on Michelangelo's naked figures in the Sistine Chapel.) It also pronounced against music that was 'lascivious' or 'seductive and impure'. But it was too late to gather up the faithful within the fold. Once opened, the divide between Catholic and Protestant continued to widen.

Getting back to basics

If Luther began the chorus of protest, it was Calvin who orchestrated it. John Calvin is widely portrayed as a hater of the arts, so it is worth examining his words and actions a little more closely. He did indeed promote a strict and austere Christianity. Churches were devoid of all decoration and artefacts, lest anything should distract the congregation from the the most vital element – the Word of God. As if making a visual statement, the pulpit became the central feature. Calvin believed singing should be praise pure and simple. The only texts he saw suitable for this purpose were the Psalms and one or two canticles. Singing in harmony and the use of instruments, including the organ, were forbidden. Dancing was classified along with visiting taverns as a moral lapse for which believers would be reprimanded in front of the congregation.

Calvin was determined to get back to the essentials of a religion that depended on faith in Christ alone. But it would be wrong to conclude that he was simply an aesthetically challenged killjoy: 'Should the Lord have attracted our eyes to the beauty of the flowers, and our senses to pleasant odours,' he asked, 'and should it then be a sin to drink them in? . . . Has he not made many things worthy of our attention that go far beyond our needs?'[15]

Indeed he stated clearly that the arts were a gift of God, and in 1546 put his money where his mouth was by springing to the defence of a miracle play on the Acts of the Apostles that was being performed in Geneva, and pronouncing it 'sound and godly'.[16]

He understood that even art created by an unbeliever could still be a vehicle for truth:

Therefore in reading profane authors, the admirable light of truth displayed in them should remind us that the human mind, however much fallen and

The invention of the arts, and other things which serve the common use and convenience of life, is a gift of God by no means to be despised, and a faculty worthy of commendation.
    John Calvin[17]

perverted from its original integrity, is still adorned and invested with admirable gifts from its Creator. If we reflect that the Spirit of God is the only fountain of truth, we will be careful, as we would avoid offering insults to Him, not to reject or condemn truth wherever it appears. In despising the gifts we insult the giver.[18]

Indeed he acknowledged that art by non-Christians could often be better, rather wistfully remarking that 'these radiations of Divine Light shone more brilliantly among unbelieving people than among God's saints.'[19]

But in understanding the power of good art, he also realised the dangers. 'For music has a secret and incredible power to move our hearts. When evil words are accompanied by music, they penetrate more deeply and the poison enters as wine through a funnel into a vat.'[20]

Playing it safe

As so often in history, the great pioneers have a courage and balance that those who come after them lack. Over the history of Protestantism that followed, all too frequently it was the perils of the arts that were emphasised, rather than the delights.

The theatre, it appears, was often considered the most dangerous of all. In 1575 the Church of Scotland banned liturgical drama, a move which arguably prevented the growth of any Scottish theatre tradition for centuries to come. In 1642 Oliver Cromwell's Parliament passed a law closing theatres altogether. Quite what effect that would have had on British culture had the Royalists not regained power is a matter of interesting conjecture. What is apparent is that thereafter theatre, abandoned by Christians, became much more superficial. Elegant comedies of manners replaced the more searching Jacobean plays with their moral and spiritual dilemmas. 'Something had gone,' comments Murray Watts, 'and it was undoubtedly a deeper sense of human value, which is closely allied to religious awareness, and can produce the greatest comedy as well as the greatest tragedy.'[21]

A closer look at these bans on theatre will reveal that it was not simply the art form itself that was perceived as threatening. In the Scottish example, it can be seen as a reaction to the theology behind the plays, whereas in Cromwell's Commonwealth it was more as a safeguard against political subversion. Perhaps it was the same sort of reasoning that today leads revolutionaries to take over the TV and radio stations before the parliament buildings. Theatre was, and still is, a powerful means of communication. Anyone aspiring to power is wise to treat it with respect, if not outright fear.

When in 1644 that same brief Puritan parliament ordered the demo-lition of 'organs, images and all matters of superstitious monuments',[22] it was theology they were tilting at, rather than the art forms them-selves. The organs and images were simply the outward symbols of an old set of ideas, and their destruction, thankfully a short-lived activity, was a show of power signalling the new to be ushered in. (In fact even the Puritans were not so averse to the arts as it might appear. One of Shakespeare's leading patrons was a Puritan, Cromwell's own officer Bulstrode Whitelock fought for operas to be allowed, and Cromwell

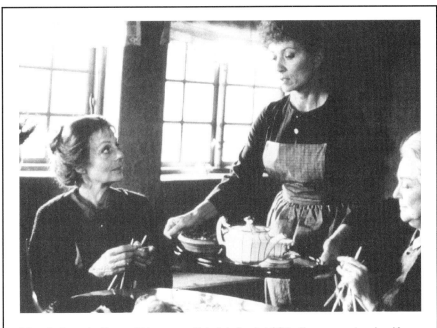

10. *Babette's Feast* (Director: Gabriel Axel 1987. From staging by Karen Blixen and Isak Dinesen)

When Babette, a sophisticated but penniless Parisian refugee, finds her-self washed up in a desolate corner of Denmark, among a strict but good-hearted religious community, she is grateful for their kindness. When an unexpected lottery win arrives for her, she decides to spend it all on one huge extravagant gesture – a feast. With reckless abandon she sends away for choice wines, meats and vegetables. With immense care she prepares her culinary masterpiece. The simple chapel folk, more used to a lifestyle of relentless austerity and dreary food, are at first sus-picious, but gradually they begin to mellow and marvel at a richness they never dreamed of.

Babette's art form is cookery and, in her hands, the feast gives glory to God and delight to a community whose theology had left them dour and joyless.

himself uttered one of the most memorable encouragements to artistic realism: 'Paint me, warts and all'!)

Church history, then, would seem to indicate that the arts have been victims of the clash of two great theologies, Protestant and Catholic, with a particular pile-up of casualties behind the Protestant lines.

By the time the newly revived evangelicals found themselves in the Victorian era, with its all-pervasive principle of respectability, no one was even questioning whether the arts really were as dangerous as they were cracked up to be. It was best to play safe, argued our evangelical forebears, unaware of what meagre cultural crumbs that policy left them with. And anyway, the emergence of Empire and advances in travel meant there were other exciting frontiers to be conquered. The 'fields were ripe for harvest' and overseas mission beckoned. No matter that the church at home was becoming progressively more bland and dull and unattractive. No matter that it reeked of what psychologist William James called 'the atrocious harmlessness of all things'. (On visiting a supposedly idyllic Christian holiday centre, he found himself longing for the outside world with all its 'heights and depths, the precipices and steep ideals, the gleams of the awful and the infinite'.)[25] No matter that, as author Garrison Keillor comments on his small town Lutheran heritage, 'The avoidance of unedifying things as the ultimate value makes us lead very strange lives.'[26] The Christian world was safe in its respectable cocoon, acting, in Calvin Seerveld's words, 'as if the Holy Spirit only shows up in straight-backed people wearing black suits'.[27]

But, of course, the Holy Spirit has a habit of turning up in all sorts of unexpected ways and times. Indeed, it may be that a longer view of history will reveal the charismatic movement as one of the vital factors in the church's return to the arts. Certainly, it has brought back movement, symbolism and visual awareness to a church starved of colour – not to mention a willingness to change. It is perhaps too soon to write that particular chapter of the church's history, but it is certainly important to look back over the longer chronicle of Christianity's relationship with the arts and draw some lessons from it. It can point out to us both the dangers of glorifying the arts and the equal dangers of withdrawing from them altogether. God grant that in a new millennium we may find a positive and healthy approach which has been conspicuously absent for so long.

. . . Protestantism –
the adroit
castrator
Of art; the bitter
negation
Of song and dance
and the heart's
innocent joy –
You have botched
our flesh and left
us only the soul's
Terrible impotence in
a warm world . . .
R.S. Thomas[23]

History repeats itself.
Has to.
No-one listens
Steve Turner[24]

Part 2

Garden, Serpent and Sacrifice:
Returning to primary sources

4

Art and the Bible

The previous section has sketched some of the conflicting philosophies with which Christians in the arts may be bombarded. No wonder so many give up thinking too deeply about what they are doing. It's all so confusing. But if we are to develop art that is thoroughly contemporary and thoroughly Christian, we desperately need a clear understanding of our mandate. And for that we will need, as in the study of any discipline, to go back to primary source material – in our case, the Bible.

The problem, at first glance, is that the Bible would seem to have very little to say that will encourage us. As Derek Kidner comments:

Your word is a lamp to my feet and a light for my path.
Psalm 119:105

> When we turn to the Bible for guidance about human art, entertainment and learning, we are struck by the difficulty of finding any recommendation to pursue these activities for their own sake. The most determined attempt to explore these possibilities is found in Ecclesiastes, but the verdict is that 'All was vanity and a striving after wind.' The whole weight of the biblical emphasis is on the dangers, not the advantages, of the leisured conditions in which the arts flourish and in which the Greeks sought to cultivate the good life.[1]

But that is, as Kidner goes on to acknowledge, very much a 'first glance' conclusion. Deeper study will show us that the arts, like every other aspect of human cultural activity, can indeed be rooted in a biblical worldview.

The first step may be to rethink the way we read our Bibles. In some strands of Christianity, we have become all too used to the 'proof-text' approach – the Bible as a source of instant ready-made instructions. If that is what we are after, then, on the arts as on many other specific issues (sport, space travel, 'laughing in the Spirit', heart transplants etc.), the Scriptures will indeed let us down. Using this approach it is a short step to conclude that the absence of instruction means absence of approval.

But the Bible is not an instruction manual. It is a book of 'God-speaking literature' and as such includes almost every variety of writing style: some instruction, yes, but also reportage, human stories, national history, myth (in the sense of a traditional story that makes sense of the world, rather than something untrue), poetry, allegory and political comment. It has many voices: the rough-hewn fury of the prophets, the highly structured artistry of Hebrew poetry, the matter-of-fact narrative of the gospels and the reasoned logic of the apostle Paul. The Bible gives us, says Derek Kidner, 'an example of art which has found its station in life: subordinate to the Spirit and shaped by truth, yet all the freer for being purposeful and unselfconscious.'[2]

To understand the Bible fully means to read it as each of its human writers intended it to be read. It also means to read it as a

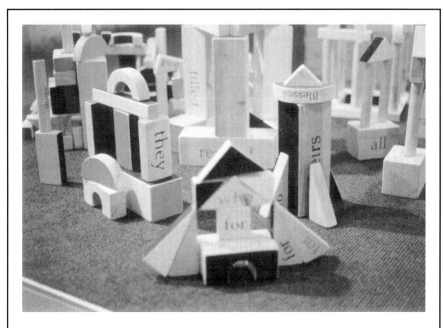

11.   Paul Hobbs, *Attitudes* (1997), wood and acrylic, 193 × 193 cm

Paul Hobbs has taken a 'hands on' approach to the Bible with his set of building bricks, each one of which bears a word from the Beatitudes, the teaching of Jesus in Matthew's gospel which begins 'Blessed are the poor in spirit'.[3] This is art without a 'Do not touch' sign, there to be played with by adults and children, allowing them to (quite literally) deconstruct – and reconstruct – the meaning of the familiar words.

The Bible is indeed a holy book, but the extreme reverence of previous generations of evangelicals has sometimes meant that we have forgotten how to enjoy it. The artist reminds us that we are allowed to be playful. It is OK simply to let its meanings puzzle and intrigue us. In fact, we might learn more if we stop feeling we *ought* to get an inspired message at every reading.

whole, assembled under the divine editorship of the Holy Spirit, in order to trace the major themes running through it. And it does mean actually *reading* it. As Franky Schaeffer comments, 'Today the Bible is widely studied but rarely read.'[4] It means allowing the Scriptures to seep into our thinking, seeing, feeling and imagining, so much so that they begin to remould them – as the apostle Paul described it, being 'transformed by the renewing of our minds'.[5] It means struggling to make all our thinking compatible with the teaching of Jesus – in another of Paul's memorable phrases, to 'take captive every thought to make it obedient to Christ'.[6] We will then discover that what the Scriptures give us is not a theology of the arts, but a biblical framework within which the arts, like all other human activity, can be evaluated and understood.

The Bible is not a collection of atomic, bullet-like proof texts to be shot at people . . . The Bible is not an anthology of lessons in piety which can be distributed, so to speak, like candy to whoever holds out his hand. The Bible does not give recipes, which when followed to the letter, make wonderful devotional soup . . . The Bible is not like a telephone book where you can find God's special number for emergency use.

Calvin Seerveld[7]

5

Art and a Playful God

With the eyes of a child

'Let's start at the very beginning, a very good place to start.' Julie Andrews' immortal dictum cannot be surpassed when it comes to understanding the Bible.

> In the beginning God created . . .
> . . . and it was very good.[2]

The doctrine of creation might seem so basic as to require little attention, but it is here, rather than with Christ and his salvation, that a Christian worldview begins.

The Lord God was playful enough to make lobsters and ginko trees, quartz crystals and red-haired girls with freckles. God wants us to laugh and enjoy the imaginative riches smiling and crying everywhere.
Calvin Seerveld[1]

Those who spend their energies pitting the first chapter of Genesis against contemporary science have missed the point. The opening pages of the Bible are not textbook science and their purpose is not to present a proven scientific account of the origin of the universe (something ultimately beyond the grasp of even the greatest scientist) but to give testimony to the power and wisdom of the God who created it. As Albert Einstein is said to have remarked, anyone who is not awed and astonished at the power and glory of the mind behind the creation of the universe is 'as good as a burnt-out candle'.[3] Both science and Genesis point out that 'it was good . . . it was good . . . it was very good'.

'Christians who have lost the overwhelming biblical sense of creation,' warns Calvin Seerveld, 'because they are so "heavenly minded", citified or just plainly insensitive to the Old Testament, soon become warped and unfaithful stewards.'[4] If we are to think and act Christianly, a vital part of the renewing of our minds is to regain a sense of wonder. Seerveld's suggested remedy is to 'go with the eyes of a child to the zoo'.[5] Perhaps those of us who live in the concrete jungle may need to step outside it for a while, if only to look into the depths of a night sky not masked by sodium lighting. Certainly wherever we are we will need to take time to stop and stare.

Whether in the power of a storm or the tiny fingers of a baby, in the darting fluorescence of tropical fish, in the stark silhouette of a winter tree, or even in the humble Brussels sprout, we need to learn to see our world, to quote Seerveld again, as 'the stunning theatre, workshop, playground of our Father in heaven, peopled by whatever his creative Word sustains'.[6]

The apostle Paul, talking about Christ as the image of God the creator says that 'by him all things were created, things in heaven and on earth, visible and invisible'.[7] It is worth noting that the invisible things include the whole realm of ideas and imagination, emotions, instincts, memory, sensitivity, intuition and the ability to dream and fantasise. These things also were made by the Creator and pronounced good.

There are only two ways to live your life. One is as though nothing is a miracle. The other is as if everything is.
Albert Einstein[8]

Divine line management

It is not just the Bible's opening chapter which speak of God's creation. The Psalms are bursting with delight in it, Job and Proverbs are soaked in it, Jesus and the prophets drew their insights from it, and Paul wrote

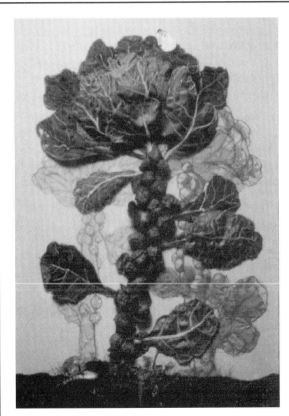

One vital role of the artist is to help others to stop and look, to remind them that there is beauty to be seen in humble things, in simple shapes and subtle colours. Ann Bridges makes even the vegetable patch fascinating in this fabric illustration.

12. Ann Bridges, *Brussels Sprouts* (1991), textiles,
63 × 45 cm

and preached about it. In one of Paul's impromptu sermons he pointed out that even those to whom God was a big unknown had an inbuilt sense of divine activity: 'He is not far from each one of us. For in him we live and move and have our being.'[10] Paul was touching on an idea, self-evident to his hearers, which we in later, more humanist, centuries have lost. God is not just the divine watchmaker, setting the clock ticking and leaving it to run by itself. God is continuously and actively involved in the ongoing life of every part of creation. Jesus, who had it on good authority, pointed to lilies, sparrows and the hairs on our heads[11] as being under God's direct supervision – a pretty intimate level of involvement.

It is also worth noting that throughout the Bible narrative as God continued his involvement with his people, gradually helping them understand more of his nature, he often used creative methods to get their attention. Not only did God use story-telling, visual aids in the sky and plenty of dreams and visions, he also instructed those he chose as his representatives to use a wide and wacky range of non-verbal techniques (see box).

Inventive image-bearers

Going back to the beginning of the story, we find at the culmination of God's inventive 'week' the pinnacle of his creation: humanity, designed 'in our image, in our likeness'.[12] What does it mean to be made in the image of God? It is a subject that has caused much debate over the centuries, and will undoubtedly provoke still more.

Let us first focus on that characteristic that defines us as artists – our 'creativity'. 'We are creative. God is creative,' the argument runs.

For further study: some of the symbolic activities God instructed his human agents to use

Interior design	Exodus 25 – 27
Dress	Exodus 28
Music	Numbers 10
Song	Deuteronomy 31:19
	Psalm 40:3
Monument	Joshua 4
Architecture	1 Chronicles 28:12,19
Poetry	2 Samuel 23:1,2
Prophetic performance	Isaiah 20
	Jeremiah 19, 27, 28
	Ezekiel 4, 5

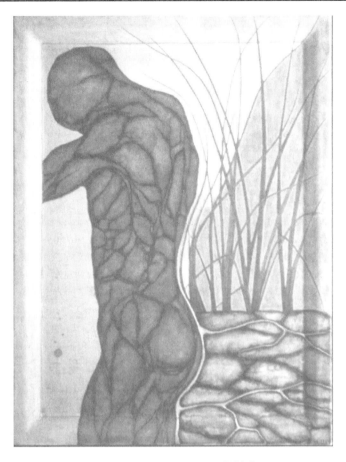

13.   Michel Burgard, *Marsh I: Witness* (1994), egg tempera, water gilding on birch, 81 × 61 cm

If we are to comprehend our place in the world, we need to understand both our role as image-bearers and our creatureliness, our connectedness with the rest of creation. To remember that we are, quite literally, stardust, the atoms of our bodies forged in long-dead stars.

Michel Burgard worked for some time on images of the wetlands, using the marsh to represent a metaphorical place origin. 'My personal vision,' she says, 'is of the human embedded in and emerging from elements . . . and being transformed through rivers of gold (spirit, light) penetrating all things.'

Reluctant to see her work as message or theology, she acknowledges it as being about God coming into the world of material reality and drawing that world closer into God's own life. She sees the work of an artist as 'one person opening another little window for someone else', offering them an image to carry with them 'that resonates with them at some point – and, suddenly, meaning comes'.[13]

'Therefore it is our creativity that defines us as being made in the image of God.' Or does it?

Human beings clearly have, like the Creator God, the ability to conceive, either by reason or imagination, an idea; to express it in language; and then to make it happen. And we clearly have a desire, some might say a drive, to do just that. However, there is good reason to be cautious before using the adjective 'creative', as applied to humans. Firstly, we must always remember that only God can create 'ex nihilo' – out of nothing; that however imaginative, intelligent and powerful we become, we remain creatures. However many gifts we possess, we must never forget that they are just that – 'gifts' given by God and not ours by right.

We must also remember that these gifts can be applied to every aspect of human activity. 'Create' in its contemporary meaning is defined as 'to bring into being by force of imagination'. By this definition, it was creativity that led Brunel to design bridges, Einstein to formulate his special and general theories of relativity, Bob Geldof to organise Live Aid, and the staff of East Croydon station to brighten commuters' lives by broadcasting Valentine messages over the tannoy on 14 February. One can have creative management, creative accounting (although perhaps this is not always so godly), and creative play with glue and cornflakes boxes and sticky-backed plastic.

The capacity to imagine, experiment and make things happen can be applied to the whole of life – education, horticulture, science, home-making etc. Artists do not have a monopoly.

We are right to get excited about this 'creative' gift. But if we claim it as the essential element of being image-bearers, we are missing the biblical point. (For further development of this argument see Chapter 11.)

Stewards and cultivators

So if it is not our 'creativity' that defines us as image-bearers, what is it? God gave the men and women he created a job to do: to 'fill the earth and subdue it', to 'rule over . . . every living creature'.[16]

An imperialist's charter, if ever there was one. Such a commission would seem to give permission for any amount of plunder and desecration. What could God have been thinking of, to give the earth into such unreliable hands? It has taken the looming environmental crisis to prompt Christians into re-examining these words. It has reminded us that humanity is part of the created order, made to be in relationship with the earth, not just to use it. The planet itself is forcibly proving to us that 'subduing' does not mean beating into submission at any cost, like a tiger pacing in a cage, or a tract of rainforest destroyed to provide grazing to feed the West's burger habit. We are beginning to rediscover that

Art is one way for men and women to respond to the Lord's command to cultivate the earth . . . Art is neither more nor less than that.
Calvin Seerveld[14]

If you and I carve wood, apply paint to canvas, pile stone on stone, or inscribe marks on paper, we are dealing with things which bear to us the most intimate of relations.
Nicholas Wolterstorff[15]

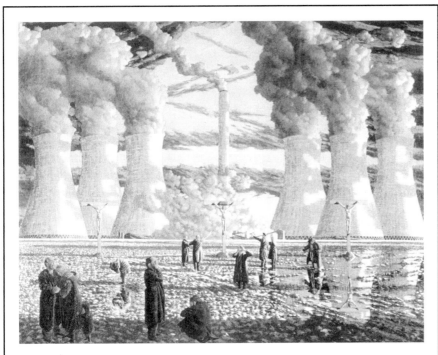

14.   Roger Wagner, *Menorah* (1993), oil on canvas, 193 × 155 cm (coll. of the artist)

Roger Wagner offers a bleak picture of humankind's stewardship of the earth, seeing in the cooling towers of Didcot, near his native Oxford, an image of our capacity to pollute and spoil. The towers form the Menorah of the title, the traditional Jewish seven-branched candlestick, and the figures in the foreground are inspired by pictures of prisoners in concentration camps.

Wagner's vision has a double-edge, however. Much as he resents the imposition of the power station on the Thames valley landscape, he also recognises its beauty. In the impersonal and slightly menacing power of industry he also finds a hint of God.

'ruling over the earth' is not a right or a privilege but a responsibility. Which, of course, is what it was always meant to be.

By 'subduing', the writer of Genesis surely had in mind the continuation of the task with which God began his creation – forming out of formlessness, then filling it with rich diversity. It was, as Nicholas Wolterstorff describes it, 'an imposition of order for the purpose of serving human livelihood and delight'.[17] It was, as Genesis goes on to describe, the act of tending a garden, 'to work it and take care of it'.[18] In other words, to 'cultivate' it.

So this, essentially, is what being an image-bearer means. It means taking on the role of steward, of managing on behalf of the Owner. It means being given the opportunity to delve and discover, preserve, develop and improve. It means accepting the responsibility to cultivate.

Dreamers and doers

And here we return to our arts theme. Culture, that catch-all word to describe the state of being civilised, is not about reading the right books and seeing the right films, knowing which knives and forks to use, or never calling napkins serviettes. It is about taking responsibility to conserve, develop and improve the world we have been given.

Improve? Yes, God actually gave us marble, knowing that, when combined with those invisible gifts of imagination and determination, it could be turned into Michelangelo's *David*. God created catgut, horse-hair and wood, knowing that human ingenuity could draw from them Vivaldi's *Four Seasons*; the cocoa pod, knowing that curiosity would transform it into chocolate; and mouldy bread, knowing that logic and the quest for knowledge would one day discover penicillin. (Of course, he also created the Grand Canyon and the Amazon jungle in the hopes that sometimes we might have the wisdom to leave well alone!)

Without this capacity to envisage a different state of affairs and to bring it into being we could not *be* responsible. Those things that mark our creativity – our sensual awareness, imaginative thinking and manual skills – are God-given tools in our task of cultivating the earth.

And, praise God, they are also gifts given simply for our delight. The biblical narrative goes on to describe how in that brief time in the perfect garden, humankind had both aesthetic sense and imaginative ability. The trees of the garden, according to Genesis 2, were 'pleasing to the eye'. God had made a world of beauty and had made humans to respond to it; to enjoy green and gold and dappled light, knobbly bark and shapely branches, as well as shade and food. We also see in the naming of the animals in Genesis 2[21] that God prompted Adam not only into scientific classification but into a bit of verbal fun! Adam had to think up his own names for all the creatures. Try it yourself, making up new names for the ordinary, everyday objects you see around you. You will soon discover how much imagination and original thinking is required!

Finally, when Eve was presented to Adam he burst into what is almost a lyrical poem:

> This is now bone of my bones
> and flesh of my flesh;
> she shall be called woman,
> for she was taken out of man.[22]

Here, right at the beginning of human history, we find the ability to play with words, to use them to create vivid images rather than make bald factual statements. He could have just said: 'Wow!'

Team players

Cultivating the earth was never optional. The cultural mandate is for every human being and covers every aspect of life. And it is meant to be fun. Nevertheless, it seems a daunting task. How could we possibly achieve such a thing?

'Let us make man in our image,' said God,[23] and the 'our' gives us a clue. The God at work in creation is a relational God: Father/Creator, Son (Jesus the Word as in John's Gospel chapter 1), and Spirit (hovering over the waters). We, God's image-bearers, are designed to function in relationship. Not just the male/female relationship of physical delight, but a working relationship, sharing together the task we have been given – with each other and with God. It is a team project and artists are just one part of the team. The good news is that the team manager is never far away.

Culture is not optional. Formative culturing of creation is intrinsic to human nature, put there purposely – God knows why.
Calvin Seerveld[24]

6

Art and a Fallen World

A deadly choice

The Bible uses story-telling (the earliest art form?) to explain a phenomenon we all recognise: we live in a fallen world. A man, a woman, a talking serpent and some luscious fruit, bound together in a chain of events that seemed innocuous yet had an all-embracing effect. No matter whether the story was told first around a flickering fire by Adam himself or some other hunter-gatherer. We cannot know. The vital fact is that this story has lasted down the ages and formed the preface to the most holy book on earth because it says something basic and fundamental about the human condition.

The first humans had a choice – to do what God said or to decide they knew better. No matter that the suggestion came from a crafty smooth-talking deceiver, it was their decision – disobedience pure and simple, says the Bible. The luscious fruit had become deadly poison, because they took rather than waiting to be given.

The Genesis story still has power because it is about far more than Adam and Eve. It is not just about the first man and woman, but Everyman and Everywoman and is retold in every generation. Humans still make the same deadly choices: making themselves the sole arbiters of right or wrong, ignoring the still, small voice of conscience, and all in order to 'take the waiting out of wanting'. And the poison still spreads.

A disordered world

The Bible teaches that this poison has seeped into every aspect of life. One of the first results of the fall was alienation. In the garden the man blamed the woman and the woman blamed the serpent. Within a generation brother was murdering brother. The first and most obvious result of our deadly choices is almost always broken relationships.

More devastating still is alienation from God. The Genesis account pictures the Lord God, the landowner, strolling through the garden in the cool of the day,[2] chatting with his estate-managers perhaps, admiring their mutual handiwork. But on that day, after the fatal taste, they were missing, gone into hiding. The relationship had passed from one of friendship to one of fear.

But the rot does not even stop there. Alan Storkey explains: 'The Bible teaches that both I and what is out there – nature – are in relationship to God. If we leave God out of the picture we leave out the binding force that holds all things in tension.'[3] The broken relationship with God means that we also live in broken relationship with the earth. 'Cursed is the ground because of you,' said God,[4] in what can be imagined as more sadness than anger, as he put Adam and Eve out of the garden for their own good. And so the disorder of human sin has its effect on the whole created world, so that as the apostle Paul describes, 'All creation groans as in the pain of childbirth.'[5] Al Wolters describes it this way:

> Not only the whole human race but the whole non-human world too was caught up in the train of Adam's failure to heed God's explicit command and warning. The effects of sin touch all of creation; no created thing is in principle untouched by the corrosive effects of the fall. Whether we look at societal structures such as the state or family, or bodily functions such as sexuality or

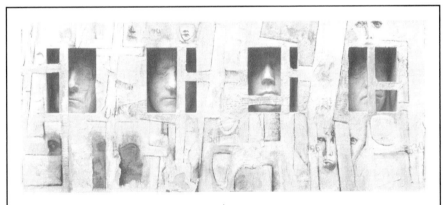

15.   Colin Riches, *Like Dreams in Sleep* (1994), mixed media, 123 × 46 × 36 cm (photo: Geoff Pigott)

Sculptor Colin Riches, who has worked for many years as an art teacher with prisoners, uses his own artwork to explore themes of alienation. The visual fragmentation of the prison with its walls, fences, gates and bars has become for him a metaphor for the psychological fragmentation and emotional pain evident in the broken lives he encounters.

'I have not found it easy,' he explains. 'I felt overwhelmed both by the evil represented in the prison and by my powerlessness to change things . . . The bleakness of prison has forced me to explore ways of saying something authentic about hope and redemption in a context of alienation, brokenness and fear.'[6]

eating, or anything at all within the wide scope of creation, we discover that the good handiwork of God has been drawn into the sphere of human mutiny against God.[7]

This, by definition, includes both artist and art. All the products of human creativity, even the finest and most glorious, are products of a sin-infested world. If Satan can masquerade as an angel of light[8] then evil can surely infect even the most beautiful art.

A distorted view

The problem is that sin is not merely the absence of goodness and truth, but the distortion of it. As Calvin Seerveld writes:

> Sin spells perversion. Sin corrupts what it titillates, dirties what it exposes, puffs up into an empty bubble that breaks what it champions. Sin wrecks things, prostitutes, wastes what could be so fresh and full of laughter.
>
> We can never localize sin, put our finger on the spot . . . because sin is like yeast. It wheedles and weasels through a man or a woman in an undercover way and quite subtly frames a whole undertaking, bends a person's life crooked. And that is the crime of it all! Some people caught by sin never sense the God-damning, God-ignoring barrenness of their self-important, warped perspective.[9]

The Genesis account highlights several aspects of life instantly distorted by disobedience. Sex, childbearing, and one which will affect us as artists – work. Forced to labour outside the garden, Adam's work became 'painful toil'. Rather than joyous service, it became something to be done 'by the sweat of your brow'. No wonder so many artists describe their work as a struggle.

A damaged image

In this fallen state two of the things that are out of skew, God as Lord, and humanity as image-bearer, have a profound effect on the nature of art. Humans are made to worship. If they cease to worship God as Lord, they do not worship nothing, but something. As the apostle Paul told the Romans, society had 'exchanged the truth of God for a lie, and worshipped and served created things rather than the Creator'.[11] Distortion again – showing itself in that very thing that Luther, Calvin and Cromwell were so wary of, the danger of idolatry.

Interestingly, the Bible uses the term 'image' to refer to both human beings and idols. And here we touch on another result of our fallen nature. 'If man is not the image-bearer of God then he is an accidental nothing,' says John Wilson.[12] One need only walk round almost any contemporary art exhibition to see this idea played out. Indeed, commenting on the 'Sensation' show at the Royal Academy, one critic remarked: 'This is how the exhibition leaves you – desperate for someone to say something positive about being human.'[13]

To look at Mark Quinn's *No Visible Means of Escape*, a hung corpse, disembodied with only the skin remaining; Ron Mueck's *Dead Dad*, a three-foot long exact replica of his naked dead father; the Chapman brothers' *Great Deeds against the Dead*, an ironic pastiche of a Goya etching with all trace of passionate anger removed; or even Jenny Saville's nudes and Damien Hirst's ubiquitous sliced cows, is to find yourself asking the same question over and over again: 'Is this all we are?'

And, of course, take God out of the picture and that *is* all – flesh, blood, bone and a few pence worth of chemicals.

But it was never meant to be so. God is *not* out of the picture and that is *not* all we are. As image-bearers we were created to be 'a little lower than the angels'[14] (or perhaps even higher). Humans retain the possibility of being 'everlasting splendours', or indeed the terrifying opposite. The fall may have masked our perception of it, but it does not make it untrue.

Major and minor

Faced with the bleak hopelessness characterised by 'Sensation', many Christian artists see their role as redressing the balance. In the words of the old song, they try to, 'accentuate the positive, eliminate the negative'. But is that really all there is to it?

The apostle Paul exhorted his fledgling Christian converts to think about 'whatever is noble, whatever is right, whatever is pure, whatever is lovely, whatever is admirable'.[16] Given the natural tendency of most of us to think about the negative rather than the positive, it is no bad advice. Unfortunately it has often produced a kind of Christian cheeriness that is both bland and artificial. Christ did not sing 'always look on the bright side of life' as he hung on the cross. To act as if he did, is as absurd and as untrue to the gospel as the Pythons' *Life of Brian*.

Neither did Paul advocate denial. He began his summary of subjects for meditation with the words 'whatever is true'. If as Christian artists we are accurately to portray 'whatever is true', it will inexorably lead us to portray a sinful, fallen world. (Of course, this refers specifically to the representational or narrative arts. Pots, textiles and typography are unlikely to show our 'fallenness' in the same way!) It will lead us to photography that exposes the ugly waste of war; poetry, like the

*There are no **ordinary** people. You have never talked to a mere mortal. Nations, cultures, arts, civilizations – these are mortals and their life is to ours as the life of a gnat. But it is immortals whom we joke with, work with, marry, snub and exploit – immortal horrors or everlasting splendours.*

C.S. Lewis[15]

*Christianity has a
major and a minor
theme. The minor is
that men are lost and
can never attain
perfection in this life.
The major dominant
theme is that there is
a purpose to life
because God is there
and man is made in
his image . . . Real
Christian art should
show both the minor
and major themes.*
    Francis Schaeffer[17]

Psalms, that plumbs the depths of human despair; stories with complex
and confusing characters; and painting that depicts decay and chaos, as
well as beauty and order. 'If you have only the major theme,' says
Schaeffer, 'no one will listen. They will know you are lying.'[18] Truthful
Christian art incorporates both major *and* minor.

Order and chaos

A little aside here might be helpful on the subject of order and chaos.
Time was when scientists and theologians agreed that the universe ran
on orderly, predictable lines. 'God does not play dice,' proclaimed
Einstein confidently.[20] Quantum physics and chaos theory changed all
that and the runnings of the universe turned out to be far more 'random'
and unpredictable than we thought.

The church, always keen to have things tidy and sewn up, found these
new ideas somewhat threatening. Wasn't this just one more argument
that God did not exist? Or that having created the universe, he abandoned it to do as it willed? Worse perhaps, God was playing a cruel
game, not only throwing dice but tossing them in dark corners? And
wasn't contemporary art just as cynical and anti-God? Even Francis
Schaeffer was suspicious of artists like Jackson Pollock and John Cage,
implying that their explorations of randomness in art were no more than
the outworkings of a nihilistic and godless worldview.

Perhaps now we are beginning to realise that unpredictability is not
the threatening thing we took it to be. This 'subtle interplay between
spontaneity and regularity, freedom and necessity' is one of God's creative mechanisms. Chaos (in this scientific sense) is not *dis*order, rather
a way of ordering that we do not yet fully understand. God's world is
even bigger, more complex and more exciting than we thought.

*Modern science has
shown that the
universe is
characterised by a
subtle interplay
between spontaneity
and regularity,
freedom and
necessity.*
    Jeremy Begbie[19]

We need to understand the distinction. Disorder, the destructive
confusion and lawlessness that sin brings with it, is to be fought. As
Christian artists we are called to expose it for what it is. But we also
worship, in Gerard Hughes' memorable phrase, a God of Surprises.[21]
Jesus described the Holy Spirit as a wind blowing where it wills. The
actions of the God of the Scriptures and the Jesus of the Gospels are
anything but predictable. Randomness, spontaneity, untidy outcomes
and unexpected twists – the unpredictability of our world can be both
positive and stimulating and as artists we should not be afraid to
celebrate and explore it. God has given us his serendipity for us to
enjoy.

Louiz Kirkebjerg Nielsen uses a calligraphy pen to lay down small sections of pattern, gradually developing the image in much the same way a town seems to grow up randomly over the years. Her art has that feel of aerial views: places of construction and wilderness, areas of rippled water or untamed vegetation, mapping out not just external landscape but the emotional spaces of relationships. The paths in this landscape lead through tunnels and gaps, into dead ends and

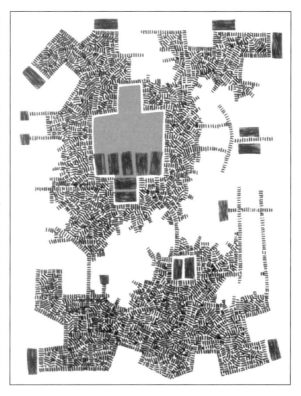

16. Louiz Kirkebjerg Nielsen, *Connecting Paths* (1997), silkscreen print on paper, 56.5 × 42 cm

through chaotic places, finally arriving at some kind of destination.

Life, both internal and external, is never as tidy as we would like it to be, but as Kirkebjerg demonstrates, it can be that very untidiness that makes it so fascinating.

Contrast and complexity

Truthfulness demands complexity. It requires that our biographies, novels or screenplays have flawed heroes. In fact it is impossible to create or portray a convincing 'good' character unless they do come complete with warts, failure and sheer bloody-mindedness. Equally important is to remember that even the worst villains are made in the image of God. Even murderers love their mothers, as *Dead Man Walking* memorably portrayed. In fact, the very best stories are those where the hero sees in his nemesis a reflection of himself, and we, the audience, see reflected in both of them the warring contradictions of our own nature.

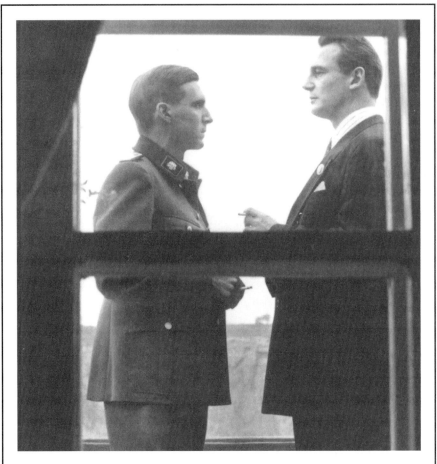

17.   *Schindler's List* (Director: Steven Spielberg 1993)

Schindler's List truthfully portrays extremes of good and evil. It refuses, however, to polarise its characters. Schindler, the German businessman out to make a quick profit from the cheap labour of Jewish prisoners, is no saint. He enjoys a lavish lifestyle and a string of pretty women. He fraternises with the Nazis and sends them presents. Yet faced with the awful reality of the Holocaust, compassion takes over and he becomes an unlikely saviour.

The Nazi commandant is an equally complex character. He feels affection for his Jewish servant, yet shoots Jews for casual sport. It is a tribute to the immense skill of writer, director and actor that we understand not only the great evil in the character but also the humanity. In the moment when he sees his own image in the mirror and is unable to forgive himself, we feel the anguish with him.

Great drama often takes the audience to places and events (such as the Holocaust) that they might rather not visit, because there the heights and depths of human capabilities are most clearly revealed.

All humanity, saint and sinner alike, is locked into the dilemma the apostle Paul describes: 'For what I do is not the good I want to do; no, the evil I do not want to do – this I keep on doing.'[22] Our art will not be true if we do not wrestle with this dilemma. It may mean creating characters who are both confused and confusing – but then the good guys never did wear white hats and the bad guys black!

Yes, there are times when the artist must deal in the stark contrasts of light and darkness: an important part of our Christian calling is to remind the world there *is* still such a thing as a spirit of good and a spirit of evil (although, paradoxically, to do so may mean following in the footsteps of C.S. Lewis and entering a genre called fantasy). There will also be occasions when limitations of time or space, or the understanding of the audience (children in particular) demand simplification.

But to portray the world truthfully as it really is to an adult audience, the artist must learn to create a complex weave of dark and light. It means learning to use the full palette of shades, confident that, if in truly skilled hands, they will not all merge into muddy grey.

Honest and uncompromising

If our commission to be truthful demands that we portray sin, our commission to be holy demands that we do not glory in it. This means treading a fine line – being brave enough to risk falling off on either side and to face the many critics who will undoubtedly disagree on where we drew it. It also means treading a narrow path between using art as an excuse to moralise and making no moral judgements at all. It means developing work with a truthfulness and clarity that shows evil for what it is, without need for pontificating or preaching.

An aside, however, for those of us whose artistic medium is words: it is all too easy to create resistance simply by the language we use. The word 'sin', for example, tends to cause a knee-jerk reaction, simply because it has picked up so many distorted connotations. As writers, our task may be to speak obliquely through creative imagery, or where necessary replace a worn-out word with a new one. We may need to call a spade a shovel: the important thing is to identify it. And this we must do. Sin and disobedience are not popular concepts in our 'If it feels good, do it' post-modern world, but then artists, like prophets, are not always called to popularity.

Our society may be resisting the Christian 'grand story', but it is still looking for answers. However much it resists the biblical diagnosis, it is increasingly aware of the condition. The earth is scarred, the seas are polluted, families are disintegrating, loving relationships bring pain, material comfort brings dissatisfaction. We no longer believe the myth of progress. We may not believe there ever was a home, but we all know we are far from it.

Talking about addiction, psychotherapist M. Scott Peck comments: 'I think that people who become slaves to alcohol and other drugs are people who want, who yearn, to go back to Eden. They are desperate to regain that lost warm, fuzzy sense of oneness with the rest of nature we used to have in the Garden of Eden.'[23] Somewhere deep within each human being is a nostalgia for how things might have been. The Christian message is that all is not lost. There remains the possibility of redemption.

7

Art and the Possibility of Redemption

God did not give up on rebellious humanity after the fall. He never has and he never does. Patiently he formed a people who began to understand and worship the one true God. Endlessly they strayed off to other gods, endlessly he punished, cajoled and forgave to bring them back on the path. Eventually when the time was right, he sent his son Jesus. In his life, Jesus taught and demonstrated what living in relationship with Father God could be. And in his death, by drawing off into himself the poison of sin, he made that relationship possible in a new way.

God in human flesh

The belief that God did not just send messages 'from afar', but took on flesh and blood and bone and walked this earth himself, is what makes Christianity unique among the world's religions. This belief – the incarnation – is a profound comfort to us as we struggle with all it means to be human. It also has profound implications for us as artists. Here was the ultimate demonstration that God could be found in matter – flesh and blood and bone, not to mention bread and water and wine. Here was the ultimate demonstration that to find holiness was not to walk away from all things earthy, but to walk among them.

This idea of God in human form did not come and go with the man Jesus. The story continued as God gave his Holy Spirit to ordinary people and commissioned them to be his body, and it continues to this day.

The chance of a new start

The message of Christianity is essentially one of redemption. Its greatest promise is of life beyond the grave. But it also promises that on this side we have forgiveness, cleansing and the chance to start again.

Redemption is personal. It gives individuals the opportunity to restore their broken relationship with God. And not only with God: 'To be authentically free,' says Jeremy Begbie, 'is to be in appropriate relationship

It is curious that of all the aspects of God which the modern writers can accommodate, it is God's dereliction that they find most accessible: not his power, certainly not his authority, but dereliction.

Ruth Etchells[1]

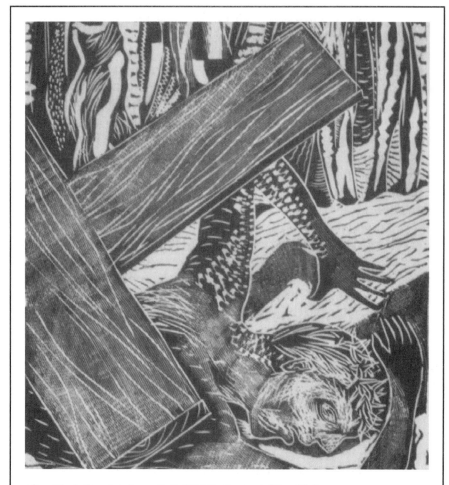

18.   Mark Cazalet, *Jesus Falls* (1990), lino cut, 29 × 21.5 cm

The idea of God as suffering and vulnerable is another of Christianity's unique offerings, and perhaps the one which resonates most strongly in a world stripped of the last triumphant shreds of modernism. Certainly the image of the crucifixion is one that continues to fascinate artists, both Christian and non-Christian alike.

For Jeremy Begbie, it was not a new aspect of God which came in with the New Testament, but one which was there by implication at the beginning.

> The act of creation *ex nihilo* can be construed as an act of suffering or sacrificial love, or at the very least, an act which lays God open to the possibility of suffering. In creating a reality distinct from himself and allowing a measure of genuine freedom, God risks exposing himself to the pain and rejection it can bring. The divine love takes the risk of getting no return for its expense. The vulnerability of the stable at Bethlehem and the ignominious death of an alleged criminal is the self-same vulnerability at the heart of the Creator.[2]

with what is outside ourselves.'[3] Through Christ we discover our true humanity by being appropriately related – to God, to others, to ourselves. Such is the distortion that sin has brought into the world that it may be only after we have experienced redemption that we are free to truly appreciate the glory of the created world around us.

But redemption is more than personal. God sent his Son not only to save individuals but, as Paul asserts, to bring back to himself *all things*. Ultimately it will mean a new heaven and a new earth. 'I am making *everything* new!' is the triumphant assertion of the last book of the Bible.[4] To grasp this cosmic scope of Christ's redemptive work we need to understand that sin can neither destroy nor become indissoluble with the created world. It can only exist as a distortion of something that is inherently good. Al Wolters explains: 'Creation and sin remain distinct, however closely they may be intertwined in our experience. Prostitution does not eliminate the goodness of human sexuality; political tyranny cannot wipe out the divinely-ordained character of the state; the anarchy and subjectivism of modern art cannot obliterate the creational legitimacy of art itself.'[5]

Just as personal redemption has a *now and not yet* aspect, so does the redemption of the material world. God has reconciled us to himself through Christ, says Paul, but it doesn't stop there. He also 'gave us the ministry of reconciliation'.[6]

In order to experience Creator God, we need to experience redemptive God.
William Mather[7]

. . . through him to reconcile to himself all things . . .
Colossians 1:20

A commission to reconcile

Before we go further, we need to make a distinction between two almost, but not quite, interchangeable words: redemption and reconciliation. Redemption means to buy back, to ransom. It is essentially the work of Christ, the only one who could pay the price. Reconciliation means to restore to friendship or union, in this context specifically with God. Again this is part of Christ's work, the final object of that costly redemption. However, now in the era between his first and second coming, it is a task that has been seconded to us, his followers. We are, as it were, to make the initial introductions; we can trust God to do the rest.

Al Wolters agrees that nothing and nowhere is outside the bounds of reconciliation:

The prefix 're-' indicates going back to an original state . . . The practical implications of the intention are legion. Marriage should not be avoided by Christians, but sanctified. Emotions should not be repressed, but purified. Sexuality is not simply to be shunned, but redeemed. Politics should not be declared off-limits, but reformed. Art ought not to be pronounced worldly, but claimed for Christ.[8]

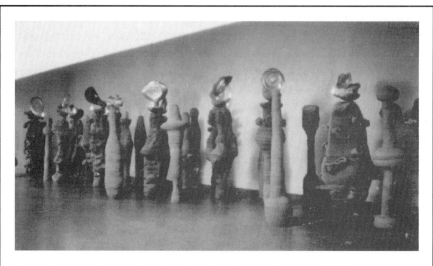

19.   Nicholas Pope, *The Apostles Speaking in Tongues* (1996), terracotta, metal, wick, paraffin and flame, 12.5 × 3 metres

The Apostles Speaking in Tongues is no usual subject for a contemporary installation, and these are no conventional saints. Nicholas Pope's installation shows the apostles as huge terracotta vessel-like figures, rough and misshapen with odd extrusions, both comic and crude. Each is topped with a primitive oil lamp backed by a halo of beaten bronze.

They conjure up a multitude of associations, not least the words of the apostle Paul to the Corinthians: 'For God . . . made his light shine in our hearts . . . But we have this treasure in jars of clay to show that this all-surpassing power is from God and not from us.'[9]

Nicholas Pope says that he is as interested in the evil as in the good. 'I've talked to my Vicar about the Apostles and he tells me they were not good people, but people who became good. People tend to think of evil as over here and good over here [pointing to opposite directions]. But I see them as here and here [very close]. Just down the middle is the meeting point.

'I'm very muddled in my thought. I often contradict myself. I find it quite important to accept that I may be wrong. I've discovered that the closer I get to being wrong, the nearer I am to being right. It happens in belief and art . . .

'Most of my sculptures are made by putting together bits of other sculptures that have failed – the good and the bad together.'[10]

The Holy Spirit alighting on awkward, earthy, misshapen people. In the possibility of reshaping mistakes into something powerful and beautiful, Nicholas Pope seems to have an understanding of redemption. He himself makes no such claim. 'The *Apostles* is about not knowing what you're talking about, and yet being understood. As an abstract sculptor, I like that.'

Reconciliation, then, means not walking away from the world as it is –
media, fine art, politics, relationships or whatever – but having the
courage to invite God's redeeming presence into it.

Our salvation is not something which takes place at the expense of
our calling to tend creation (see previous chapter). The purpose of salvation is the healing of all creation, which includes using our artistic
talents as an offering to God. Chris Gidney, director of Christians in
Entertainment, recalls the reaction of his church when told he was going
into the theatre:

> They said it was a place where sinners were. I said, 'That's absolutely true
> and that's exactly why I'm going.'
>
>   The church has abandoned the entertainment industry, and all too often.
> Satan has claimed it as his own. To our horror, we've found it has grown
> into one of the most influential areas in our society and we have little say
> over it. We've got to chip our way in and say: 'Sorry, this belongs to Jesus.'[11]

Being salt and light is not an optional extra.[12] Salt to the Jews meant both
a seasoning to enrich flavour and a preservative to prevent food going
mouldy. Light is intended for dark places. If we withdraw into the Christian ghetto the world will be darker, more tasteless and rotten for our
absence. Certainly, there may be times when individuals need to with-
draw for a while in order to build new patterns of living, but Christians as
a body have no mandate to abandon any section of society, certainly not
one so vitally important as arts and media. There may be a place for alter-
natives – creating so-called Christian art or theatre – but not at the expense of believers being right in there in the mainstream world of the arts.

'What difference can I make?' will often be the question of a lone
Christian operating in a world with very different values – and it may be
the price of our calling that we ask the question over and over again. We
can be thankful, however, that both the Bible and history are littered
with examples of isolated believers swimming against the tide of their
culture and perhaps even turning it.

*To 'reconcile' means
to pull out of
unrighteous forming
hands whatever they
are busy with and
bring it back to the
Lord. Where the
cultural action is, its
most current market
place, that is the very
place where the Holy
Spirit must be called
into forceful play.*
  Calvin Seerveld[13]

Redemption as subject-matter

Our task as Christian artists is not to portray God's plan of salvation in
three easy stages. Very rarely indeed will we be called upon to tell the
Gospel story in its completeness. What we can do is give plenty of hints.

Often the way we will hint will be to show the redemptive power of
the human spirit – a spirit, as Genesis tells us, that is made in the image
of God. We will show that redemption can come in the darkest places
and via the most unlikely people. Examples of this from Hollywood
include *Schindler's List*, *The Shawshank Redemption* and *Dead Man
Walking*.

In *Dead Man Walking* (director: Tim Robbins 1995),[14] based on a true story, Sister Helen Prejean struggles with the horror of what the condemned man, Matthew Poncelet, has done and with his apparent lack of remorse. She doggedly perseveres, confronting him with the reality of his actions, believing that only by admitting his part in the murders will he gain redemption.

Chaplain's office

CHAPLAIN	The boy's to be executed in six days and is in dire need of redemption. Are you up to this?
PREJEAN	I don't know, Father, I hope so. I've been praying for guidance.
CHAPLAIN	You can save this boy by getting him to receive the sacraments of the church before he dies. This is your job – nothing more, nothing less . . .

Condemned cell

PREJEAN	You been reading your Bible?
PONCELET	I tried to last night. Made me wanna sleep . . . I try to stay conscious . . . I appreciate you tryin' to save me. But me an' God, we got all things squared away. I know Jesus died on the cross for us an' I believe he's gonna be there to take care of me when I appear before God on Judgement Day.
PREJEAN	Matt, redemption isn't some kind of free admission ticket because Jesus paid the price. You gotta participate in your own redemption. You got some work to do. I think maybe you should look at the gospel of John, chapter eight, where Jesus said, 'You shall know the truth, and the truth shall set you free.'
PONCELET	I'll check it out. I like that bit. The truth shall make you free. I like that. If I pass that lie detector test, I'm gonna go free.
PREJEAN	Matt, if you do die, as your friend I want to help you die with dignity and I don't see how you can, unless you start to own up to the part you played in Walter and Hope's death.

*   *   *   *

Condemned cell – before the execution

| PREJEAN | You did a terrible thing, Matt, a terrible thing. But you have a dignity now. No one can take that from you. You are a son of God, Matthew Poncelet. |

It is worth emphasising, however, that while redemptive moments can be powerfully portrayed in film and theatre, they will lose their power if they look too easy. The Christian message is that grace is free, but it is not cheap. Cheap grace will not convince anyone. The Greeks in their tragedies had a typical ending, known as *deus ex machina*. The gods came down in a sort of cage out of heaven, tied up the loose ends and put everything back to rights. A modern audience instinctively, and rightly, balks at this kind of simplistic ending. We know that is not the way things are. Christians, in their desire to communicate the wonder of the gospel, are rather inclined to *deus ex machina*: the main character is converted in the final chapter or last act and everything is suddenly all right. Then they wonder why the critics pan their work. It is true that conversion is indeed miraculous and often apparently simple. But, says screenwriting teacher Bart Gavigan, 'We cannot simply show what is true, we have to show what is believable.'[15] To make an audience believe in the possibility of redemption, it is necessary to dig under the surface and show the cost.

Costly grace is believable – it strikes a chord in those who all too often see Christianity as shallow and hypocritical – and grace is an attractive quality in our brittle hard-edged world. Not for nothing was *Dead Man Walking* put up for several Oscars. Cheap grace – ritual and empty words – impresses no one, but costly love and painful honesty have the power to touch even the most sophisticated Hollywood heart.

But what of those artists whose medium is not story-telling? Is it possible to portray God's saving work in other ways? Redemption itself may be a difficult concept in, say, painting or music, but even the most non-figurative art form can still display its accompanying emotion – hope. In a society increasingly devoid of meaning, hope is a precious commodity. If redemption and hope are deep and genuine experiences in our own lives, the hints will be there. We will take them with us wherever we go – and that includes into our art.

Part 3

Worldview, Worship and the Work of Art:
Applying the Bible to some basic art issues

8

Art and an Integrated Worldview

There are many biblical passages relevant to art which we have not yet discussed, but in working through the most central plot of the Bible's 'grand story' – creation, fall and redemption – we have put in place the beginnings of a worldview. Through these spectacles we can begin to view and perhaps question the many assumptions that are tossed in our direction. Questioning assumptions is, of course, very much the spirit of the post-modern age, but it is also the spirit of Christ. One of the reasons both the Jewish and Roman establishment found Jesus so threatening was that he refused to take for granted many of the 'givens' of his day.

Looking through our biblical spectacles at two of the apparently opposing views we began with – the secular world's quest for the spiritual through art and the Christian world's suspicion that art is too worldly to be spiritual – brings them into clearer focus. We can begin to see why the first gives art too high a role, the second too low.

Strangely enough, both viewpoints lead us back to the same philosophical blind alley: dualism. Dualism is a word that can be applied to any split-vision worldview. It separates God's creation into distinct and opposing realms, one representing good, the other representing evil: holy versus profane, sacred versus secular, material versus spiritual. So it is dualism at work in the abstraction of Kandinsky, Mondrian and Brancusi, believing that to get through to something pure and spiritual, one must strip away all objective representation. It is dualism we see throughout church history, banning organs, dancing, bonnet ribbons, or the 'sinema', as being too worldly. It is dualism we hear in the church that subtly suggests being a full-time Christian worker is more worthy than being a reporter; in the art college that implies fine art is higher than graphics.

However, a truly biblical worldview will not let us get away with such simplistic divides. The Bible frequently speaks in paradox, explaining truths not in terms of *either/or* but *both/and*: creation is both gloriously beautiful and tainted by sin; humanity is both made in God's image and fallen; Jesus is both fully human and fully divine; Christians are both redeemed from the curse of sin and still suffering its consequences. This does not mean that God contradicts himself. Rather these are literary paradoxes, inviting us to dig deeper. If we do so, we will discover that these apparent contradictions are, in fact, all part of a coherent picture of God at work in the world.

There is a *duality* (as distinct from dualism) at the heart of the Christian message – a very real battle between opposing forces of good and evil. But it is not played out in endless legalistic divides: Rembrandt good, Rothko bad; guitars good, organs bad; headscarves good, nose piercing bad – or whatever the latest rule-maker happens to decree. The problem comes when the line is drawn *compartmentally* rather than *spiritually*, putting certain aspects of culture inside the Kingdom of God and others outside. Rather we need to understand that the battle-lines between good and evil run across *all* aspects of culture and *every* facet of life.

Jesus reserved his fiercest invective for the rule-makers and instead used paradox to point the way of discipleship: 'The first will be last',[1] 'Whoever loses his life for me will find it.'[2] Again, it is part of a coherent picture: true status and value (the dignity of being God's image-bearers) lies in fulfilling our role as responsible stewards in willing submission to God. In essence it is simple. But it is never simplistic.

The heresies that dualism encourages are attractive. They are safe and uncomplicated. We know where we are. In contrast, living a life that is both fully committed to our art and fully committed to Christ can seem like a precarious balancing act. Jesus never promised his followers a comfortable life. For the Christian artist that may mean a continued struggle for a biblical path, trying to find the rightful role of both art and artist in our world.

9

Art as a Valid Christian Activity

It's all Greek

As we continue to nail those particular dualisms which are the speciality of the church, we soon encounter another character whose influence has spread over centuries of church history, which is odd considering that he lived and died long before Christianity was even dreamed of, and had not one drop of Jewish blood in his veins.

Plato, one of the noblest philosophers to tread the marble streets of Athens, taught that the material world is just the shadow of a much higher, and eternal, reality in the world of ideas. He saw the soul, immortal and infused with the divine, as being held in the 'prison-house' of the mortal body.[1]

All of this might have become just an interesting example of ancient logic, had it not been taken up by Augustine of Hippo some eight hundred years later. Augustine had dabbled in the beliefs of the Manichaeans, a sect with even more pronounced ideas of the evil nature of matter, before he was converted to Christ. As a bishop he became one of the greatest Christian leaders, but he also embraced many of the ideas of Neo-Platonism and integrated them into his Christian thought. Such was his influence that they have lasted to this day.

Augustine saw the the Kingdom of God as at war with the Kingdom of the World, believing that sensory perception might be real but had no ultimate worth and could give no genuine knowledge. His greatest mistrust of worldly activity was reserved for sex which he saw as shameful even within marriage. Modern psychologists might have a field day with Augustine, who was heavily influenced by his pious mother, and abandoned his common-law wife when he converted. Be that as it may, it was through him that a Platonic worldview became so integrated with Christianity that subsequent generations somehow assumed it was biblical.

Of course, there were texts that could back up this worldview. 'Do not love the world or anything in the world,' said the apostle John. 'For everything in the world – the cravings of sinful man, the lust of his eyes and the boasting of what he has and does – comes not from the Father but from the world.'[2] But we need to be careful to understand what the

I desire to know God and the soul.
Nothing more?
Nothing whatever.
  Augustine of Hippo[3]

It is the Platonist and not the Christian who is committed to avoiding the delights of the senses, to taking no joy in colours, to avoiding the pleasures to be found in sounds.
  Nicholas Wolterstorff[4]

Bible means by 'world', a word with as many shades of meaning in the original Greek *kosmos* as in the English. It can mean variously earth, universe, creation, humanity, or the theatre of history. But the New Testament frequently gives it another distinct meaning: 'the present condition of human affairs in alienation from and opposition to God'.[6] It is to this meaning that John refers when he says we should not love 'the world'. He is warning that sin has permeated all of life, and if we cling too tightly to any human longing it will master us and destroy us.

However, in contrast to those who counsel shunning all the delights of the created world, John also records, in his gospel, that Jesus said he had come 'that they might have life, and have it to the full'.[7] Jesus also told us to trust a heavenly Father who gave his children good gifts,[8] and warned of the criminal waste of burying our talents.[9]

Lord of all

In stark contrast to the position of dualism is a Christian view which sees Jesus as Lord over all areas of life. 'All things were created by him and for him,' claims the letter to the Colossians, and 'in him all things hold together'.[11] It might seem to be Paul carried away by his own rhetoric, had not Jesus himself make the astonishing claim, 'All authority in heaven and on earth has been given to me.'[12]

Unfortunately, many Christians have been taught much more about Christ's lordship of their personal life than their working life. (A recent survey revealed that 75 per cent of Christians have never been taught a theology of work or vocation and 50 per cent have never heard a sermon about work.[13]) They have been encouraged to get very excited about his lordship of the church, but find it somewhat harder to recognise his lordship over the structures of society. The secular world is more easily understood as territory that rightfully belongs to Jesus but is currently in enemy hands.

The problem is right there: it is seen as the *secular* world. A dualistic worldview splits life into two clearly divided realms – sacred and secular – and most human culture becomes identified as the realm of the secular. We have seen how Augustine kick-started this view with his emphasis on opposing kingdoms, but it is a division which really took hold around the beginning of the eighteenth century, when the Age of Reason led to a tacit stand-off between religion on the one hand and science, politics, commerce on the other. Since churches operated by faith it was not felt appropriate for them to meddle in other matters best decided by reason alone. It was not a conscious pact but an unspoken acceptance that society would work better if each power group retreated to its own territory.

And for a while it did work. 'All manner of good came from it,' claims

M. Scott Peck: 'the Inquisition faded away, religious folk stopped burning witches, the coffers of the church remained full for several centuries . . . democracy was established without anarchy, and, perhaps because it did restrict itself to natural phenomena, science thrived, giving birth to a technological revolution beyond anybody's wildest expectations.'

However, as Peck goes on to say, this 'unwritten social contract' proved unworkable and was, in a literal sense, 'diabolic', the word coming from the Greek *diaballein* meaning 'to throw apart, or to separate, to compartmentalise'.[14] The problem is that, under this 'unwritten social contract', life became separated into compartments: sacred and secular. That meant it was perfectly possible to go to chapel on Sunday and make huge profits from a dark Satanic mill on Monday. It still is possible for Bible-believing, hand-raising Christians to work in arms manufacturing, exploitative trading, sensationalist tabloid newspapers, or élitist art galleries and see themselves as having no responsibility for the structures or working practices that surround them. It is regrettable, they tell us, but what choice do they have? 'I don't make the policies. I'm only doing my job. Trying to keep my head down and earn an honest wage.' Such justifications have been used to excuse some of the worst atrocities on earth. This is why an understanding of what it means to be God's image-bearer – to be *responsible* for God's earth – is so important. That is why we need to grasp the subtle damage dualism can wreak.

The word which stands in opposition to this dualism is *integrity* – a state of entireness, of wholeness. For Christians, it is a state that can only be reached when every aspect of our human existence is submitted to the lordship of Christ. If Christ is Lord over all the earth then no structures or practices are outside his concern. If we are his Body, his image-bearers on earth, then none can be considered outside our concern either. Our Christian obedience extends beyond our personal spirituality and into the nitty-gritty of every choice we make each day of the week.

A quick final warning: integrity is not the sole province of Christians. Franky Schaeffer comments, 'Having lived in both communities, I can honestly say I have found as much integrity, or as little, in Hollywood as in the evangelical world of radio, TV and publishing media.'[15] Sadly, his experience is far from unique!

Into all the world

Having unveiled just how far his authority extended, Jesus went on to give what has come to be known as the Great Commission, telling his disciples to go into all the world and make disciples. It is a command that surely encompasses more than geography. It includes the world of science, the world of politics – and the world of the arts.

The more exclusively we acknowledge Christ as Lord, the more wide the range of his dominion will be revealed to us.
Dietrich Bonhoeffer[16]

Most Christians today identify the sacred solely with their personal and individual life, so that their faith has less and less to do with the culture 'out there'. Christians have little influence in shaping culture because their worldview precludes such an influence. If, by chance, Christians do find themselves in positions of cultural leadership, often their Christian faith plays only a minor role in guiding their decisions.
Brian Walsh and Richard Middleton[17]

This command is rightly seen as one for all Christians. The difficulties come when it is seen as negating God's original commission to culture the earth. 'Salvation is not something going on at the expense of tending creation,' points out Calvin Seerveld. 'Salvation is not a makeshift plan God thought up for an unforeseen contingency; it is not something we must suddenly adopt as a crash-plan, and give full-time to, making our original creaturely task impossible, or at best something for our spare time.'[19]

Indeed, it is an irony of church life that those who give themselves most ardently to what they see as fulfilling the Great Commission – leafleting, street preaching, Bible study, intercession – are usually those who end up with having the least point of contact with their non-Christian neighbours. In a recent survey non-Christians assessed Christians as, among other things, 'more boring, more isolated, more unfashionable, having fewer interests, less involved in the real world, less happy'.[20] And then we suggest they come and join us!

Some preachers have got wise to this, and suggested their flock might need to make some forays into enemy territory. (Rarely, however, do they sanction non-attendance at church events in order to do so!) Propping up the bar of the pub, perhaps, or taking up some activity: the art club or the poetry group maybe, 'just to witness, of course'. Who do they think they are kidding? If the would-be evangelists do not actually enjoy real ale and bar stool politics, if they are not passionate about light and colour and form, if they do not love, in W.H. Auden's memorable phrase, 'hanging around words listening to what they say',[21] they will be about as convincing as a fish on a bicycle. But people with an enthusiasm, be it for dance or dahlia-growing, Restoration comedy or restoring old aircraft, are engaging people, even to those who do not share that particular interest. If they have a genuine Christian faith which they take with them into the activities they love, then fulfilling the Great Commission will be a natural activity and not the cringe-worthy turn-off it so often is.

By all means save some?

It sometimes seems that nowhere is the Christian cringe-factor more apparent than in the making of art. The secular world is all too often scornful rather than impressed, particularly with artists who invoke God as an ally. 'I am surprised and disappointed that God should choose so feeble a painter as his instrument,' commented critic Brian Sewell on Cecil Collins' assertion that his art attempted to 'manifest the Face of the God of life'.[22] Murray Watts tells a story, 'doubtless apocryphal', of Sir John Betjeman being handed a poem by a Christian writer with the words, 'The Lord has given me this poem.' 'Scanning the appalling

For his neighbours' sake if for no other reason, the Christian should beware of becoming a person of so few earthly interests that he cannot sustain a conversation, let alone a friendship with anybody outside his religious circle. To have a genuine and discriminating pleasure in some human pursuit is to be halfway toward deserving human confidence and without confidence people cannot be led towards the knowledge of Christ, they can only be prodded.
Derek Kidner[18]

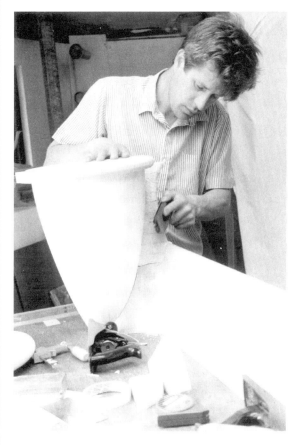

Stephen Owen's love of his chosen craft is engaging and infectious. 'The power, strength, beauty and delight of wood is a renewable resource that God has planned for us. The red-wine fragrance of ash being sawn, the taste of walnut as its timber is worked, the penetrating aroma of cedar of Lebanon is a trip for anyone with a nose. The delicate form of a shaving or the solid mass of a tree – wood as a material gives us so much. No wonder the Lord came as a carpenter.'[23]

20. Furniture-maker Stephen Owen (photo: Hilary Brand)

Working with wood is a passion as well as a lifetime's journey for Owen. Some of his commissions are prestigious and complex while others are more mundane and repetitive 'as a way to pay the rent'. Stephen feels it is as important to be 'thoroughly Christian and thoroughly professional' in the smaller jobs as in the big ones. 'We are God's creation, living for him.'

doggerel, Sir John threw it in the bin with the reply "The Lord has given and the Lord has taken away, blessed be the name of the Lord."'[24]

But if God is with us, our art should be better, shouldn't it? Why is it that so often it seems to be worse? One of the reasons we have already touched on: the lack of a history. The failure of Protestantism to engage with the arts means many of today's believers are starting out disadvantaged by several generations' lack of cultural understanding.

But beyond that, another major factor is undoubtedly the evangelical emphasis on the Great Commission and its preoccupation with the message and the 'word'. The arts in church are all too often seen as little more than 'a colourful wrapping to attract people's attention',[25] a slightly frivolous lead-in to the 'real' activity of communication – the big preach.

There is no doubt that we have a message worth delivering and that the confused world of Generation X is in urgent need of it. However, half-baked art is not a good means to feed the world, however desperate its hunger. *Using* art to convey a message, without understanding the form, structure, materials, techniques and history of the medium, is rather like setting out on a rescue mission on a foggy ocean in an unsea-worthy lifeboat with no navigational skills. Screenwriter Bart Gavigan believes that Christians in the media do have a missionary calling, but points out:

> In the last century missionaries to the third world really believed they were the ones who were giving, they were the rich ones. In our century, through the terrible mistakes, which have been many, missionaries have found a humility that almost no other Christians have achieved. All the great missionaries in our century understand that they're bringing a gospel, but they're also learning from the culture. They understand that if they do not enter into a dialogue with the culture, they cannot bring the gospel.
>
> But I've still had people say to me: 'We now understand the need for dialogue in a missionary situation, but surely here in the first world we can use the media to preach?' I'm appalled. Don't you understand? You're in a missionary situation here. You're called to enter into a dialogue with the world.[26]

Gavigan points to another truth that at first sight seems a contradiction. To establish ourselves as a power and a presence, we must first learn to listen. To bring a message of salvation, we may need years of obscurity and a great deal of uncomfortable wilderness experience. In order to communicate effectively through our art, we may need to let go of all attempts to do so for quite a long time. We must also learn to love and respect our medium. We must earn the right to be heard.

All things work together . . .

A proviso is needed here. God is the ultimate Master Craftsman, and as his apprentices, the more we understand and love both the Master and his work, the more we too will aspire to excellence in our own handi-work. But the biblical God is also the one who 'chose the foolish things of the world to shame the wise',[27] whose 'power is made perfect in weakness'.[28] If in our pursuit of excellence we conclude that God can only work through the highest art, we will be drawing a false conclusion. 'This is too facile,' warns Derek Kidner:

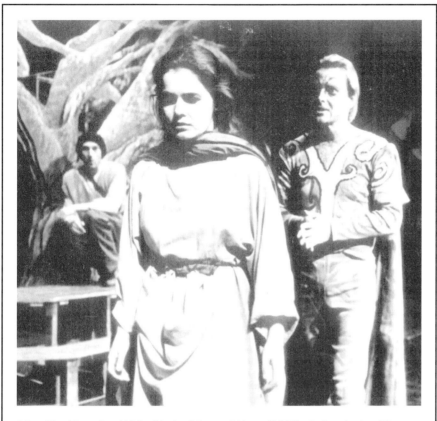

21.   *The Tree that Woke Up* by Murray Watts (1988); Riding Lights Theatre Company (photo: Gerry Murray)

Murray Watts was a co-founder of Riding Lights Theatre Company, a Christian group for whom much of his early work was written. Some of it, published in books of sketches such as *Time to Act*, was widely used by Christian drama groups. Watts, however, has his reservations about some such church activities. Whilst he praises the work of good amateur theatre, he comments that, 'Many Christian groups by contrast, have no particular love or dedication to the art; they are merely intent on "putting over the message" . . . Marshall McLuhan's famous dictum, "The medium is the message," could be adapted to read "The message without the medium" for many Christians.'[29]

Watts' own love and dedication to his medium has won him both awards and critical acclaim. His play *The Fatherland* was winner of the 1989 London Weekend Television Plays on Stage Competition and, despite some critics' initial misgivings about a white man venturing to write about a black family in Soweto, was pronounced 'utterly convincing'; 'a convincing picture of a real society'; one that dealt in both 'tragedy and comedy, poetry and political commitment' and, above all, hope.

It makes the mistake of prescribing for God what He should have, instead of discovering what He prefers – as a child might prescribe for a king nothing but crowns and state robes and be shocked to discover him in tweeds. For there is no doubt that, however we account for it, God has often used the poorest of equipment: not only obscure and weak men, but often their equally unprepossessing products – ugly mission halls, second-rate pictures, bad tunes, illiterate tracts. All these He has so often made to be the gate of heaven to people of all kinds that we might even be tempted to think that the gospel needed the help of bad taste and sentimentality.

Thankfully, Kidner does not end here, but concludes that

We find then, not that God insists on good art or bad, but that he does not restrict himself to either. The connoisseur and the Philistine both need to weigh this fact well.[30]

All things bright and beautiful?

Addressing the question of why Christian writing is so often bad, both T.S. Eliot and Flannery O'Connor reached similar conclusions: both pointed to an observable tendency in Christians to try and make things neater and tidier than they really are. Again this is probably related to our misguided attempts to fulfil the Great Commission. How can we convince people of the truth of Christianity (or so the logic runs) if we express how we really feel? How can we ever bring them to a point of conversion if we leave our stories hanging with inconclusive loose ends?

This is not only an unconvincing tactic, but a false logic, and one that is certainly not borne out by our source literature, the Bible. The Psalms are full of the most (christianly) politically incorrect feelings: 'If only you would slay the wicked, O God . . . I have nothing but hatred for them'; 'May his children be wandering beggars'; 'All our days pass away under your wrath; we end our days with a moan'; 'Why, O Lord, do you reject me and hide your face from me?'[33]

The Old Testament is full of stories that end in the most unsatisfactory ways. Noah is so wise and obedient he survives the destruction of humankind, managing a floating zoo in the process. What happens then? He goes and gets plastered.[34] Moses turns a ramshackle group of slaves into a nation with an identity and a legal system, and leads them to the promised land. What happens then? Um, well, he dies before they actually get there.[35] The New Testament provides us not so much with inconvenient endings as no endings at all. What happened to the rich young ruler, or Lazarus, or the woman by the well? Did Peter really fulfil his promise as the church's rock, or did he just fade out in favour of Paul? Where did Paul get to in the end anyway?

*Why, I would ask, is most religious verse so bad and why does so little religious verse reach the highest levels of poetry? Largely, I think because of a pious insincerity . . . People who write devotional verse are usually writing as they **want** to feel, rather than as they do feel.*

T.S. Eliot[31]

The sorry religious novel comes about when the writer supposes that because of his belief, he is somehow dispensed from the obligation to penetrate concrete reality . . . and that his business is somehow to arrange this essential vision into satisfying patterns, getting himself as little dirty as possible in the progress.

Flannery O'Connor[32]

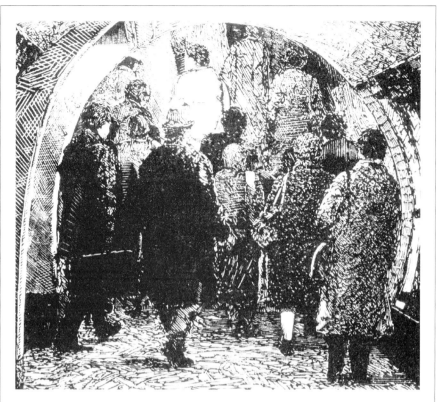

22.   Peter S. Smith, *Leaving* (1984), wood engraving, 13 × 10 cm

Peter Smith's work is unpretentious, the antithesis of 'in-yer-face' shock art. It is the kind of work another artist has described as 'playing with a very small idea, but hitting on its significance and creating a specialness about it'.[36] Or as Schaeffer describes, being 'true to what is there'.

Smith himself refuses to be drawn into making art with a message. 'Once the pressure is there to make a painting "message-orientated" there is a strong tendency to undervalue or ignore the reality of a painting as a painting . . .'

'The question "What does it mean?" often hides a plea for a verbal substitute of the visual experience.'[37] But paintings cannot be decoded verbally, says Smith, and in that sense have no 'meaning'. What they can do is draw our attention to an area of experience and invite us to understand it more. An apparently simple observation – a shuffling crowd in a subway – invites us to a clearer perception of the experience of being human.

Once we understand that Christianity is true to what is there, true to the ultimate environment – the infinite personal God who is really there – then our minds can be freed. We can pursue any questions and be sure we will not fall off the ends of the earth.
Francis Schaeffer[38]

Mixed emotions. Loose ends. The Bible is like this because life is like this. And if life is like this, then our art had better reflect it too. God does not need us as his spin-doctors.

Into all the world

But he does need us as salt and light. Jesus' metaphors for the role of the believer seem more than ever applicable in a post-modern society. Our media are so filled with violence, sexual perversity and profane language that we have been rendered almost unshockable. Our contemporary galleries show an art that is characterised by what one art historian has described as 'disaffirmation and negation'.[39]

Salt played a vital role in peasant society as a preservative and a disinfectant. If Christians are not in there to stop the rot, no wonder contemporary culture has more to say about decadence and disintegration than health and wholeness. If Christians keep what light they have hidden inside the churches, no wonder our arts portray such a dark worldview. What can you expect, asks Calvin Seerveld, 'if no redemptive, imaginatively rich alternative has been engaged in by Christ's body for sustained years of work? . . . We must come to see the unwisdom of having run as far away from plastic art and gritty literature as our sanctified legs can run.'[40]

Jesus does not tell his followers to *do* salt and light, simply to *be* them in the right place. If genuine believers, committed to integrity, are living their faith 'out there' in contemporary culture, they will by definition *be* salt and light. Their life-enhancing properties will flow inevitably 'to the art, through the art, and from the art'. That means that, as they go into the world of the arts, they will quite naturally share their Christian story with those they meet and apply the radical standards of Jesus to the situations they encounter. Their faith will be so much a part of them that it cannot but come out through the medium of their art, whether or not overtly stated. And should their art make them famous or respected, the wider world too will be curious about the 'different drummer'[41] that orders their steps, and they will have earned the right to tell them.

10

Art as a Means of Worship

This chapter is an aside, rather than a main focus of our thoughts, but since many Christian artists will at one time or another be asked to use their art in the service of the church, it it worth examining what, if any, principles are involved.

Graven images

The first biblical reference which comes to mind is naturally the third of the Ten Commandments. The edict against what used to be known as 'graven images' has sometimes been used to prohibit any representational art, and indeed the Jews (and Moslems) have always had a tradition of non-representational art. But any argument that that was the intention can quickly be demolished by a further look at Exodus.

In the same instruction session while Moses is still up the mountain, he is given, direct from God, detailed commands about the Tabernacle. This first Jewish place of worship – the most elaborate marquee ever – contained not only rich ornament, but some works of art that were unmistakably representational. The ark of God was to have two cherubim carved, one at each end,[1] clearly a form of something in heaven. The lampstand was to have cups like almond flowers,[2] and the priests were to wear garments with tassels like pomegranates round the hem. Not just pomegranates, but blue, purple and scarlet ones – imagination was not restricted here![3]

So it was clearly not the making of *images* that was forbidden, but the making of *idols* – something which would be worshipped as a symbol of allegiance to anything or anyone other than the One Almighty God. The same instruction not to bow down to idols appears throughout the Old Testament, most notably immediately after Moses came back down the mountain. He arrived, triumphantly bearing the framework of a new society, a new legal system and a new religion, only to find his fledgling nation in chaos and his second-in-command doing what every politician would do when faced with people power – going with the flow. Aaron had channelled the Israelites' rebellious energy into a powerful image – a golden calf. Was it a symbol of the lush lands of the Nile they had left, or the fertile promised land they dreamed of? It was clearly not an act of trust in the bleak desert God in whom Moses seemed to have invested so many hopes. It seemed more an act of defiance toward Moses himself, and the incident ended tragically in a bloody reassertion of control.[4]

When we encounter idols in the Old Testament we are almost always looking at them as symbols of another worldview, one which threatened to turn the Jews away from their fragile understanding of the One God to a multiplicity of other beliefs and practices. We are also looking at

You shall not make for yourself an idol in the form of any-thing in heaven above or on the earth beneath or in the waters below. You shall not bow down to them or worship them; for I the Lord your God am a jealous God . . .
Exodus 20:4

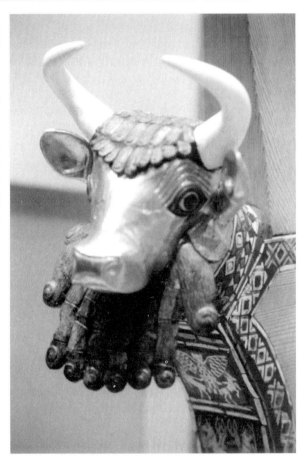

23. Bull's head in gold and lapis lazuli, detail of the Queen's Lyre, Sumerian 2600 BC (British Museum) (photo: Hilary Brand)

Even as the command was being given, the Israelites, tired of waiting, were busy fashioning a golden calf in a desperate attempt to emulate the more powerful nations around them and create their own talisman. Bulls and calfs are common sacred motifs in the early civilisations of the Middle East.

power struggles between the emblems of one tiny nation or another, because that, very often, is what idols were. It is not the idols themselves but what they represented that caused the threat.

Moses kept his people rigorously away from these local gods, but he knew there were times when a symbol was needed. The book of Numbers finds the Israelites still in the wilderness and still rebellious: tired, hungry and thirsty and dying in numbers from venomous snake bites. Moses made a bronze snake and put it on a pole. The people were to look at it, not as something to worship, but more as a symbolic way of standing up to the evil they were facing – a kind of 'face the fear and do it anyway'.[5]

It worked at the time, and the bronze snake was kept for generations as a memorial of triumph over adversity. But in another era, when the worship of other gods once more threatened, its original purpose was subverted and Hezekiah, King of Judah, knew he had to take drastic action.[6] However holy the bronze snake had once been, it was now a danger. He took it and broke it into pieces. No matter how successful a practice has been in the past, no matter how God has used it, it can all too easily take on a life of its own and become something quite different from its original purpose. Sometimes there is no alternative to a little therapeutic idol-smashing.

A fully biblical view must find a way of affirming both the artist Bezalel and the idol-smashing Hezekiah.
Gene Veith[7]

Glittering Prizes

It is interesting to note as a further aside that Jesus never once mentioned images or idols. Even when the Pharisees tried to draw him into controversy about paying taxes with a coin bearing Caesar's portrait, he refused to be drawn. 'Giving to Caesar what was Caesar's' was a necessary evil of an occupied land and did not imply allegiance. The coin was a symbol of another value system that Jesus simply had no part of. He cared about the Jews as people, but he was not going to be drawn into nationalism – his kingdom was not of this world.

What Jesus *did* reserve his anger for, however (Christian record producers, publishers, and concert organisers, please note) was the commercialisation of religion. If there was any smashing to be done it was of money-changers' tables. This is not to say that anything religious should never be sold at a proper commercial rate; rather that the profit motive can easily downgrade religion to anything from twee to downright evil. Neil Postman in *Amusing Ourselves to Death* writes:

One creates not necessarily what one wants to create, but what sells, what is being published, what is fashionable. The concern is to present something that will gain peer approval rather than what one really believes.
Gene Veith[8]

> You shall wait a very long time indeed if you wish to hear an electronic preacher refer to the difficulties a rich man will have in gaining access to heaven. The executive director of the National Religious Broadcasters Association [in the USA] sums up what he calls the unwritten law of all television preachers: 'You can get your share of the audience only by offering people something they want.'

You will note, I am sure, that this is an unusual religious credo . . . As a consequence what is preached on television is not anything like the Sermon on the Mount. Religious programs are filled with good cheer. They celebrate affluence. Their featured players become celebrities. Though their messages are trivial, the shows have high ratings, or rather, *because* their messages are trivial the shows have high ratings.[10]

The profit motive remains one of the great idolatries of our post-modern age. Perhaps we have passed the eighties peak with its credo that 'Greed is good',[11] but shopping remains our favourite Sabbath activity. Whereas in Victorian times the great railway termini were temples to the god of progress, shopping malls are undoubtedly the twentieth-century temples of consumerism.

Art too has its temples, as a glance at the frontages of the National and Tate Galleries will remind us. And was there ever a greater cathedral to art than the Guggenheim in Bilbao? Go inside any gallery and the atmosphere is hushed and reverent. If you dare to touch any exhibit, so swift are the attendants' reprimands that you could almost imagine a punishment of instant death, like the unfortunate Uzzah who reached out and touched the ark of the Lord![12] (The irony, of course, is that as art museums become more like churches, so churches in their turn become more like museums. 'Not one person in 500 goes to the Brancacci chapel in Florence to pray in front of the Masaccios,' points out Robert Hughes.[13])

If worship can be defined as what we give worth to, then a visitor from another planet might conclude that we have a very strange value system indeed. When Damien Hirst can spend eight minutes throwing paint at a colour wheel and get £40,000 for the result, while a teacher in an inner-city school gets £14,000 for a year of developing underprivileged young lives, you don't have to be an alien to wonder if there is something badly wrong.

Jesus called his followers to live by his value system, a very different one from the world's. For some of us that may mean working to overturn an élitist and consumerist set of values – believing that as Christ's body we *do* have the power to turn the world upside down. For others, it will mean quietly going on dancing to a different tune, ignoring the glittering prizes of fame or recognition, or at least holding them very lightly. For that in itself can be a subversive act.

Once a mere collection, the art museum is by way of becoming a sort of shrine, the only one of the modern age . . . Though this art is not a god, but an absolute, it has like a god, its fanatics and its martyrs . . .

André Malraux[9]

Gilded icons

In our earlier dash through church history, we focused only on the Western streams of Roman Catholicism and Protestantism. It is time now to visit briefly that other great strand – the Orthodox tradition – for it is

This temple of the arts and muses is dedicated to Almighty God by the first Governors in the year of our Lord 1931 John Reith being Director General. And they pray that the good seed sown may bring forth good harvests that all things foul or hostile to peace may be banished hence and that the people inclining their ear to whatever things are lovely and honest and whatsoever things are of good report may tread the path of virtue and wisdom.

Inscription in the
foyer of
Broadcasting
House

Television is about the production of needs and wants, the mobilisation of desire and fantasy, of the politics of distraction.

David Harvey[14]

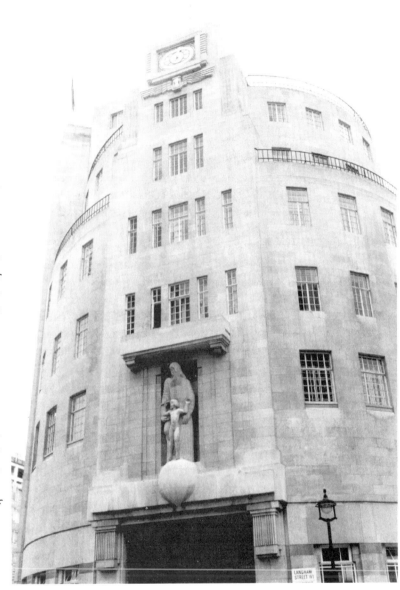

24.   BBC Broadcasting House, London (photo: Hilary Brand)

The BBC of Lord Reith, with its cut-glass accents and announcers who wore dinner-jackets on radio to read the evening news, seems a far-off age. The BBC of John Birt seems run in the service of a very different god. Is it inevitable, or could the broadcast media become once more a temple dedicated to Almighty God?

here we meet another type of religious image, the icon. Usually small painted panels, but occasionally frescoes or mosaics, icons depict holy personages, Christ, Mary and the saints, in a highly stylised manner.

The twentieth century has seen a huge revival of interest in icons. The non-Orthodox world has discovered their power and beauty – but also their strangeness. Drawing on an ancient tradition that has completely bypassed both Renaissance innovations and the Romantic view of the artist, icons are dauntingly and mysteriously different by Western standards of religious art. This is a subject of which we can only scratch the surface, but it is worth digging just a little to try and understand how those differences originated.

It was at the end of the seventh century that the Eastern church formally recognised icons and placed them on a par with the cross and the Holy Scriptures as objects of veneration. But gradually their making spiralled out of control. A rival system of local shrines and local saints grew up across the Byzantine Empire, and for many ordinary people there was no distinction between the holy image and the spiritual reality behind it. It was clear that icons were veering into idolatry and in 730 AD a controversy broke out that was to last for a hundred years.

Behind what came to be known as the Iconoclastic Controversy was a much deeper debate about the person of Christ. It was John of Damascus, a monk in far-off Palestine, who gave the definitive defence of icons. When Christ came, he argued, God's prohibition of graven images was abolished, because God had chosen to be seen in human form.

In contrast, the iconoclasts claimed that Christ's humanity was totally subsumed by his divinity; therefore icons *were* idols. Their opponents countered that to deny icons was to deny the Incarnation of Christ, thereby denying Christianity.

John of Damascus made it clear that to venerate icons was not to venerate the object itself but the person represented. It was wrong to worship an icon, said John. Worship belonged to God alone, but the presence of an icon could instruct and assist the believer in worship.

Eventually in 843 AD his view won the day. Icons became an integral part of Eastern worship, as vital as the words of the liturgy.

But the controversy, in one form or another has never died away: are icons sacred pointers to something beyond, or objects of worship in their own right? Orthodox theology puts icons clearly in the former category and many Westerners are now discovering for themselves their value as windows to a spiritual presence beyond.

There is, however, a fine line between reverence and idolatry – and one that can be crossed in any religious culture. (The adulation given to some preachers in the evangelical tradition seems dangerously near the mark.) Each Christian needs to beware that they do not overstep the line. They should also beware of drawing it across any tradition of which they have only a shallow understanding.

Since the invisible One became visible by taking on flesh, you can fashion the image of him whom you saw. . . I do not worship matter; I worship the Creator of matter who became matter for my sake, who willed to take his abode in matter, who worked out my salvation through matter.

John of Damascus[15]

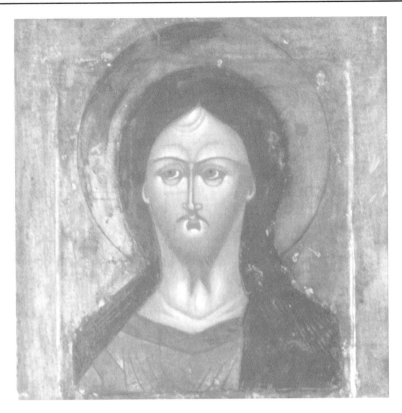

25.   *Icon of Christ* Russian, late eighteenth century (Courtesy of the Antipa Gallery, London)

The great icon painters of the Orthodox tradition have much to teach all Christian artists in their approach to their work. Firstly, it is work steeped in prayer. Secondly, it is essentially humble: most icon painters remain unknown. Thirdly, and controversially, it cuts right across our assumptions about the autonomy and individuality of the artist and the contemporary notion that great art must always create something *new*. There are strict rules about every aspect of icon painting; they are not to come solely from the imagination of the artist and every newly painted icon should resemble as closely as possible those that came before.

Icons are a far cry from the 'one glance' art of the contemporary art world. They are made by a long and complex process: layers of gesso are built up on a wood base, then incised with the image, then gilded, then painted, again with many layers. Icons represent real people but with an air of mystery. They are two-dimensional, devoid of shadow, and lacking or even reversing normal perspective in order to point to something deeper outside time and space. They are about the light behind the image and are made for long and repeated contemplation. If ever art was made to point beyond itself it is the icon.

Help or hindrance

The debate about whether art in worship is a help or hindrance is clearly one that will run and run. Those of us who love the arts may find it difficult to come to terms with those churches which have about as much aesthetic quality as a warehouse. (For some of the newer churches, warehouses are quite literally their homes.) Ugly exteriors, unadorned interiors, movement limited to 'charismatic hopping', music confined to banal songs. Surely the Creator God deserves something better than this?

A crucifix exists in order to direct the worshipper's thought and affections to the Passion. It had better not have any excellencies, subtleties or originalities which will fix attention upon itself. Hence, devout people may, for this purpose, prefer the crudest and emptiest icon. The emptier, the more permeable; and they want, as it were, to pass through the material image and go beyond.

C.S. Lewis[16]

For others, bringing the arts into worship is simply a distraction. A great aria may be a poor tool, points out Derek Kidner, because 'its own radiance and symmetry steal some of the attention due to the message . . . Picture and frame, so to speak, are in competition.'[17] Moreover, worship is not an élite activity. It is one in which all levels of society should be able to come as equals. Highly sophisticated music in this setting can sometimes act as a divide. Isaac Watts, the great hymn-writer of the eighteenth century, made a conscious decision to create hymns that were within the reach of every worshipper: 'I would neither indulge any bold metaphors, nor admit of hard words, nor tempt the ignorant worshipper to sing without his understanding.' It was not an easy decision: 'It was hard to sink every line to the level of a whole congregation, and yet to keep it above contempt.'[18] Watts is a good role model here, writing music and lyrics that were simple without being simplistic, accessible without being trite. The Shakers too provide us with a good example. Simple design need not be bad design.

Those who prefer their worship plain and unadorned are not necessarily Philistines and art-haters. For some, worship is all about coming aside from everyday life, both its drudgery *and* its delights. As we have seen from our trawl through history, those who were most concerned that the church be stripped of its distracting artistry – Luther, Calvin, Cromwell *et al.* – often had a healthy enjoyment of the arts in their daily lives.

Perhaps all we can conclude in this quick look at the subject of the arts in worship is that it will always be 'different strokes for different folks'. Maybe, when we move between the rich adornments of Orthodoxy and the uncompromising plainness of the Brethren, we can only give a hallelujah for the rich diversity that makes up the body of Christ, and add a hearty '*Vive la différence*!'

And maybe we need to remember that the church is the *body* of Christ – it is people not buildings. God has called human beings to be his image-bearers. It is our lives, not our art, that will always be his most potent image.

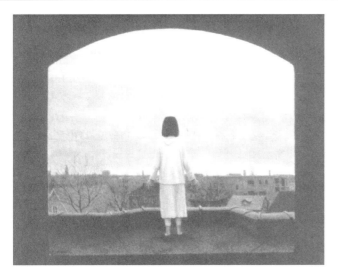 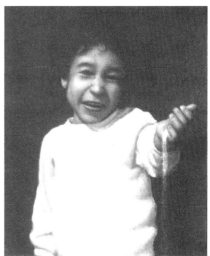

26.   Tim Lowly, *Reba Chapel Paintings* (1993), tempera on panels, 43 × 48 and 23 × 18 cm

These two paintings form an altar-piece for a church in Evanston, Illinois. In the first a woman is looking out over the city from the roof of the church. The second, on the reverse like many icons, is the Lent altarpiece, a boy letting wheat (or is it ashes?) slip through his fingers; a child-like God, holding mortality in his hand. They provide powerful evidence that Christian art need not be restricted to the same old familiar symbolism.

Tim Lowly says: 'I want to make art that one can live with . . . Art that one can come back to repeatedly . . . I hope to communicate on a variety of levels to a variety of persons. No art is entirely accessible to all people, yet the idea of most contemporary artists that the public must climb their aesthetic ladder is unrealistic, élitist and self-handicapping.'

Lowly has written of his interest in working in the icon painters' tradition, creating work that acts as a vehicle for the viewer's imagination and a doorway through which God can enter. 'The images I strive for are those that speak "icon" – towards kingdom, towards God – and are simultaneously non-didactic. They have a life/presence of their own, yet have/are nothing apart from God.'[19]

11

Art in its Rightful Place

In our whistle-stop tour of art history we looked at some of the ways in which art is considered spiritual. These could be summed up as:

- art used in the service of the church
- art containing religious subject-matter
- art as a bridge to the spiritual realm
- art as a reflection of divine beauty
- art as an echo of divine creativity

The first two are more to do with art fulfilling a specific function or containing specific subject-matter and need not concern us here, but the last three deal with the very nature of art itself. We are now in a position to turn the biblical spotlight on these ideas and examine them more thoroughly in the light of our creation–fall–redemption framework.

A bridge to the spiritual

For me, music in particular has given my life a shape and purpose, a spiritual dimension which the more fortunate find in religion.
David Mellor[1]

We have already noted the growing number of people who look to the arts as something which gives them a sense of transcendence – the experience described by one-time Member of Parliament David Mellor when he was Minister for the Arts. It is interesting to note that he sees art as a second-best to religion. As we have commented before, humans are made to worship and if they cannot or do not fill that need with religion, they will find something else to fill the gap. If 'God is dead' but they must still worship something, then art and beauty at least get close.

Is that all this phenomenon of 'art as transcendent' is about – just one of the many manifestations of idolatry? Strange, then, that some Christians also espouse the idea of art as having a special connection with the spiritual realm. For example, C. Nolan Huizenga, in a book of essays on Christian imagination, proposed that 'art is a bridge between the natural and the supernatural, between the earthly and the spiritual. Many of the things we associate with art – beauty, permanence, mystery, perfection –

are qualities that are equally characteristic of God in heaven.'[2] We can deduce from this that 'Sensation' and *Trainspotting* were not the kind of art he had in mind. We can probably identify with him, however, in the experience of more traditional art forms lifting us for a while above our mundane existence.

But we must be careful. The view of art as a bridge brings us very close to dualism once more, with the idea that to experience God we must leave behind our normal existence. It may be that the more abstract arts, music in particular, have a capacity to still the mind and allow time for reflection in a frenetic world. It may be that stopping to contemplate, using our senses rather than our intellect for a while, can awaken some deadened spiritual awareness. It may be that bathing our senses in glorious colour, movement or sound does evoke in us some memory of a lost homeland. It may well be that art, *like any other facet of God's wonderful creation*, can point beyond itself to the Divine Maker. But we dare not claim for art too high a role.

Firstly, we must remember that the whole of creation is full of pointers to the Maker. If we have eyes to see, we will discover him in the pounding waves, in the laughter of children, in the whiteness of a sudden snow flurry, or simply in the work colleague who takes the trouble to ask how we're feeling.

But we must also remember the spreading infestation of sin. Art, like every other human activity, cannot but be broken and flawed. It may not appear so, but sin is deceptive. The line between a *spiritual* experience and an *aesthetic* one is very fine, and the two are easily confused. The very feelings of tranquillity and delight that art gives us can lull us into thinking that we are right with God. The good is all too often an enemy of the best. No doubt there were officers of the Third Reich who felt uplifted listening to Mozart and Beethoven on their wind-up gramophones, after a hard day in the concentration camps. For them it was a welcome *escape* from the cruel activities of their day.

Art can create a longing for God or an awareness of God, but it cannot give us a life lived under God. That involves more than a pleasurable aesthetic experience. A life committed to God can involve difficult choices. It is about our relationships and our work, about what we do with our lives alongside and through the experience of art.

Art is mainly about wrestling with material reality, not striving after a spiritual ideal.
Calvin Seerveld[3]

I see no compelling reason why we should construe art as constantly moving us beyond this material world to some higher realm.
Jeremy Begbie[4]

A reflection of divine beauty

The idea that beauty is an essential feature of art is almost laughably unfashionable in the contemporary art scene. It is still, however, a common assumption in the world at large, and certainly not one to be discarded. However, in the church it is sometimes taken a stage further, as a pro-art argument. Art is beautiful: therefore art reflects the beauty

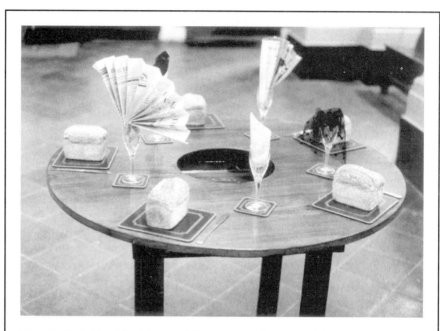

27.   Paul Hobbs, *Hard Hearts Waiting for a Miracle* (1989), bread, fish and mixed media

The table is set in anticipation. Each of the five place settings has a loaf and in the centre two goldfish swim in a bowl set in a bowl set into the table. At the bottom of the bowl, the words 'Hard hearts waiting for a miracle' appear. In the wine glasses the 'napkins' are formed from pages of the *TV Times* and *Financial Times*, a horoscope, a map of a conflict zone and a pair of knickers! The piece questions where people draw their sustenance in life, and reminds of Jesus' frustration that the crowds were so quick to seek a miraculous experience, but so slow to seek the true bread of life.[6]

Beautiful things are those which please when seen. Hence beauty consists in due proportion; for the senses delight in things duly proportioned . . . beauty includes three conditions: integrity or perfection, since those things that are impaired are by the very fact ugly; due proportion or harmony; and lastly brightness or clarity, whence things are called beautiful which have bright colour.

Thomas Aquinas[5]

of God: therefore art is a valid Christian activity. It would seem a reasonable argument, but it is one that demands a little cautious chewing over, rather than swallowing whole.

Beauty, of course, is in the eye of the beholder, but our main focus here is on the traditional notions of beauty: harmony, balance, rhythm, symmetry, proportion, and order. Using these definitions we can easily see why Bertrand Russell saw in mathematics 'a supreme beauty . . . cold and austere . . . sublimely pure and capable of a stern perfection'.[7] We can also see why these kinds of definitions, Greek in origin, have their attractions. They certainly inspired the great medieval philosopher Thomas Aquinas and his contemporaries. They fit somewhat uncomfortably, however, with the Christian view of a fallen world. At best they limit beauty to certain classical notions of composition and design, or a bland 'niceness' of subject-matter. At worst, their emphasis on streamlined perfection brings us back to the Nazis and the horrifying consequences of their obsession with an Aryan super-race. Misfits have no place in this vision of beauty.

Richard Harries, Bishop of Oxford, claims that 'a sense of beauty is essential for belief in God'. His justification for the claim is a valid one: 'Unless a person still has the capacity to be drawn out of themselves to appreciate and praise earthly things, they will no longer be able to pray or love. If they are so locked in on themselves in cynicism that they are unable to appreciate the worth of anything, they will not be able to acknowledge the worth of God.'[8] It is possible for the human spirit to be so deadened that it loses the capacity to wonder. But, it is a short step from Harries' statement to one that says 'an *experience* of beauty is essential for belief in God'. Those who follow this tenet will worship with magnificent music and splendid surroundings, but probably dislike the presence of children and the muddle and noise they inevitably trail in their wake. The person with disability who sings loudly and blissfully out of tune will not be too welcome in their midst either.

The main problem with this claim, however, is not its intolerant consequences, but the fact that it simply isn't true. People in disorder and deprivation cry out to God in their desperation, not because they experience beauty but precisely because of its absence. Conversely, those who are dependent on an experience of beauty in order to believe and pray may find that exposure to a fragmented and violent world will make belief and prayer unsustainable.

If we equate the idea of God too closely with one of beauty we may search for him in vain. Rock musician Bryn Haworth wrote a song about his experience of meeting God in an evangelical fellowship: 'It's a good job I know just what I'm looking for, I never would have guessed I'd find it here.'[9] The Jews expected a Messiah to come and save them. They never expected he would come in the guise the prophet Isaiah described, the suffering servant who we now know was Jesus: 'He had no beauty or majesty to attract us to him, nothing in his appearance that we should desire him. He was despised and rejected by men, a man of sorrows, and familiar with suffering.'[10] We may not only miss God by searching for him in beauty alone, we may be dangerously misled. Francis Schaeffer reminds us that art forms can be used for any message: 'The fact that a great artist is saying it, does not make it any more true than the most lowly man speaking the most awful prose.' Moreover, he points out, 'A beautiful art form can be even more dangerous. It heightens the destructiveness of the message.'[11]

Just because something is beautifully written, it does not mean it is true.

Francis Schaeffer[12]

The Bible has its own warnings about the transitory and unsatisfactory nature of beauty. The cynical (and remarkably post-modern) 'Teacher' of Ecclesiastes discovered that creating a beautiful environment for himself ultimately failed to satisfy. It was 'meaningless' (or in the older and more familiar translation 'vanity'), 'a chasing after the wind'.[13] Ezekiel had the cheery job of delivering a lament to the people of Tyre, one of the most splendid cities of its day. Tyre had claimed (in an early example of PR?): 'I am perfect in beauty.' Pride comes before a fall,

---

Poet Jack Clemo gives the lie to the idea that experience of beauty is necessary for belief in God. Blind and deaf from an early age, he retained a fierce faith in God, whom he found amid the rain and mud and industrial machinery of the bleak Cornish claypits near to his remote cottage.

> . . . I feel exultantly
> The drip of clayey water from the poised
> Still bar above me; thrilling with the rite
> Of baptism all my own,
> Acknowledging the might
> Of God's great arm alone;
> Needing no ritual voiced
> In speech or earthly idiom to draw
> My soul to His new law . . .
>
> . . . All staining rhythms of Art and Nature break
> Within my mind, turn grey, grow truth
> Rigid and ominous as this engine's tooth.
> And so I am awake:
> No more a man who sees
> Colour in flowers or hears from birds a song,
> Or dares to worship where the throng
> Seek Beauty and its old idolatries.
> No altar soils my vision with a lax
> Adult appeal to sense,
> Or festering harmonies' magniloquence.
> My faith and symbol shall be stark.
> My hand upon these caterpillar tracks
> Bogged in the mud and clay,
> I find it easier to pray:
> 'Keep far from me all loveliness, O God,
> And let me laud
> Thy meaner moods, so long unprized;
> The motions of that twisted, dark,
> Deliberate crucial Will
> I feel deep-grinding still
> Under the dripping clay with which I am baptised.

from Jack Clemo, 'The Excavator'[14]

reminded the prophet, predicting: 'You have come to a horrible end and will be no more.'[15]

The Hebrew authors, far from seeing earthly beauty as a 'privileged entry point' to a higher spiritual realm, recognised that beauty is as much part of our broken reality as anything else. The biblical view of our world describes it as one in which a battle between good and evil cuts right across every stratum of heaven and earth. Art and beauty, like every aspect of creation, are caught up in this spiritual battle.[16] That is why they are never neutral and can never automatically be seen as stepping-stones to another spiritual world.

An echo of divine creativity

An argument in support of Christians in the arts is often made as follows: we are made in the image of Creator God, therefore we are made to be creative. Therefore those who make art their main calling bear the image of God more closely than others. It seems such a plausible argument. Yet biblically it is deeply flawed. We may also meet God's image in the exuberant hug of a Down's syndrome child, in the nursing auxiliary who takes the trouble to clean the teeth of her terminally ill patients, in the tuneless singing of a person with severe cerebral palsy, in the way the beggars in the subway look out for one another.

Art is a simile of creation.
Paul Klee[17]

It *is* true (as we discovered in our examination of the Genesis account in Chapter 5) that humanity stands in a special relationship to God, one intended to be both responsive and responsible. It is also true that to exercise those faculties we have been given 'creativity'; the capability and desire to imagine, experiment and make things happen.

But *all* human beings are image-bearers, those the world counts weakest just as much as the high-powered, multi-talented ones. If we find ourselves with both artistic skills and the opportunity to exercise them, then we are fortunate indeed, but we are not higher mortals than any other.

It is a marvellous task and a wonderful gift, to take the vast array of materials God has given us (wood, stone, metal, fabric, silicon, language systems, logic, joints and muscles, facial expressions, young plants, young lives or whatever) and from them 'to bring into being by force of imagination' something that has never been seen or heard before. But it is such a wonderful gift and such a mammoth task – this 'image-bearing' – that to see it as the sole province of the arts is to place an 'unlawful burden' on its back. To elevate artists to the position of mini-'creators' is to lift them above their station.

The important thing is to create. Nothing else matters, creation is all.
Pablo Picasso[18]

It is interesting that the roots of this idea of the artist as creator do not lie in Christianity at all. The first evidence of a comparison between God and the artist appears only in the late fifteenth century, in writings on poetry by Christophoro Landino. Up to that time, and for a long while after it, claiming any similarity was seen to be impious, almost blasphemous. The Christian view was identical to an earlier Greek one. The artist did not make or shape, but merely imitated what was already there in nature. And because nature was already perfect, the artist's main virtue was in his (*sic*) ability to learn and apply the rules by which nature could be duplicated.

It was in the seventeenth century that the word 'creativity' first became used for artistic activity, when the Polish poet Sarbiewski wrote that the poet 'creates in the manner of God'.[21] From then on the concept of the artist as creator became more common, but it was only in the eighteenth century that it really took hold. It was in the age of Enlightenment, and the Romantic movement which was both part of and counter to it, that the cultural climate shifted to emphasise the autonomous power of the human mind. It was a philosophy encapsulated by Immanuel Kant who urged that humans should no longer derive laws *from* nature, but rather prescribe them *to* nature.

At the root of all creativity, one finds the possession of something that is more than earthly fruit.

Igor Stravinsky[19]

It is a long and winding road from Kant to conceptual art, but one can begin to understand how we got from there to here. If it is the creative act that is all important then, as a speaker at a 1967 congress on 'Art in today's society' pointed out, the process matters more than the end result: 'It does not matter what is created as long as creation proceeds. The point is not to have works of art: we have enough of those . . . the object is to have artists, those incarnations of imagination and freedom.'[22]

Making the creative act the focus of artistic activity also accounts for the assumption, particularly in the fine art of this century, that the only art worthy of the name is that which is *new*. It is an idea that has led to many exciting developments, but also to a sad loss. It has brought with it a refusal to learn from the past, or accept anything done in traditional technique as valid art. And it is by definition an accelerating tendency, so that 'traditional' starts to mean anything more than a decade or so old. One begins to wonder whether post-modernity, with its constant ironic 'references' and 'borrowing' from older artworks, signals that *newness* is running out of steam.

The avant-garde poet or artist tries in effect to imitate God by creating something valid solely on its own terms.

Clement Greenberg[20]

What is it that has made 'creating' and 'creativity' take on such cosmic significance for the artists of the last couple of centuries? The Polish aesthetician Wladislaw Tatarkiewicz answers: '. . . because in producing new things, it expands the framework of our lives; and also because it is a manifestation of the power and independence of the human mind, a manifestation of its individuality and uniqueness . . . But above all the cult of creativity is a cult of the superhuman – so to speak divine – capability of man.'[23]

We can now begin to see how the word 'creative', as applied to the artist, carries with it some baggage which is far from Christian. At its worst it elevates the artist to some God-like role as maker of his own world. Even at its best it carries the unspoken assumption that art is a

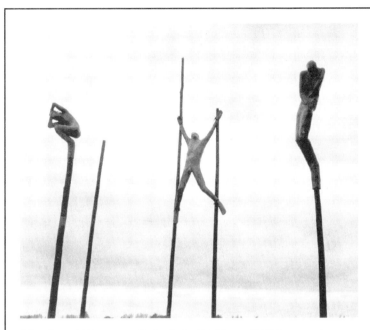

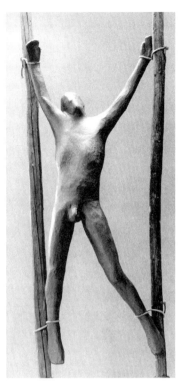

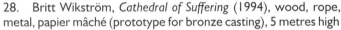

28.   Britt Wikström, *Cathedral of Suffering* (1994), wood, rope, metal, papier mâché (prototype for bronze casting), 5 metres high

Britt Wikström took the raw materials of wood, rope and metal and mixed them with an understanding of the violence, persecution and torture of twentieth-century history, together with her own experience of fear, pain and passivity, and used the force of her imagination to form a three-dimensional image that had never been seen before.

It is not 'beautiful' in any traditional sense of form and colour, nor is it pleasing in its subject-matter. It is about humanity at its worst and ugliest, rather than its beautiful and best. Yet it is steeped in compassion and, because of this, points to something higher. To those with even the faintest folk memory of the crucifixion, it reminds of a God of dereliction who suffers with us.

higher activity than lorry driving or accountancy (although, and here we meet one of the contradictions of this high view of the artist, the pay will undoubtedly be better for the number-cruncher, and probably for the trucker as well).

'The artist in our society is in a very peculiar position,' comments Hans Rookmaaker. 'On the one hand he is regarded very highly, almost like a high priest of culture who knows the inner secrets of reality. But on the other he is a completely superfluous person whom people like to think quite highly of, but are quite ready to allow to starve.'[24]

It is time that Christians at least got the balance right between this high and low view of artists. Art is a responsible job of work, like any other.

It is not wise to perpetuate the myth of artist as 'creator', for it puts an unlawful burden on the back of any serious, young Christian who wants to be an artist.

Calvin Seerveld[25]

Part 4

Seeing, Weighing and Interpreting:
Some attempts at definition and pointers
for assessment

12

Art and a Way of Seeing

If the activity of art is a life's calling, and even (or perhaps especially) if it is not but is something we simply yearn to pursue, then it is vital that we feed that side of ourselves we describe as the 'aesthetic'. The aesthetic is at best a slippery concept, so we must first attempt a definition.

Three people stand in a grove of old oak trees. The ecologist explains that the trees will have to come down to make way for a by-pass approach road. He tells the others how at least 30 different wildlife species have made the grove their home, in particular a rare and miniscule beetle that is his particular study. To his eyes it is a veritable eco-city, teeming with insects, birds, plants and tiny organisms each dependent upon the other.

The second person sees none of this activity. She sees the land bull-dozed and bare, and alongside it a streamlined factory rising. She thinks she can attract Japanese investment to this site, a business venture that will bring employment and much-needed economic regeneration to the region. She is calculating how high a price to offer for the land and what development funds to tap.

The third stands back. He hears the soft rustle of wind and the crunch of last year's leaves under his feet. He drinks in the green glow of the dappled leaves, the dancing shadows, the gnarled lines of the grey-lime trunks. Automatically he reaches for his camera.

Three entirely different responses are evoked by the same trees. All are valid dimensions of the same reality. For the last person it is not economy, politics or ecology that interests him, but the *aesthetic* dimension of the trees. He is not analysing or calculating, but focused on sensing and feeling what is before him.

It's all right, baby . . .

The third person in our scenario is using, psychologists tell us, the right side of his brain. Research suggests (despite many unknowns) that it is the left hemisphere of the brain which is predominantly verbal and analytical, the right which is non-verbal, intuitive and capable of imagination and visualising. Some people are more disposed to use one side than the other when processing information, but no one is limited to only one side. Aesthetic awareness can be cultivated and learned.

In the introduction to her book *Drawing on the Right Side of the Brain*, Betty Edwards extols the benefits of a little artistic activity:

> Many artists have spoken of seeing things differently while drawing and have often mentioned that drawing puts them into a somewhat altered state of awareness. In that different subjective state, artists speak of feeling transported, 'at one with the work', able to grasp relationships that they ordinarily cannot grasp. Awareness of the passage of time fades away, and words recede from consciousness. Artists say that they feel alert and aware, yet are relaxed and free from anxiety, experiencing a pleasurable, almost mystical activation of the mind.[2]

Interestingly, the same experience is often reported by sports-people when in peak performance. At such moments they feel a sense of seemingly effortless achievement. However, the use here of terminology such as 'mystical' and 'feeling transported' may give some clues as to why so many find links between art and spirituality. Both are predominantly right-brain activities, very different from the functional activities which of necessity govern most of our days.

Even if we are not consciously using our right brain, it is still hard at work for us, a fact of which advertisers are all too aware. Aesthetic experience is not, of course, limited to art, nor to the natural world. It is at play in the colour of the detergent packet we pick off the shelf (bright blues and whites work well) and in the music that accompanies us around the supermarket aisles (up-tempo to keep us moving on busy Saturday mornings, softer and slower to tempt us to linger on the late-night round). It is there in the sensuous curves of the coffee jar and the elegant lettering on the shampoo bottle. It is also there in the wording which tells us it is made from 'fresh mountain herbs' and is 'therapeutic and revitalising'.

The aesthetic dimension not only bombards us but defines us. What we put on our mantlepiece, what colour we paint our walls, the texture of the clothes we wear, the shape of the fork and the flavour of the meal – each of these both expresses something about who we are and plays a part in shaping it.

If of thy mortal goods thou art bereft,
And from thy slender store two loaves alone to thee are left,
Sell one and with the dole
Buy hyacinths to feed thy soul.
Gulistan of Moslih Eddin Saadi[1]

The traditional wisdom is that this has nothing to do with moral or spiritual concerns – it is an optional extra, a matter of taste. Calvin Seerveld has another view: 'My point is: the flowers in your life, the plastic a man or woman associates with, the drag or tempo alert to one's singing is the place to look for discovering whether there be an obedient or disobedient aesthetic life exercised before the face of God.' He acknowledges that it is not a life-or-death matter: 'I know that the Lord

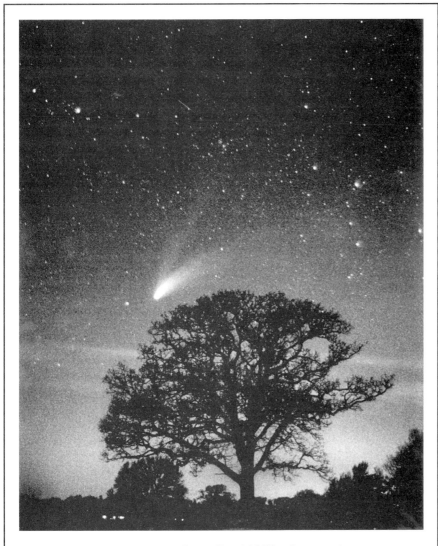

29.   Tricia Porter, *Hale-Bopp Comet* (April 1997), photograph

The power of photography lies in capturing just that decisive moment when a juxtaposition of light, shapes and atmosphere make magic happen. For Tricia Porter it meant patiently tramping through dark fields to find just the foreground for the comet in the evening sky – a combination of the familiar with the mysterious that evokes a sense of wonder.

shall save some without a cultural deed to their name, as if by fire,' but he is unequivocal as to its importance: 'Creaturely life is what the Lord wants redeemed . . . bearing obedient fruit in *all* facets of our existence . . . I am talking about sanctification that is gritty and concrete.'[3] Seerveld believes aesthetic health is as vital to our well-being as physical health.

This brings us back to our earlier look at worldviews. A worldview, fully integrated, will affect all our choices, down to what we pick from the supermarket shelves or how we blow our nose. It also brings us back to the playful Creator and our responsibility as stewards, daily tending the garden he has given us.

But why is this nurturing of the sensory dimension so important? After all, doesn't more good get done by the ecologist and the developer than the person who photographs the trees?

True, a photograph of a tree will not of itself change society. But, returning to our hypothetical oak grove, it may play its part in persuading the locals that it is a cause worth fighting and the politician to divert the by-pass. It may convince the industrialist to plant new trees around her factory, put geraniums on the window-sills and a sculpture in the forecourt. It might even, in keeping before the ecologist a wider picture than his dearly loved beetles, spur him on to lateral thinking or collaborative research that results in some amazing scientific breakthrough. Or it might just remind scientist, politician or industrialist to make time to take their child by the hand and go searching for acorns and conkers.

Of course, since none of these decisions will be consciously linked to the photograph, neither photographer nor publisher will get the credit. Like the vast majority of artists, their contribution to society will be unheralded and unsung.

The aesthetic dimension of life feeds and enriches every other facet. Right-brain aspects of thinking – dreaming, humour, metaphor, play, ambiguity, hunch, fantasy, paradox, intuition – are as likely to help form a good and wise society as are the left-brain ones – logic, deduction, definition, analysis, calculation, focus.

It's all in the game

Talk of aesthetics tends to bring to mind exquisite and expensive good taste. But a healthy aesthetic life is not about being able to afford antiques, designer clothes, or evenings at Glyndebourne. It is just as much about being able to play – not just play as an antidote to work, a quick diversion before going back and working harder; nor just competitive play – be it football, ping-pong or Trivial Pursuit – which can end up being even more serious and determined than work itself.

What we mean is an attitude of playfulness, an approach to life which can permeate even the work itself: taking a few minutes to write someone a silly birthday poem, arranging colourful vegetables in a bowl when there's no money for flowers, paddling in a fountain, making popcorn. Painters having a go at tap dance, dancers dabbling with paint, journalists telling kids stories, film directors making wobbly clay pots – becoming like a little child is a good way to approach both the kingdom

Aesthetic life is not something sophisticated – that's a humanistic lie. Aesthetic life is as integral to being human as building sandcastles on the beach and giving your children names.
Calvin Seerveld[4]

I am convinced that we Christ-followers need an understanding of playfulness if we are going to take sanctification by the Holy Spirit seriously.
Calvin Seerveld[6]

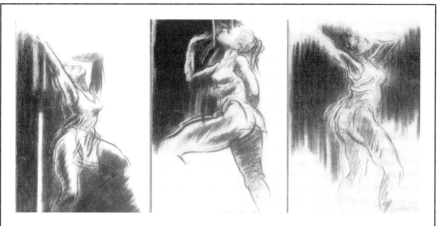

30. Ben Ecclestone, *Just Dancing* (1997), charcoal on cotton duck, triptych, each panel 80 × 50 cm

'I love to capture moments of exuberance and playfulness in my work,' says artist Ben Ecclestone, 'especially dancing. It's one way for me, as a non-dancer, to participate in the sheer enjoyment of movement.'

He also likes drawing children. 'I love the way they come rushing into things with no preconceived ideas of how you are supposed to behave.' Ecclestone appreciates the uninhibited way children approach the making of art. 'I would never want to instruct a young child *how* to draw or paint. The important thing is to give them encouragement and stimulus. When you start insisting, "Do it this way," you will kill all that freshness and expression.'[5]

of God and the business of making art. Children have much to teach us world-weary and inhibited old grown-ups about exuberance, enjoyment and having a good giggle. Laughter has always been the best medicine and being able to see the funny side of our great artistic endeavours may save us from the pain of many a pratfall.

Every child is an artist. The problem is how to remain an artist once he grows up.

Pablo Picasso[7]

It's only make-believe

There are those, sadly often Christians, who say that there is no virtue in reading, watching or listening to fiction. 'It isn't true,' they say, 'so what's the point?' They have, it hardly needs saying, missed the point. Like Picasso's art, there is more truth in fiction than in many a history, biography or documentary. 'Fiction may be perfectly serious,' points out C.S. Lewis, 'in that people often express their deepest thoughts, speculations, etc. in a story.'[8]

One can rarely be fully honest about one's own life. There are always too many people who could be hurt, not least ourselves. And besides,

Art is a lie that makes us realise truth.

Pablo Picasso[9]

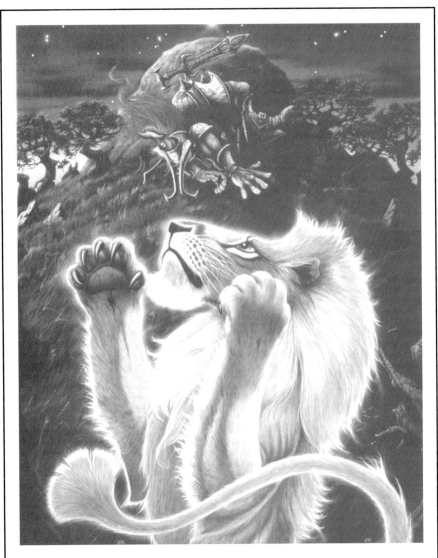

31.   Rodney Matthews, *Aslan and the Dwarf* (1991), inks, 48 × 30 cm (based on *Prince Caspian* by C.S. Lewis)

Fantasy artist Rodney Matthews became a Christian after a narrow and miraculous escape from a bomb blast. He turned away from his previous lifestyle of drink, drugs and women, but did not turn away from the art style. He finds the inspiration for his fantasy landscapes in the Welsh countryside around his home. Gnarled roots become dragon lairs, poppy heads are transformed into sci-fi dwellings, beetles become apocalyptic monsters.

Having had such a dramatic conversion, he has a vivid sense of the opposing forces of good and evil at work in real life, forces that swirl with wild imagination and stunning draughtsmanship around his work.

however genuine and intense our own pains or triumphs, when translated to the page intact, they can somehow turn out incredibly boring or infuriatingly priggish. Nor can one give an accurate account of anyone else's life. There is so much of it that is lived only on the inside. We can recount the facts, but only the barest sketch of the motivation, thought processes, struggle. We cannot get inside the bedroom door, let alone the brain.

If we want to understand what makes other people tick, if we want to get inside the mind of someone of another gender, race, age, or religion, we can do it best by fiction. We can experience circumstances we have never encountered. We can empathise with villains and saints. We can see both sides of the story.

Where does our nation do its ethics these days? Certainly not in the church. Not in the debating chamber or the library. No, the place where our ethics are discussed and refined is the soap opera. Should Peggy accept Mark at the Queen Vic now she knows he is HIV-positive? Should Bianca have her baby with spina bifida aborted? Whether this is the best place for it is arguable. But for better or worse it is the arena where our nation's ethics are being thrashed out and Christians ignore it at their peril.

There is an extension of the 'no fiction' argument which abhors fairy tales. Witches, wolves and wicked stepmothers – what kind of stuff is this to feed into children's minds? 'We want our children to believe that, inherently, all men are good,' says psychoanalyst Bruno Bettelheim, writing on the meaning and importance of fairy tales. 'But children know that *they* are not always good; and often, even when they are, they would prefer not to be.'[10] In fairy stories, the child can confront the monsters within and without.

Traditional fairy stories are not *safe* stories. They are about journeying out into the world, battling against terrible odds but finding help when it is needed. In ancient Hindu medicine a fairy story giving form to the patient's particular problem was offered for meditation to someone going through mental stress. 'The fairy tale is therapeutic,' says Bettelheim, 'because the patient finds his own solutions, through contemplating what the story seems to imply about him and his inner conflicts.' The world of make-believe is far more than trivial escapism. It is a vital right-brain tool helping us to face up to the 'giants' in our life's path.

Poetry emotion?

One of the recognised roles of fiction, be it book, stage or screen, is that of *catharsis*. The word means a purification or purging, and it is a term first introduced by Aristotle. In identifying with the drama, the viewer vicariously feels those emotions which have hitherto been buried deep below. It provides a safe place to draw out feelings – anger, fear, pain, lust – which, exploding into another context, could be dangerous. The same could be said of many other art forms – Francis Bacon's *Head VI* (screaming pope), Samuel Barber's 'Adagio', Leonard Cohen's 'Bird on the Wire', Sylvia Plath's 'Poppies' – articulations of feeling in pigment or sound, that leave us no doubt that the act of making was a catharsis for the artist as well. To 'name' a feeling is to gain a hold over it.

It is one of the great arguments between scholars of the arts as to whether this emotional interaction between artist and audience is the primary one, leaving reason disengaged, or whether the arts mainly engage our faculties of reason. Novelist Flannery O'Connor champions the rational aspect: 'St Thomas called art "reason in the making". This is a very cold and very beautiful definition and if it is unpopular today, this is because reason has lost ground among us. As grace and nature have been separated, so imagination and reason have been separated and that means an end to art.'[13]

It is a nonsense (and perhaps another dualist heresy) that engaging with something emotionally means one cannot engage with it rationally. All great art carries with it both aspects. The examples mentioned above are not simply outpourings on to page or canvas; they are crafted and refined, they engage with us precisely because intellect and emotion are fused.

Of course, as any propagandist knows, it is possible to stir the emotions without the audience recognising the shallowness of the content. Oliver Sacks tells a story of a group of mental patients watching Ronald Reagan make a speech on TV. The patients had aphasia, a condition which renders the sufferer unable to comprehend words as such. Nevertheless they can still understand tone – the way the words are said – and in fact this faculty is enhanced. Watching Reagan, these patients were convulsed with laughter, hearing in his tones nothing but false sincerity and crafty histrionics. One other patient also watching the speech had a different condition: tonal agnosia, where words and grammatical construction are perfectly understood, but all sense of tone and expressive qualities disappear. She too was unconvinced by the President's speech. 'He is not cogent,' she said. 'He does not speak good prose. His word use is improper. Either he is brain-damaged or he has something to conceal.'

'Here then was the paradox of the President's speech,' says Sacks. 'We normals – aided doubtless by our wish to be fooled – were indeed well and truly fooled . . . And so cunningly was deceptive word-use combined with deceptive tone that only the brain-damaged remained intact, undeceived.'[14]

As we engage in makng art (and rhetoric has always been listed as one of the classical arts) we need God-given integrity so that we do not wrongly use our emotional power. And when as audience we engage with the arts that are offered us, we need to make sure we do not leave any of our brains at the door.

I want to make people feel so much they can't help but think.
Murray Watts[12]

Chirpy chirpy, cheap cheap

There is one kind of art that specialises in shallow emotion – kitsch. It is a hard concept to define: one man's kitsch is another man's irony, perhaps. But Chambers dictionary defines it as 'trash, work in any of the arts that is pretentious or inferior or in bad taste'. It comes from a German word meaning 'to put together sloppily', but is most often used not of artefacts that are shoddy but of those that ooze sentimentality – plastic virgins, ducks wearing bonnets, lakeland calendars with sunset views, posters of cute puppies saying 'Smile, Jesus loves you'.

Milan Kundera memorably describes kitsch as art in which there is an absolute denial of shit.[15] Kitsch offers a cosy, comfortable world, a world that is chirpy and cheerful and emotionally cheap. Kitsch trivialises human experience, never enlarges it. It deals in cliché, never new ways of saying something. It is art that is immature, often deliberately babyish. It is high on nostalgia and glitter and low on realism.

The problem with talking about kitsch is that it risks criticising objects which can mean very much to people. The attachment is often based not on the aesthetic qualities of the object but the associations and memories it evokes: a gift from a child, a souvenir of a happy holiday. There is, of course, nothing wrong with that. Any dogmatic condemnation of such items is merely snobbery. In any case, today's kitsch may well be tomorrow's antiques!

However, if Christian artists produce art which is shallow, sentimental and low on realism, they not only produce bad art, they also misinterpret the full Christian experience of living in a broken, albeit redeemed, world – an experience which may contain more lows than highs.

Sadly, many Christian bookshops prefer their pictures shallow, as can be witnessed by their posters and greetings cards. The only way to counter such a trend is to produce more compelling and convincing Christian art which is true, not only to life as people experience it, but also to biblical wisdom.

One final thought to ponder: using the dictionary definition of kitsch as art that is 'pretentious', could it be that there is as much kitsch in degree shows and smart London galleries as in any Christian bookshop?

It is hard to talk with Christian care about kitsch because those who love it are naive about it, unaware they are identifying with something fake and inferior, and those people deserve supportive help, not a sophisticated put-down. It is those who know better, who are making a fast buck on it, or should be deepening aesthetic life Christianly – not fastidiously! – that deserve our righteous remonstrance.

Calvin Seerveld[16]

Memories are made of this

Cliché is a real danger for any artist. Stereotyping, mimicking, repeating a successful formula – making art is such hard work that any short cuts are tempting. There are many ways to reduce this tendency – ruthless editing, soliciting honest opinion, co-working, to name but a few. But

20 December, New York. A sign on Seventh Avenue at Sheridan Square: 'Ears pierced, with or without pain' . . . 14 March. Two nuns in Marks and Spencer's studying meringues . . . 2 September. A young mother passes the house wheeling a pram. She is wearing headphones. The baby is crying desperately.

Alan Bennett[17]

these can only slice out the slip-shod. They cannot replace it with fresh insights if the artist is stale and no longer has anything new to give.

One vital way for the artist to guard against this is in keeping a note-book. It may take the form of a sketchbook or a written journal. It may be a collection of newspaper cuttings, snippets of textiles, snapshots or even sound recordings. The vital thing is that the artist has built up a habit of daily observation and with it an invaluable resource to call upon on that day when the manna of inspiration is thin on the ground, or the work cries out for this or that forgotten detail. Playwright Alan Bennett gives some revealing glimpses of how he does this in his collection of essays and diary entries *Writing Home*. Simple incidents which would pass most of us by are, for Bennett, the raw material of his brilliant and closely observed plays. Look in any newspaper, says another writer, and you will find an idea that can be developed into a story. Record a quarter of an hour of someone talking, suggests yet another, and then transcribe it. At the end of the process, that character and their speech patterns will be inside your head. Every artist and arts discipline will have their own favourite techniques. Each depends on habits, meticulously built up by the artist over a period of years.

Another habit to build up is that of finding out from friends, or from the arts pages of newspapers, what is worth seeing or hearing in art forms other than your own; then making a point of seeing or hearing for yourself that which is most highly recommended, or perhaps most con-troversial. (We are assuming that you not only keep abreast of, but also analyse, developments in your own art form.) No one can have an encyclopaedic knowledge of every development across the arts, but a magpie approach, picking up things here and there, will go a long way to inform and stimulate the artist's own work.

Sounds of silence

It is always worth asking established artists for their tips. One that comes up frequently from many Christian artists is to give yourself space for spiritual reflection – to build up a habit of retreat. It may be in snatched days here or there, one week per year, or a sabbatical month every few years; but for all of us there are times when we need to with-draw. It may be a monastery or convent and formal time with a spiritual director; it may be a country walk or a remote cottage. Whatever form it takes, if we are to recharge both our aesthetic and spiritual batteries, it is an idea worth considering.

Writer Ben Okri has written about why silence is such an important component of the artist's experience:

> Yet the highest things are beyond words. That is probably why all art aspires to the condition of wordlessness. When literature works on you, it does so in

silence, in your dreams, in your wordless moments . . . Art wants to move into silence, into the emotional and spiritual conditions of the world. Statues become melodies, melodies become yearnings, yearnings become actions . . . The greatest art was probably born from a profound and terrible silence – a silence out of which the deepest enigmas of our lives cry.[18]

In similar vein, but with an added Christian dimension, theologian and author Henri Nouwen advocates silence. He speaks of words, but we can safely apply his meaning to any of the many symbol systems that make up the arts:

A word with power is a word that comes out of silence. A word that bears fruit is a word that emerges from the silence and returns to it. It is a word that reminds us of the silence from which it comes and leads us back into that silence. A word that is not rooted in silence is a weak, powerless word that sounds like a 'clashing cymbal or a booming gong'.

   All this is true only when the silence from which the word comes forth is not emptiness or absence, but fullness and presence, not the human silence of embarrassment, shame or guilt, but the divine silence in which love rests secure.[19]

I can see clearly now . . .

In whatever way we can, whether it is in order to produce art or simply to live life to the full, we need to develop a Christian way of seeing. For each of us, growing up into spiritual and aesthetic maturity will mean developing disciplined habits, an alert mind and a playful spirit. It sounds almost impossible, but it is not. God, who wills us to become 'filled to the measure of all the fulness of God',[20] has sent his Holy Spirit to help us turn a task into something that will bless us at every turn.

In fact he enables us not by making us supernaturally strong, but by opening our eyes. The Holy Spirit is that power which opens eyes that are closed, hearts that are unaware and minds that shrink from too much reality.

John Taylor[21]

13

Art and Blurred Boundaries

What is art?

'If all this is art,' griped art critic Brian Sewell in one of his more exasperated outbursts on the avant-garde gallery scene, 'I know no word that fits the work of Michelangelo and Titian.'[1]

One can see his point. Is it really possible to describe the contents of the Sistine Chapel and the Serpentine Gallery with the same word? Has art changed out of all recognition, or do any of the old definitions still hold? How do we know that when two people talk about art these days they are even on the same planet, let alone in the same country? Is there any conceivable definition that can explain what this mysterious beast called 'art' really is?

And why does it matter anyway?

Is there really any point in this quest for definition? After all, artists, scholars and critics have spent the last century or so trying in vain to arrive at even a vague consensus. Why run through all the arguments again?

There are only questions in art – no answers . . . The question is where are we now? But there's no answer.
Norman Rosenthal[2]

The main reason is precisely because this state of flux exists. There is a general recognition that the old concepts are past their sell-by date and that there are no new ones which provide genuine answers. Of course, taking this recognition to its ultimate post-modern conclusions, one might decide that everything is relative, that any view of the nature of art can only be subjective, and what does it matter, anyway?

For Christians who believe in a God-given and God-ordered cosmos, such conclusions are not good enough. Our biblical worldview and our spiritual experience tell us that God *has* put structures and patterns into the universe. Our understanding of them may be challenged by new discoveries; our unfolding knowledge and changing technologies may leave us groping for new patterns – sometimes in the dark – but still we believe there are certain constants in reality for humans to discover. We can and should bring this Christian trust into the world of the arts.

A new understanding will not arrive overnight, but that is no reason to assume there will never be one. It will take a great deal of debate, and it is vital that Christian believers take part in it. Some may claim that the debate is an esoteric one amongst fine artists and academics with nothing better to do. It is true that it centres around fine art – that amorphous mass evolved from the once clearly defined disciplines of painting and sculpture. But it is not esoteric. The same issues, whether overtly or subconsciously, are being worked through in almost every aspect of the arts. Indeed, one of the main issues is this very divide between 'fine' and 'popular'. Knocking down some artificial divisions there can only be a good thing. In any case, the growth of electronic media and computer manipulation means that the map is being redrawn whether we like it or not.

One very non-esoteric and highly practical reason for defining the nature of art is the thorny issue of funding. Public outrage is quickly expressed at anything that is considered 'bunk', be it Carl Andre's firebricks, Rachel Whiteread's house or John Cage's four minutes of silence. No one wants to limit the production of art to only that which is commercially viable, but if it is to be funded from the public purse, then there has to be some means of evaluation. The history of art is peppered with new developments that have shocked people, and we have no reason to believe that will change. But surely there has to be some objective means of deciding what is valid, and surely a bemused public deserves some kind of explanation?

Those artists lucky enough to scrape a living from their art may counter that they are far too busy getting on and doing it to worry about defining it. After all, the argument goes, you can wire up a house without being able to explain what an electron is. True, but suppose someone comes along and tells the electrician with great authority that leaving bare wires now no longer matters. What if someone trained thirty years ago is told that it is now possible to draw electrical energy from the sun? How is our imaginary electrician going to know what is true if he or she has no understanding of how electricity works?

In our rapidly changing culture, many conflicting claims are made about the nature of art. They are often assumed or trotted out without explanation. Some may be absurd. Others may sound absurd but turn out to have more than a grain of truth about them. Christians who are taking their responsibility as artists seriously need to ask some hard questions, and perhaps make some unfashionable statements.

It could be argued that Christians are so marginalised and have so tiny a voice that what we say can have no effect anyway. To answer that one, we must return to our biblical view and one of its recurring themes that God very often chooses the foolish to confound the wise (1 Corinthians 1:27). It may be just *because* Christians come to the art world with such a different perspective that, like the little boy pointing out the emperor's new clothes, we have something worthwhile to say.

The fact that so many books are published that deal with the arts is not a proof that people are sure what art is about, rather the opposite. This quest for meaning in the arts is a sign of crisis in the arts.
    Hans Rookmaaker[3]

. . . words fail us; the glossary dissolves, there are no more terms that really work.
    New York art critic[4]

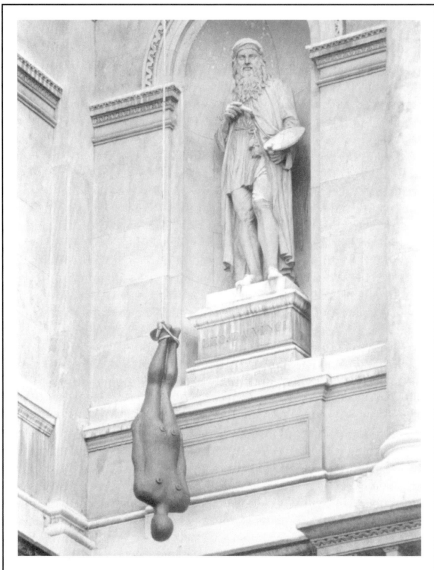

32.   *Gormley meets Da Vinci*. Detail of *Critical Mass* by Anthony Gormley, in the Courtyard of the Royal Academy, London, 1998 (photo: Hilary Brand)

What would Leonardo make of it? Can Anthony Gormley (who creates his figures by taking casts of his own body) have anything in common with the great Renaissance artist–craftsman?

And if Leonardo was baffled by Gormley, what would he make of Hirst, Lucas, the Chapmans and co.? Gormley's work is at least representational, beautiful, made to last and easily appreciated by society at large.

One can go to the Royal Academy and see within the space of a year: Braque, Russian icons, 'Sensation' and the water-colourists of the Summer Exhibition. But can one possibly apply the same criteria to them all?

What art isn't

In order to kick off our investigation, let us look at some statements that have been made about the nature of art, and some of the arguments that counter them.[5]

A work of art is something that makes you see life in a new way. Yes, but taking an ecstasy tablet or going to the Natural History Museum might make you see life in a new way, and neither of those is an art experience. A well-designed office building does not make me see life in a new way. Does that mean architecture cannot be called one of the arts?

A work of art is something that is made with craft and skill. Did Jackson Pollock's action paintings have craft or skill? Surgeons and mechanical engineers have craft and skill. Does that make them artists?

A work of art is something that is beautiful. Sunsets and roses are beautiful, but they are not art. The Sydney Harbour Bridge or Concorde may be said to be beautiful. Are they art? Could Damien Hirst's *A Thousand Years* (featuring a rotting cow's head and thousands of flies) ever be described as beautiful? Does that mean it can't possibly be art? What about Irvine Welsh's *Trainspotting*, Picasso's *Demoiselles d'Avignon*, Bosch's *Garden of Earthly Delights*, or Stockhausen's *Stimmung*?

A work of art must have been intended as such by the person who made it. Rublev's icons, Michelangelo's *Pietà*, Byrd's masses, and African tribal masks were made as artefacts of worship. The makers would have had no concept of them as works of art. Does that mean they are not? A fully plumbed-in lavatory, a jumble sale in a subway, the contents of a student's desk-drawer – all these and many weirder have been exhibited as art. Does that mean anything an artist says is art, must be art?

If it's in a gallery, it must be a work of art. What if you take Carl Andre's firebricks and put them in the corner of a builder's yard? Are they still art? What if the cleaner leaves his mop and bucket in the corner of the gallery? Does it become art? Such confusions have been known!

Where does that get us?

We can see already that while each of these statements defines some aspects of art, none of them will do as a catch-all. Perhaps the best we can do is to adopt the philosopher Wittgenstein's approach when trying to analyse a similar problem. He concluded that: 'We see a complicated network of similarities overlapping and criss-crossing: sometimes overall similarities, sometimes similarities in detail. I can think of no better expression to characterise these similarities than "family resemblances".'[6]

If we are to understand just what the connections are between the motley band of relatives that makes up twentieth-century art, perhaps we had better go back and look at the family tree.

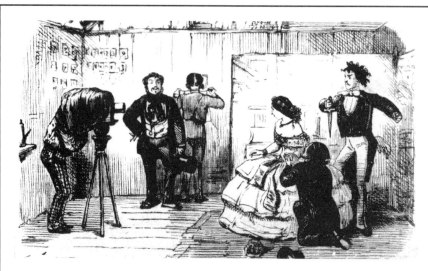

33.   *The Artistic Studio* (1857), print (Mary Evans Picture Library)

When the amazing new art form of photography burst on the scene, an instant reaction was to use it to mimic painting. Eventually the realisation dawned that photography could simply be used to do what it did best – capturing faithfully a real moment in time. Thus painting was released from the need to produce 'exact replicas' of reality and freed to become anything it chose.

The history of art in six and a half concepts

From the classical Greeks to the time of the Renaissance, the word 'art' meant simply a skill or technique. Those activities we group together as 'arts' today were seen in very different categories. Activities requiring mental effort were called *liberal arts*: grammar, rhetoric, music, astronomy and so on. Those requiring physical effort (and therefore deemed inferior) were the *common arts*: painting, pottery, tailoring, building etc. Each of these activities followed laid-down rules. Poetry, interestingly, was originally not an art at all. Requiring inspiration, and therefore not rules, it was on a par with philosophy and prophecy.

It was during the eighteenth century that the concept of 'the arts' as we know them arose. They became known as the *fine arts*, noble and refined activities and entertainments for leisured gentlefolk. Under their elegant umbrella came music, dance, painting, sculpture, poetry, architecture, and the one that somewhere along the line got lost, rhetoric.

Throughout all this long stretch of history the defining characteristic of these fine arts was undisputed: they were all about *beauty*. And beauty in turn had its own characteristics: order, harmony, unity in diversity, symmetry, proportion, balance. But around the time of the Romantics, a new idea was jostling for position. It was that of *the sublime*, a vehement emotion of awe and veneration, both terrible and wonderful, something far more overwhelming and undefined than the measured classical idea of beauty.

It was the philosopher Hegel who took this idea to its logical conclusion. Since some art clearly needed to depict horror and ugliness (medieval crucifixion altar-pieces, Shakespeare's plays), the ugly became part of the beautiful. The upshot of this was that 'beauty' became an extremely vague and eventually almost useless concept as a defining characteristic of art.

During the nineteenth century some other assumed characteristics of art began to be challenged. Since Plato, it had always been assumed that the main purpose of art was *mimesis* or imitation: that is, to copy nature in as convincing a way as possible. But photography, followed swiftly by cinematography, challenged all that. It became clear that painting, which anyway by then was stuck in a shallow rut, was not going to be able to compete. Set free from the need to imitate, painting could do anything it chose.

Art is not a copy of the real world. One of the damn things is enough.
Virginia Woolf[7]

These new technologies posed another question: who was to say they weren't arts anyway? Debate ranged long and hard on the subject. Other innovations – sound recording, radio, television – were hard on their heels and posing the same questions. What was an art form and what was not? If these were included, then what about newspapers, posters, product design? These developments, and other social ones – free libraries, galleries and further education – meant that the arts were no longer the sole preserve of the privileged classes.

The fine arts held their ground with remarkable tenacity and have continued to do so. But the boundaries had disappeared. The arts were no longer the prerogative of refined gentlefolk. They were no longer a matter of beauty, or, since God was dead, even of the sublime. They were not about imitating nature. They did not fit within certain clearly defined disciplines. And so the flood-gates opened on a series of claims and counter-claims as to what this business of art could now possibly be about.

The funny thing was that, even though no one was quite sure how to define it, art was now more important than ever.

Who do we want to be seen with?

Like most families, there are some relatives in the contemporary art world we rather wish we did not have. How are we to decide which of them we want to associate with? Which of them are good role models, and which are the black sheep?

Here are just a few statements made by some of our artistic kith and kin over the last century or so. This is not a comprehensive list and there are many other seminal ideas that are not covered. However, by briefly examining each of them in the light of both a biblical worldview and a long-term perspective of art history, we hope we may be pointing towards a Christian method of evaluation.

Art is for art's sake alone

> Today's real art makes no direct appeal to the emotions, nor is it involved in uplift, but instead offers itself in the form of the simple, irreducible, irrefutable object.
>
> Catalogue of minimal art exhibition[8]

> A poem must not mean, but be.
>
> Archibald McLeish[9]

The *l'art pour l'art* (art for art's sake) movement of the last century claimed that art did not need to justify its existence. It did not need to have a proven purpose or meaning – it simply *was*.

We need to be careful before refuting this. Art can be there for no other reason than to be enjoyed and its 'meaning' is often so subtle as to be indefinable. But there is an arrogance displayed by the 'art for art's sake' purists that is incompatible with a biblical approach. It is the uncompromising distain that states, 'This is my art. Whether you like it or not, whether you understand it or not, really isn't my problem. I couldn't care less.' Hardly the view of a responsible servant.

Art is for contemplation

> The most evident characteristic of a work of art may be termed uselessness.
>
> Paul Valéry[10]

> [What I am saying is:] 'Have a look at this. What do you feel? What do you think?' If people go, 'Ooooh', that's it.
>
> Helen Chadwick[11]

As we have seen, until almost two hundred years ago, art always did have a use – monument, decoration, worship, communication etc. Therefore the Bible, as a product of this earlier age, by definition, always sees art in the service of some other function. Does this mean that art that exists purely to be contemplated is unbiblical? A return to our view of God as creator suggests otherwise. Creation is full of a richness far over and above what is purely functional. The garden that humankind was set to tend was full of all kinds of trees – 'pleasing to the eye' as well as being 'good for food'.[12]

But a biblical perspective also asks some hard questions of the 'art as contemplation' approach. If our task is to be responsible stewards, will we not want our art to serve the world in some broader way? Could it serve better by informing, adorning, commemorating, provoking into action?

The Bible is shot through with what is described as 'a bias to the poor'. As Christians we need to wrestle with this. How can we justify producing work that is seen and appreciated only by a small élite? Shouldn't our work be on subway walls rather than framed in galleries? Shouldn't we be making music in schools rather than concert halls, in the market rather than the opera house? Maybe we need to adapt our artistic 'language' to communicate to the many rather than the few.

On the other hand, the financially and culturally 'rich' may be deeply impoverished in spirit, and God needs his people to be salt and light in every stratum of society.

No easy answers here then, but some questions that we dare not ignore.

Art has no meaning

> Everything is purged from this painting but art, no ideas have entered this work.
>
> John Baldessari[13]

> If you want to know all about Andy Warhol, just look at the surface of my films and my paintings and me and there I am. There's nothing behind it.
>
> Andy Warhol[14]

> [My aim is] to try and do paintings without a state of mind.
>
> Niele Toroni[15]

It's impossible, of course. One cannot do paintings without a state of mind, even if it be numbing boredom. (Each one of Toroni's installations from 1967 to at least 1990 has been done by 'applying patches of paint with a No. 50 brush at eleven and three quarter centimetre intervals', so it seems a fair assumption that he is rather bored with it by now.)

Nor can anyone claim to have created work with nothing behind it. There always is something behind it: a human being with thoughts and feelings, a cultural heritage and a worldview. It was precisely *because* John Baldessari was thinking so hard about art that he created a canvas, blank but for the message above. (His conclusion, incidentally, was to turn his back on painting altogether, staging a ceremony in which all the canvases he had produced between 1953 and 1966 were burned.)

Warhol had, of course, a huge amount of intelligence and creative genius behind his poseur facade, although maybe by the time he made the statement above, he was so consumed by his own publicity that he

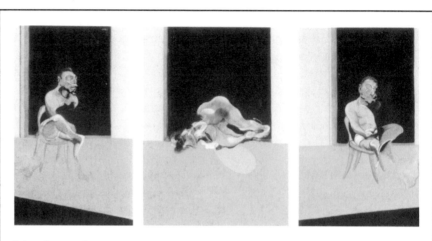

34.   Francis Bacon, *Triptych – August 1972* (1972), oil on canvas, 198 × 147 cm (London, Tate Gallery)

> *All art has become a game by which man distracts himself.*
>
> Francis Bacon[16]

If you believe, as Francis Bacon did, that 'Man now realises that he is an accident, that he is a completely futile being' then it is a perfectly logical conclusion that art is a meaningless game, a distraction to pass the time before the inevitable nothingness of death. Even so, it was a game played in deadly earnest. Bacon believed that the artist's job was now more difficult, 'because he must really deepen the game to be any good at all'.

Bacon himself claimed merely to celebrate the wonderful aesthetic qualities of raw human flesh. But there is something about his figures that is less than human. They are often deformed versions of real images – old masters, film stills, or photojournalism. Caged and alone, they epitomise horror and fear. For the three male figures of *Triptych* there is nothing but the revulsion of their own selves and the black void beyond.

It was not only the futility of life that had turned art to a game, according to Bacon, but the advent of photography. 'Velasquez believed that he was recording the court at that time . . . But a really good artist today would be forced to make a game of the same situation. He knows that particular thing could be recorded on film; so this side of his activity has been taken over by something else.'[17]

really believed it. Often that art which claims to have the least meaning has the strongest philosophical approach behind it. Its meaning is that there is no meaning.

To be Christian is to be convinced that, however inexplicable it can sometimes appear, ultimately life has a meaning and a purpose. For the Christian, human actions are not conditioned reflexes, but choices in which the whole person – body, intellect, emotions and spirit – plays a part. Art, for the Christian, can never be meaningless.

Art can only go forward by negating what has gone before

In this period, if a picture looked like a picture, i.e. something you already knew, it was no good. We tried to make a clean slate, to start painting all over again.

John Ferren[18]

By practice of negation, I mean some form of decisive innovation, in method or materials or imagery, whereby a previously established set of skills or frame of reference – skills or references which up till then had been taken as essential to art-making of any seriousness – are deliberately avoided or travestied, in such a way as to imply that only by such incompetence or obscurity will genuine picturing get done.

Timothy Clark[19]

Art historian Timothy Clark describes one essential feature of the contemporary art scene as a 'practice of negation' – the implication from many quarters being that only by stripping away any vestige of previous convention can anything new be achieved. But the history of art, and indeed the history of the human race itself, would seem to belie this, resembling more a leapfrogging relay than a continual return to the start line.

The author of the book of Ecclesiastes would have had little sympathy with the 'clean slate' approach, writing several thousands of years ago that 'there is nothing new under the sun' (Ecclesiastes 1:9). Perhaps John Ferren, an Abstract Expressionist painter, soon discovered, along with the world-weary biblical writer, that 'what has been will be again, what has been done will be done again'. Possibly he also discovered that the total negation of everything that had gone before ultimately turned art into a dissatisfying activity.

Timothy Clark gives a list of negative techniques which could hardly be described either as responsible stewardship of talent or as challenging creative activity: 'deliberate displays of painterly awkwardness . . . the use of degenerate or trivial or "inartistic" materials; denial of full conscious control over the artifact, automatic or aleatory ways of doing

things, a taste for the vestiges and margins of social life; a wish to celebrate the "insignificant" or disreputable . . . the rejecting of painting's
narrative conventions, the false reproduction of painting's narrative
genres; the parody of previously powerful styles . . .'[20]

The whole 'clean slate' approach makes two rather arrogant presumptions: that new must necessarily be better, and that advancing art
for its own sake must be every artist's goal. For the Christian, whose
prime aim is humbly to serve God and neighbour, neither of these
presumptions fits the bill.

Art is against the system

> I think all the great artistic discoveries and insights have been made in a
> condition of fearlessness on the part of the artist and that's not possible
> where there is subservience to whatever social norm seems to be prevalent at
> the time. In fact, all the artist has got to offer is the ability to dive within him-
> self and not to be afraid to look at society with a very cold eye and to see
> what he sees.
>
> David Cronenberg[21]

> It's self-explanatory, isn't it? Rock'n'roll, by definition, is against
> Thatcherism. And if it isn't, it's not rock'n'roll . . . I'd say rock'n'roll should
> always be anti-establishment – whatever the establishment is.
>
> John Brennan[22]

It is true that the Old Testament prophets were often called upon to
denounce the evils of the establishment of their day. The Bible constantly tells us to fear God and not man, and to stand up for justice.
However, the assumption that great art can *only* be made in opposition
to the social norm is not born out by art history. There is no evidence,
for example, that Shakespeare, Botticelli, Haydn or Christopher Wren
set out to be socially subversive.

Jesus was a pretty anti-establishment figure, so the view of John
Brennan, an eighties rock musician, would seem to have a good prece-
dent. However, it begs some rather obvious questions. Rock'n'roll stars
are not noted for their simple, non-consumerist lifestyles, nor are those
who promote them. In fact, it could be said that the entire rock industry
is Thatcherism exemplified.

Also, as the followers of Jesus Christ have proved many times over,
what started out as against the establishment has almost always ended
up becoming part of it. As Adrian Searle observed, ' "Sensation" at the
Royal Academy is now widely regarded as the moment when
the anti-establishment became the establishment.'[23] Anyone who
assumes it will not happen to them, is on very dangerous ground.

Christians should be prepared to depict and denounce what is bad, but they also have a role in portraying and affirming what is good. They may well be called to question and challenge the establishment, although not necessarily from the outside, and never without a positive alternative to offer.

How do we know?

It seems we have arrived, at the end of the chapter, back where we began – with more questions than answers. Rather than end it there, let us narrow it down a little more and make sure we are asking the right question.

We began by asking *what* is art? Perhaps Polish aesthetician Tatarkiewicz offers us the working definition that gets closest to the *what*. His definition has several advantages: it is open to accommodate all kinds of art, it encompasses different artistic functions and it is free from evaluative terms such as 'beautiful' or 'sublime'. However, although it defines what the intention of the artist is and what is the effect on the audience, it tells us very little about the why and how.

Art is a conscious human activity of either reproducing things, or constructing forms, or expressing experience, if the product of this reproduction, construction, or expression is capable of evoking delight or emotion or shock.
Wladyslaw Tatarkiewicz[27]

Leland Ryken defines art's purpose thus: 'The function of the arts is to heighten our awareness and perception of life by making us vicariously live it . . . There can be no doubt that the arts are one of the chief means by which the human race grapples with and interprets reality.' One way it helps us cope with life, says Ryken, is by allowing us to encounter our own problems at a safe distance, another is simply by 'temporarily removing us from it and then sending us back to it with renewed understanding and zest'.[24]

Hans Rookmaaker, however, was more cautious about defining art by its function. His booklet *Art Needs No Justification* was no defiant 'art for art's sake' tract but a reminder that art cannot be understood simply by asking 'why?':

We cannot try to 'justify' art by saying that it fulfils this or that function. This has been tried in many ways. But even if art fulfils one or another function, that cannot be its deepest meaning. When times change and old functions become obsolete, we put art works in the museum; they have lost their function, but they are still works of art and, as such, are meaningful.[25]

Nicholas Wolterstorff also argues that 'what for?' could be the wrong question: 'The question assumes that there is such a thing as *the* purpose of art. That assumption is false. There is no [one] purpose which art serves, nor any which it is intended to serve. Art plays and is meant to play an enormous diversity of roles in human life.'[26]

But for Calvin Seerveld, it is the 'how?' question that gets us closest to our goal. He asserts that much theory has taken the 'how?' question and twisted it into a 'what?' question, and adds: 'But definition, rightly conceived, gets at only *one*, albeit crucial, *factor* of what may be several necessary ingredients.'[28] For Seerveld that essential factor is found by asking *how* art works, which in the next chapter is exactly what we will do.

14

Art and How it Works

Elusive allusivity

For Calvin Seerveld the characteristic that best defines a work of art is allusivity – a state the dictionaries define as 'hinting or referring indirectly, referring to without explicit mention, referring to in a covert, or passing way'. Art, says Seerveld, can never be, and never has been, simply a carbon copy of reality. Even if it is a film, photograph, sampled sound recording, or a painting using photorealist techniques, what makes it art is that it carries with it this quality of allusion. It suggests, or hints at, something beyond itself. It depicts the subject-matter *as experienced*.

Art: a sensible object or event whose identifiable structure is determined by human construction that is typically allusive in quality.
Calvin Seerveld[2]

Art can evoke a certain mood – sombre, ominous, tranquil, bright or funny – or the feelings of the artist – anger, pain, joy, fear. In doing so, it can hint at ideas: for instance, that progress is good, or that everything is subject to decay. It may simply allude to other events and memories: the potato harvest, the basketball championship.

To illustrate this, let us examine some variations on the theme of shoes. Van Gogh once painted a worn pair of shoes. It was pretty much an accurate representation of the actual leather objects he had in front of him, but in van Gogh's hands they became much more. As philosopher Martin Heidegger described it, 'You are immediately alone with it as though you yourself were making your way wearily homeward with your hoe on an evening in late autumn after the last potato fires have died down.'[1] For him, the picture alludes to a whole way of life: hard and repetitive, humble and uncomplaining, careworn and yet calm. It even raises questions about the nature of life itself. The continual cycle of nature, endless toil – is this all there is?

In contrast, think of the sort of drawing that comes on the end of a shoebox. It does its job efficiently enough, helping the shop staff quickly identify the right product. As a drawing it is accurate enough, showing skill and technical mastery. But it is completely devoid of allusion and therefore would not qualify as art. It merely serves the purpose of efficient communication.

As a further example, look at what happens to trainers in the hands of the advertisers. Nike, Jordan and the like are not simply selling a comfortable product of leather, rubber and fabric. They are selling street-cred and a dream that you too can be a champion. Even if you never go near a basketball court or an athletics track, you can excel, you can be someone, their allusions suggest, simply by wearing these shoes. Although adverts are commercially motivated communication and therefore not, as such, 'art', they nevertheless make use of that same allusive and suggestive character which qualifies art.

Evocative memories

A work of art does not normally make a direct or literal statement. If you try to reduce it to such, you will destroy its power. It communicates symbolically, allusively.
　　　Jeremy Begbie[3]

Representational art can be allusive, but so too can more abstract forms, sound, shape, colour and movement bringing echoes of feelings and forms in the natural world or in ourselves. Such 'echoes' often only emerge when we give ourselves time to look at a work. They also demand an open attitude. As is well known, children often excel in 'seeing' things in abstract works where adults miserably fail. Interestingly, Leonardo da Vinci is reputed to have encouraged his pupils to cultivate this childlike way of looking by inviting them to see battlefields in the stains on damp walls, or elephants and lions in cloud formations.

This way of looking reveals another important principle in art. Contrary to common belief, artists do not usually give form to preconceived meanings, but instead discover meaning in forms. It is through playing and experimenting with materials, be it paint, clay, sounds or computer images, that the artist creates forms which turn out to represent, or *allude* to the way we experience the world. This is most simply illustrated by drawing a basic circle, which by the mere addition of two full stops and a semi-circle – hey presto – transforms into a smiling face. Or similarly, by dividing a blank space with a horizontal line, adding a tiny little stripe on the line and, in an instant, having the beginnings of a Turner seascape. This different way of seeing can suddenly transform a two-dimensional space into a multi-modal virtual reality with infinite possibilities!

Even simple decorative motifs can fulfil such an allusive function. An elementary zigzaggy curving line covering the wall of a primitive tribal mud hut can, in a strange way, bring that wall 'alive'. In fact, as William Morris discovered, decorative devices and design, rather than being at the fringes of artistic practice, are really at the core of it. Most of our commonly accepted motifs, such as flowers, foliage or animals, arose out of purely decorative experimentation. For instance, returning to our mud hut, merely putting one dot at the end of the curved line transforms our abstract decoration into a snake, a symbol of danger, sexuality or cunning. Decorative devices, like dead metaphors, may eventually become so common that they no longer arrest our attention. Some of them may turn into 'picture language' symbols, like the sign on a toilet door. They become 'transparent', unremarkable and unnoticed except for their role in passing on information.

The artist, however, continuously seeks new forms which are arresting in themselves – what Clive Bell, influential critic at the turn of the twentieth-century, called 'significant forms'. Bell never clearly explained what made one form significant and another not. We would suggest that their significance lies precisely in their ability to articulate elusive perceptions and feelings.

Good art creates forms which not only concern an artist's incidental private associations, but which tap into the deeper stock of common human sensations and feelings. It is this that accounts for great art's so-called 'universal' or 'timeless' quality, something which breaks through geographical, historical and social boundaries. It is there in the powerful bulls outlined on the cave walls of Lascaux, the wry wit in Shakespeare's plays, the aching loveliness of Mozart's melodies and the sense of floating in Matisse's paper collages.

I often find, when a story's finished, that actually there are universal truths in there that people can relate to.

Nick Park[4]

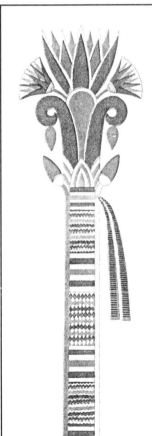

A study of ornament shows how flowers, animals and ribbons emerge in an instant out of simple curved lines. It shows too the rich variety of design in different cultures. Persian, Hindu, Celtic and Egyptian: each embodies some of the characteristic themes of its society – mystery, power, sensuality, the cyclical nature of life. With the benefit of hindsight, even the simplest of shapes can evoke a whole culture, so that the curve of lotus flower carries with it a jumble of associations: Cleopatra, Tutankhamen, Moses and, of course, the mighty river Nile, throughout history the source of Egypt's strength.

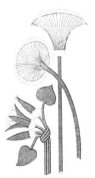

35.   Owen Jones, *Egyptian Lotus Flowers* from *Grammar of Ornament* (1856)

All of us experience sensations which we are unable to grasp because they operate at a subconscious level and, hence, defy verbalisation. The artist manipulates a particular medium in such a way that it can somehow allude to those feelings, making them visible or audible to herself as much as to her potential audience. This explains why there is often a 'surplus of meaning', beyond that which the artist herself originally intended to convey.

Subsidiary ambiguity

The obvious problem with this allusiveness is that it is so hard to capture. It is never a straightforward statement: 'Life is endless toil', 'Young black men can achieve superiority.' Its hinting nature means that it is always multi-signal, oblique and ambiguous.

As we saw, it takes two – maker and audience – for this quality of allusivity to appear. But, maintains Seerveld, that does not mean that the quality is 'intermittent', only there when the audience makes it there. It is a quality inherent in the object itself. However, by its very nature it is one that is capable of a million different responses.

The German Heidegger interprets van Gogh's boots via his memories of the potato harvest – cold and mud and mist. For someone living in Mediterranean climes, it would probably evoke memories of olive groves and vineyards – dust and the beating sun. For an insurance broker, trapped in the city rat race and dreaming of an escape to a country cottage, the boots are a romantic symbol of simplicity and peace. For the teenager who has lived all his life on a remote Welsh hill farm, they epitomise boredom and cultural insensitivity, everything from which he wishes to escape. These reactions to van Gogh's boots will probably not be articulated or even consciously realised. The city broker and the Welsh teenager may both be impressed by the quality of drawing and painting. They will say that they 'like' the painting, or do not, without stopping to analyse why.

In fact, many, if not most, of our normal sensations and feelings *in life* take place at a subconscious level. Jeremy Begbie illustrates this with some concepts from philosopher of science Michael Polanyi. Polanyi describes our perception in terms of 'focal' and 'subsidiary' awareness: 'When hammering a nail into a block of wood, I am focally aware of driving in the nail, but only subsidiarily aware of the feelings in my hand and palm as I hold the nail. I rely on the feelings in my hand in order to perform the task, but I am not aware of them focally.'[7]

Even though such sensations and feelings rarely surface consciously, they nevertheless play an important role in the way we experience life. On a simple level, we may feel uncomfortable in an unheated room, but unaware of the chill until someone comments on it. On a more complex

Art rightly has a suggestion-rich character; art is defined neither by analytical distinctness nor lingual clarity; nevertheless, it presents specific, reliable knowledge for others to grasp.
Calvin Seerveld[5]

In a certain sense, paintings have no meaning, if what is meant by the word is a simple, one-to-one verbal explanation of each element in a painting. A visual statement often brings together a whole bundle of meanings and in that sense is meaningful.
Peter Smith[6]

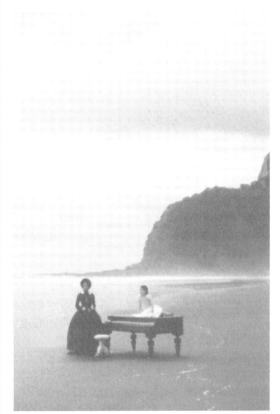
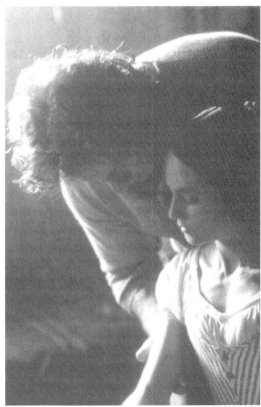

36.   *The Piano* (Director: Jane Campbell 1993)

Films, be they art house or Hollywood, have a convention of 'image systems': recurring images that carry within them one of the themes of the movie. There are often several within one film and they are never intended to be consciously noticed or understood by the audience. In *The Piano*, for instance, the piano itself is not an image system but a more overt symbol – it stands for Ada's lost voice, expressing what she cannot or will not say in words.

But there are other symbolic images which are far less obvious. The whalebone frame of the crinoline, left on the beach, becomes the image of a cage, the conventions of society and marriage in which Ada finds herself trapped, both protecting and imprisoning. The beach itself is a place of freedom and hope, in contrast to the misshapen trees in the oppressive forest where the little community lives in stunted and stifling Victorian propriety.

The music too communicates allusively the characters' feelings, especially so in this story where it quite literally substitutes for the heroine's voice. Michael Nyman explains how he went about it: 'Once I had the perception that since Ada was from Scotland, it was logical to use Scottish folk and popular songs . . . the tone and language of the score then fell into place . . . The sound of the piano becomes her character, her mood, her expressions, her unspoken dialogue, her body language . . .'

One of the characters in the film captures the allusiveness of music when he describes Ada's piano playing as 'like a mood that passes through you . . . a sound that creeps into you'.[8]

level, a mother at home with young children may find her feelings of being undervalued and trapped suddenly brought to the surface by a poem, novel or TV programme. This aspect of art is, of course, heavily used in art therapy.

This does not mean we can put these responses into exact words. Indeed to try and do so would reduce art to a pictorial sign. But they do give us a basis for further reflection and evaluation of the way we experience the world. Polanyi developed the idea into a catch-phrase: 'We know more than we can tell.'

A work of art, then, functions in a way that is both subconscious and ambiguous. Its hints and nuances exist whether or not an audience is present to interact with them, but they *are* interactive, dependent for their power on whether someone is open enough to take the hint, sensitive enough to discern the subtle shades of meaning and feeling, self-aware enough to even notice the memories and feelings the artwork evokes.

Unconditional generosity

The painting, as it truly opens our eyes, will have resonances and echoes which are unpremeditated, unsought and unrecognised by the artist himself.
Peter Smith[9]

If we take allusiveness as our defining factor, we can now begin to see why Christians can sometimes produce such bad art. On an urgent quest to present a message, the tendency can be to dive immediately for a specific symbol, metaphor or allegory as a vehicle for literal meaning. Allusiveness, with its possibility of being understood in many ways, perhaps misunderstood, or perhaps never consciously assessed at all, appears to be not good enough. And if what you want to do is put across a clear message, an article of faith or a statement of dogma, then it is not. You will end up trying to cram into your art form something that cannot ever quite fit comfortably into the frame. Art forms can be used for propaganda of all sorts and frequently are. But they work best as propaganda of the allusive Nike-trainer-type, not the up-front 'Repent and be saved' variety.

Perhaps we can also begin to see why the Christian artist must be a servant. We invite our audience to explore our art with its hints and nuances as they see appropriate. It is an unconditional and uncontrolled gift, entrusted to them with the knowledge that they may use it in more ways than we ever anticipated or intended.

Unnecessary hierarchy

One of the valuable aspects of 'allusiveness' as a definition is that it breaks through the barriers between 'high' and 'low', or 'fine' and 'applied', art.

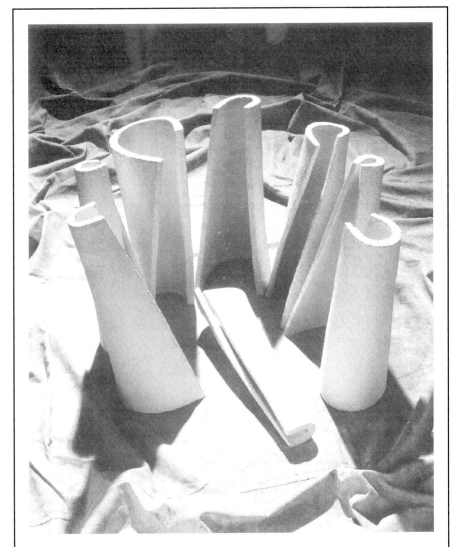

What associations does this work evoke in you? Try a little test by working out your own thoughts before you read on to see the work's title
and the artist's own thoughts.

Whether a work is heard in the concert hall or on *Top of the Pops*,
whether it is installed in a gallery, built to house a newspaper office, or
worn to a party, it can still carry this quality of allusivity.

Allusiveness is not, of course, a criterion for good or bad art. There is
good allusive art and bad allusive art: even if the technical execution of
the work is poor, it is still possible to see within it some allusive qualities.
Allusiveness will also come in varying degrees of subtlety, although this
does not necessarily divide along the fine/applied, high/low fault lines.

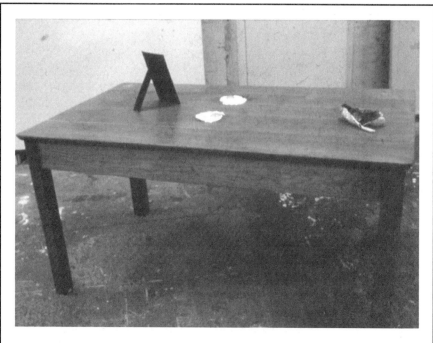

37.   Sarah Lucas, *Two Fried Eggs and a Kebab* (1992), photograph, fried eggs, kebab, table (courtesy of Sadie Coles HQ, London)

Sarah Lucas parodies the schoolboy tendency to see sexuality in everything from mattresses and melons to fried eggs and kebabs. By highlighting the absurd side of allusion, she has a serious point to make about the cultural representation of women.

One could hardly call the visual puns of installation artist Sarah Lucas subtle, even when they are to be found in the Royal Academy. It is true that the more clichéd and conventionalised examples of allusiveness are probably to be found at the popular and folksy end of the art spectrum: as we discovered when we examined kitsch, there is a big market for art that is undemanding.

But it can be in these popular and familiar art forms that the greatest allusive skills of the artist are at work. It is often called 'subverting the genre', taking an art form people think they know – classical ballet, action thrillers, soap operas, photojournalism, pantomime – and slipping into it those little suggestive barbs that point the audience towards new perceptions they never expected to find. P.D. James could serve as one model. Into her detective novels, respected as classics within the genre, she slides insights on the nature of good and evil and the workings of the human psyche, so that her books have a spiritual edge one might never expect to find in something so supposedly 'trivial' and entertaining.

Evolutionary history

The thread of allusiveness can be traced throughout the history of the arts, albeit cloaked in different styles. Whether it was classical allegory, medieval symbolism, Romantic expressionism or surrealist absurdity, the styles changed but the vital task of allusion remained, articulating the way people saw and experienced life in its nuanced complexity. Piecing together the allusions in the artwork of a particular era or comparing similar works in different eras can give compelling insights into the spirit of the age. William Edgar describes how both Rembrandt and Francis Bacon painted a side of beef:

> The comparison is revealing. While both paintings are highly competent, the feeling is very different. Rembrandt's side of beef exhibits a coherent whole. The colours, the composition tell us that this object fits into an orderly world. Rembrandt is fascinated by the object because it allows him to explore the folds, the lines, the intriguing shapes of this totally ordinary thing. It challenges his craft. Bacon's painting carries a very different meaning. One sees only an absurd ensemble of intestines, blood, horror. It is 'more' than a side of beef, it is a symbol of the torn, irrational world which the painter believes to be the real one.[10]

An interesting further comparison might be made here with Damien Hirst's sliced cows.

Seductive subtlety

Allusiveness, of course, comes in many different degrees – everything from the 'Nudge, nudge, wink, wink' species, which makes sure the hint cannot go unnoticed, to the totally baffling and obscure variety. Much contemporary art seems to seesaw alarmingly between the two.

There is plenty of the former, from the likes of Hirst, Lucas, and the Chapman brothers. (As Nigel Halliday comments on the Chapmans' tableau of child mannequins adorned with genitalia: 'The challenge is "Go on, admit it! This is what goes on in your head, isn't it?" . . . The Chapmans seem to make a gratuitous accusation without offering any hopeful solution.'[11]) It is, as Sister Wendy Beckett memorably described it, one-stop art. As an 'in-yer-face' shock tactic, it has a powerful effect, but once you've seen it, that's it. And although sometimes we are reluctant to admit just how baffled we are, there is all too much of the latter.

Allusion is pretty pointless if the audience can find no way of relating to it. This is not to say that they have to share the artist's world, or recognise every suggestive element. They may, on a conscious level be unable to identify what it is that strikes them about the piece, they might never articulate it, but still something strikes a reverberating chord. But one does not pick up a poetry book or walk into a gallery, cinema or theatre and disengage the analytical powers of the mind. The left brain will still be doing its job, trying to pick up the signals and concepts it is convinced must be being sent. 'I'm sure this must be saying something,' it tells itself, 'if only I could understand the language.'

There are two solutions to this problem. Either the left-brained punter must hang around long enough to begin to learn the language (and discern which pieces really are just gobbledygook), or the artist must modify his or her vocabulary.

Well, no, there are three solutions. The third is the most common. 'I don't understand this stuff, so I might as well give up.'

If we don't want the third response, and one assumes that most artists don't, what can we do to make sure it doesn't occur? Art that works, says painter and teacher Iain McKillop, is that which creates an image strong enough to grab attention and then keep the audience intrigued:

> *Not all art has to be profound. Some of the best art can be playing with a very small idea, but hitting on its significance and creating a specialness about it.*
> Iain McKillop[12]

The image needs to be more special than the idea . . . An image needs to be arresting without giving you the meaning instantly – the meaning should gradually appear through it. Therefore, the image has to be one which will hold your attention or stay in your memory long enough for the meaning to unravel. Good art needs allusions that are not hidden but take time to unfold.

He cites T.S. Eliot as an example of 'phrases that go on rolling round your tongue'.[13]

It may be that this haunting longer-term effect is achieved with images of rich complexity – there is simply a lot to digest. But it can also work with essentially simple images, like the effect that an exhibition of Braque's paintings had on Germaine Greer: 'I felt as if I wanted to take my duvet and sleep there, so I could wake up and look and go back to sleep again.'[14]

It may be that true appreciation of the most simple images demands a certain simplicity of spirit. *Observer* reporter Tim Adams, commenting on an exhibition of Ellsworth Kelly's bold abstract shapes, noted the reactions of visitors – a few giggles, some outrage, some indifference: 'A woman in a green and blue hooped shirt exclaims indignantly and predictably: "I could do that," and her friend in a back-to-front cap suggests glumly, "Yeah, but he thought of it first, stoopid." The only viewer who seems to share the enthusiasm of the New York art world is a four-year-old boy. "Wowww, Dad!" he yells to his parent. "*Come and see this!*" '

Kelly himself comments on his work: 'People say, "Oh, what does it mean?" But what I want is an ambience . . . Because our eyes are open all the time, we get so used to thinking we know what we can see . . . When I have an exhibition I want people to move round the paintings and see different things in them. This one [a blue arc] can be all the curves you've ever seen in that colour.'

Adams himself remarks that a visit to Kelly's studio made him begin to 'see Ellsworth Kellys even where they are not'. Which, of course, is the point.[15]

Appropriate vocabulary

Consider the following words: *fit, wicked, cool, gay, let*. When the lads at the nineties disco say a girl is *fit*, they do not mean she is in good health. They mean she is attractive, or perhaps a *peach* (forties), *dishy* (sixties), or *foxy* (eighties). Slang changes rapidly. It may fade out or become part of the language. *Cool* as a 'term of approval' has long joined 'slightly cold' in the dictionary pages. *Wicked* is well on the way, totally reversing its meaning from bad to good, depending on the inflection and tone of voice. *Let* has already reversed itself: several centuries ago it meant to hinder, now it means to allow. *Gay*, of course, has so changed in three decades or so that even if it is used in its original and technically accurate form of 'lively, bright and merry', it has lost its innocence. It can never now shake off its other allusions.

It is not just time that affects language, but also place and worldview. Missionaries of the last century going to some countries, such as Japan, found it difficult to preach the Christian message. Some of the words they needed simply weren't there.

Words are just one type of language or symbol system. The arts have many others, all of which emerged from specific historic contexts to help formulate our perceptions of life. Certain shapes, colours and sounds, for instance, come to represent particular feelings or moods. Dark colours represented the dangers of the night and became associated with fear and gloom. Bright colours represented the warmth of the sun and carried a cheerful meaning. Such 'meanings' have gradually become part and parcel of our stock communication, even when the origin is long forgotten. However, as with words, such associations are not static and can change in different cultural circumstances.

With colour, for instance, in Britain black signifies mourning and white traditionally stands for bridal purity. In some Eastern countries it is white that signifies death (possibly because death is viewed more philosophically?) and brides are decked out as colourfully as possible. Indeed, the changing use of words may also dictate the changing symbolism of colour: in a society which has adopted 'black' as a proud description for Afro-Caribbean races, the Western tradition of 'black' as a word symbolising evil is necessarily under review.

We [Christians] have the dilemma of using a symbol system, that was not made for our worldview, to give our worldview . . . I think the thing we're waiting for is a genius to come forth who can either make a new symbol system which is still modern, or more properly, as symbol systems don't come overnight, a group of people to modify the symbol systems of our day so that we can use them for our Christian message without a disadvantage.

Francis Schaeffer[16]

It quickly becomes clear that artists should approach symbolism with respect and caution. Christians should perhaps take extra care.

We have already commented that Christians love symbols. We are saturated with them from baptism onwards. But we have a problem. Many are universal symbols, such as bread, wine, rainbow, water; even those who have not the slightest Christian heritage can understand something of their meaning. But others, including cross, water, vine, lamb, are linked to a period of Roman history, a Mediterranean climate and a farming culture.

You may notice that water appeared in both lists. It is indeed a universal symbol and one need only look at films like *Rain Man* and *Shine* to see its potency. But when the Psalmist originally sang, 'He covers the sky with clouds, he supplies the earth with rain' it was in parched, dusty, unirrigated Israel where even the wells would sometimes run dry. When the church choir sings it on a drizzly British February morning, to a congregation who take for granted their sinks, baths, showers and hosepipes, the allusions are very different. This does not mean that rain can never be used as a metaphor of blessing, but it does mean you may first need to set up a contrary metaphor of desert, or water as a hostile force. (*Shine* makes an over-the-top but wonderful use of water as an image system. What is fascinating is how it progresses from rain storms, signifying pressure and tension, to swimming, signifying freedom and release.)

What of the cross, that most central of Christian symbols? After two millennia of Christendom, it can never regain the stark shame and horror it evoked in first-century Palestine. It would take a gibbet or an electric chair to do that (although, according to C.S. Lewis, 'the Crucifixion did not become a frequent motive for Christians until the generations that had seen real crucifixions were all dead'[17]).

But for better or worse, the cross now carries a host of other allusions – authority figures, power structures, jewelry, ornamentation, tradition, guilt. Again, that does not mean we can no longer use it as a symbol, but it does mean we need to think through carefully just what it is saying to a secular world.

And a whole lot more study

The court of appeal is an ongoing return to examine painting, sculpture, theatre, music and poetry, looking for what defines that kind of cultural artefact.
Calvin Seerveld[18]

Indeed, 'thinking it through' is something that is going to have to characterise Christians a whole lot more if we are to be heard as a credible voice both *to* the art world and *through* our art to society as a whole. And by 'thinking' (despite the fact that this is a book of theory) we do not just mean theoretical speculation. One never comes to a 'definition' of art by theorising about it. The only way to arrive satisfactorily at an understanding of art is to *look* at it, over and over again.

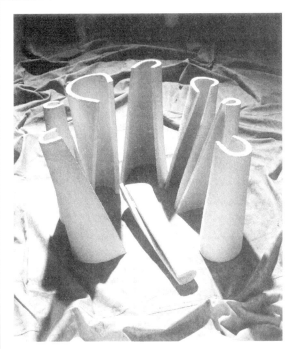

38. Henny de Klijn, *Mourning* (1992), ceramic, 70 × 42 cm

'I have grouped seven abstract figures in a circle around a dead figure. The way in which the pieces of clay are folded expresses the various ways in which people respond to the death of a loved one.'[19]

Did this work evoke in you the associations the artist intended? A straw poll of random opinions by the authors demonstrated how unsuspected allusions can creep in. Several observers of this piece said it reminded them of Stonehenge, a very English connection that may never have occurred to the Dutch artist.

Although none mentioned the word 'mourning', they were aware of a sense of fallenness, separateness and something shrivelled about the lying shape. They saw that the surrounding uprights were clearly focused on the fallen figure and found them both protective and detached, sheltering and distant.

We have focused on one concept, Seerveld's 'allusiveness', in an attempt to carry our thinking further, but as Seerveld himself comments, it is only one 'entrance to the aesthetic woods'. It is not 'the whole forest'. In our next chapter we will be taking a different route through the trees, looking at some of the component parts and multiple layers of a work of art, in a further attempt to map out the forest.

15

Art and Interpretation

Basic instincts

The only way to understand art is to *look* at it, we pronounced at the
end of the last chapter. But when we look, what is it we see?

It is very rare for anyone, and especially anyone involved in the arts,
to approach an artwork with no knowledge whatsoever. In fact, if we do
so, our first reaction may be to feel rather embarrassed and assume that
therefore we cannot evaluate the art in question.

In some ways the opposite is true. The more we are able to approach
the work unencumbered with preconceptions – with the eyes of a child
– the more we may be able to understand. After all, looking at art is
essentially a personal, private, sensory and emotional experience.
Much art can be appreciated on its own, not needing any background
information in order for it to do its work.

But in other ways there are many differing kinds of knowledge
which may help us to appreciate more fully what we see. Without the
right information we may lack some vital clue to the nature of
the piece. Art can be approached in a whole host of different ways and
analysing these approaches will help us understand why we react as we
do to a work of art. It may also help us see why others come at the
same art with such differing opinions and reactions. We need not
worry that analysis of art will destroy its magic. Over time an awareness of these different approaches will become second nature. It will
not destroy our enjoyment, only enhance it.

Misleading assessments

Obviously there are better and worse ways of approaching art. In each
of the three following approaches, the aesthetic quality and communica-
tive power of the work can come dangerously close to being missed
altogether.

When people appreciate different things about art, it can provoke mystification and sometimes open hostility, as this opening scene from the play *Art* by Yasmina Reza[1] demonstrates:

Marc alone

MARC   My friend Serge has bought a painting. It's a canvas about five foot by four: white. The background is white and if you screw up your eyes, you can make out some fine white diagonal lines . . .

      On Monday I went to see the painting; Serge had actually got hold of it on the Saturday, but he'd been lusting after it for several months. The white painting with the white lines.

At Serge's
At floor level, a white canvas with fine white diagonal scars. Serge looks at his painting, thrilled. Marc looks at the painting. Serge looks at Marc looking at the painting. Long silence: from both of them, a whole range of wordless emotions.

MARC   Expensive?

SERGE   Two hundred thousand.

MARC   Two hundred thousand? . . .

SERGE   Well?

MARC   . . .

SERGE   You're not in the right place. Look at it from this angle. Can you see the lines?

MARC   What's the name of the . . .?

SERGE   Painter. Antrios.

MARC   Well-known?

SERGE   Very. Very!

Pause

MARC   Serge, you haven't bought this painting for two hundred thousand francs?

SERGE   You don't understand. That's what it costs. It's an Antrios.

MARC   You haven't bought this painting for two hundred thousand francs?

SERGE   I might have known you'd miss the point.

MARC   You paid two hundred thousand francs for this shit?

The dollar-signs and column-inches approach

This approach depends on price, rarity or the power of a name. Strictly speaking the artwork itself could be replaced by any other if we had been told the same things about it.

We all know the *Mona Lisa* is considered a masterpiece. But had we come upon it without prior knowledge, would we have picked it out as the jewel of the Louvre or passed it by with hardly a glance? How would we feel if we were told that Leonardo's original had got lost but this was a clever fake? Will the fact that we have been told it is a masterpiece mean that we approach it with reverence and awe, or will we be somewhat disappointed when we see it 'in the flesh'. *But it's so small!* Whatever our reaction, if we come at art purely from the point of view of its economic or celebrity status, we are likely to miss the point.

Even if we think we are free from such prejudices, it is worth pondering how pervasive this approach is. If a work of art is exhibited in the Tate, must it not by definition be better than something in the local art society exhibition? If it is performed at the National Theatre, we will expect it to be more exciting or refined than something at the Haymarket, Basingstoke. At its extremes it comes down to 'If I've heard of it, it must be better than something I've never heard of' – an approach that instantly justifies self-aggrandisement as a vital part of artistic activity.

The techno-wizardry approach

'Wow, that whole five-minute sequence was one long moving camera shot.' 'Of course, this is classic three-act story structure.' 'Have you considered the brushwork on this? Magnificent.'

What is inspiring us here is the artist's mastery of craft. We are right to be impressed and will undoubtedly learn a great deal by analysing technique. The danger is that we may end up so fascinated by the technical skills that we forget to consider the art as a whole. Both photorealist painting and computer-generated effects often evoke this response. The audience marvels at the skill of the artist so much that aesthetic, content and communication elements are forgotten.

The naughty words/nice subject-matter approach

Similarly mistaken is an approach which bases its likes and dislikes entirely on the subject-matter. This is the kind of approach which rejects Martin Amis' *London Fields* because it is about a despicable character, but accepts Stubbs' paintings because the viewer happens to love horses.

It is an approach which sadly has led many Christians to reject good art because it contains the odd swear-word or sexually explicit scene. For Disgusted of Tunbridge Wells, the moral content is *all* that matters. *The Waltons* are more suitable company than *The Boys from the*

Blackstuff. It is morality by numbers, judged on how much naked flesh is shown, how many swear-words are uttered, what the body count is, and what time of day it is.

It *is* important that someone keep a tally of such things, because taken together they do offer some sort of reading of society's mores. And there *are* issues of censorship that need to be addressed (a complex debate that is outside the remit of these pages). But as a way of evaluating the ethics and edification of any individual artwork, it is a limited and misleading approach.

One other, perhaps not wrong but ultimately limited, response is that which is based on the circumstances surrounding the work. In this associative approach we will treasure a particular painting simply because it was given us by our dear grandfather, or be moved by Verdi's *Requiem* because it reminds us of Princess Diana's funeral. Although it is sometimes hard to separate out private memories and associations from the merit of the work as such, it is nevertheless important to distinguish between the two.

Useful knowledge

Having outlined some inadequate approaches to art, we will now focus on some which can greatly deepen our understanding and appreciation. Each in its own way involves background information and at least a modicum of study.

The socio-historical approach
At times, especially when dealing with non-contemporary art or art from other cultures, it is necessary to know something of the situation the artist was trying to portray. It may be circumstances that were well-known at the time but are now lost in history. There is often information contained in the title to help us, or we may have to refer to promotional blurb, programme notes, or catalogue.

In Millet's painting *The Gleaners* of 1857, three women are bent in the foreground of a recently harvested corn field, apparently picking up or searching for something on the ground. If one knows what gleaning is, it presents no problem, but gleaning is a lost custom in the twentieth-century Western world. These women could be collecting bedding for their pet rabbits, working on an ecology field project, or plain clothes detectives searching for murder clues.

But gleaning is for these poor women a matter of survival, long back-breaking toil in order to gather up enough scrapings of corn to make their bread. When we know that, we can understand the power of the picture – a harsh reality set in a pastoral idyll.

The iconographical approach

This is a very similar situation to the above, but concerned more with understanding symbolism and metaphor than historical or circumstantial background. Most Christians seeing Holman Hunt's painting of the *Light of the World* will relate it to the words of Christ in John's vision: 'Behold, I stand at the door and knock.'[2] But to anyone else, whilst still admiring some of the qualities of the painting, it may make little sense. Why is this strange man knocking on such a neglected door while staring straight out at us?

To understand this picture we need to recognise its symbolism: the door represents the soul, the ivy and brambles stand for sin and the lamp for redemption. If we see it as religious allegory, it will not worry us that the man looks slightly unnatural and is wearing an odd head-dress.

The biographical approach

Some study of the life or writings of the artist can quickly transform our understanding of what they were about. Van Gogh and his self-portrait with bandaged ear is a classic example. He could have fallen into a bacon slicer, he could have got in a fight. But if we know that he cut his own ear off, we begin to glimpse something of the tortured mind that drove his genius.

A little biographical light shed on van Gogh's boots, referred to earlier, turns out to reveal a completely different scenario from the potato harvest imagined by Heidegger. The boots, in fact, belonged to the city-dweller van Gogh himself. Moreover, as became known via his friend Gauguin, they were the very boots he had worn when he preached to the miners in Borinage in Belgium. As such, comments the art historian Meyer Shapiro, the shoes served as a sacred relic of his own life.[3]

A more recent example concerns the use of fat and felt in the work of installation artist Joseph Beuys. They make little sense until we know of his dramatic experience in the Luftwaffe during the Second World War. When his aircraft crashed on the Russian front, Tartar tribesmen saved his life by covering him with fat and felt to keep him warm. These materials became to him emblems of healing and nurture.

Similarly, we might guess that film director Oliver Stone had a bit of a thing about Vietnam simply by watching his films, but once we know he is a veteran of that war and what a seminal experience it was to him, we understand a little more about what drives and informs his work.

The worldview approach

In this approach we need to know not only that van Gogh was emotionally disturbed or that Holman Hunt used Christian symbolism, but what were the wider motives and beliefs that shaped their thinking. We need to know Millet's approach to the role of women, and Joseph Beuys' political views. This approach looks at the worldview behind the work of art, not simply the worldview of the individual artist, but of society as a whole at that time.

A worldview, as we have seen, is the set of assumptions and values which shape our lives in all their aspects, from the way we look after our cat to the strategies we devise for our business. As such it is an inescapable ingredient of all works of art. This is not to say that all artworks wear their worldview on their sleeve. For most it is far more subtle.

Of course it works best if it *is* subtle. Christians who agonise over how to put their worldview into their art are asking the wrong question. It is more a question of whether they *could* erase, even if they wanted to, that which is inevitably in there somewhere.

The art-history approach

If Picasso showed his *Demoiselles d'Avignon* at this year's Royal Academy Summer Exhibition, would it be remarked upon? Probably not. By now, we have seen such anarchic composition, disjointed figuration, African influence and rejection of naturalism many times before. But when it was painted in 1907 nothing had prepared people – even his closest friends who saw it in his studio – for such a shock. Now with the benefit of hindsight, we can label Picasso's brothel vision as the first modernist painting, a true watershed in the history of art.

The same is true of the *Unité d'Habitation*, which at first sight would appear to be just one more run-down and discoloured concrete apartment block in the suburbs of Marseilles. Its inhabitants are none too impressed with their box-like apartments and have tried their best to prettify them with 'plastic chandeliers, imitation Louis XVI bergères and Monoprix ormolu'.[4] But to a student of architecture the *Unité* has great significance since it was designed by the pioneering Le Corbusier, the only opportunity given him in his native France to translate his grand vision of mass high-rise housing into what turned out to be a disappointing reality.

We can learn a great deal from a study of how different styles evolved and how one 'ism' developed out of another. (Conversely, with this as with all aspects of background knowledge, it is always possible to stuff our heads full of facts and figures and still be no nearer a true appreciation!)

Essential elements: The aesthetic-form approach

All of the previous approaches have their uses, but still none of them comes near to evaluating that vital ingredient that makes art *art*.

No evaluation can be complete without looking at the *form* or *aesthetic surface* of the piece. In the end what matters most is whether the work *works* – whether this particular collection of colours, shapes, sounds or movements comes together in an entirety that is satisfying, striking, fascinating, or beautiful (in its broadest sense). Does it do its job so well that it draws us to watch or listen? Does its form fit its function? Do its component parts fit together so well as to create a meaningful and memorable whole?

'A picture, before being a warhorse, a nude woman, or some sort of anecdote,' said Maurice Denis, in what became a rallying cry of the early modernists, 'is essentially a surface covered with colours arranged in a certain order.'[6]

Form is what you are left with when you turn the painting upside down and screw up your eyes. It has ceased to be a virgin with child, a view of the Thames or a Brillo pad box. It is shapes, lines, areas of light and dark.

We do not necessarily need knowledge to appreciate form. There is something in us that instinctively responds to aesthetic excellence, something that can never quite be defined in rules of composition or theories of perception. But learning the rules and theories does help. It helps us understand *how* the work weaves its aesthetic magic – all the more fascinating when the rules are broken.

In an assessment of the aesthetic surface of a piece, subject-matter and worldview are often put to one side. It is, perhaps, for this reason that some Christians have too often ignored form or considered it of secondary importance. In doing so they show a basic misunderstanding of the way art works. It is this aesthetic dimension that turns something into art, as opposed to a purely functional form of communication. Considering what a work of art communicates must involve looking at *how* it treats its subject-matter.

The form of a work of art conveys meaning which goes beyond that of its subject-matter. It can convey a general sense of, for instance, order or disorder, balance or imbalance, warmth or coldness, cheerfulness or gloom, fluidity or rigidity. The whole point about art is how this form transforms the subject-matter. Hence, any interpretation of art which does not take the aesthetic surface into account seriously misses the point. As Christians we may not agree with Oscar Wilde's provocative epigram. Form is not *all* that matters, but we would do well to acknowledge that it is pretty darned important!

There is no such thing as a moral or immoral book. Books are well written or badly written. That is all.
Oscar Wilde[5]

Shifting emphasis

Armed even with all these layers of knowledge, there are still more ways to approach art, as those at art colleges will know all too well. Feminist, Marxist, semiotic, structuralist, post-structuralist, deconstructionist, psychoanalytical and socio-political critiques: it just boggles the mind. Interestingly though, what all these approaches have in common (even

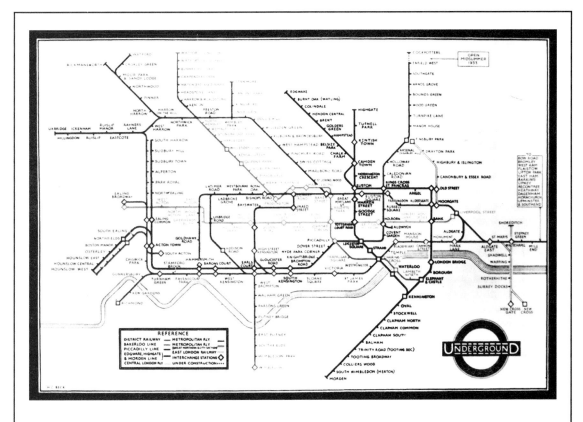

39.   Henry C. Beck, *London Underground Diagram* (1933) (courtesy of London Transport Museum)

The schematic representation of the London Underground was first made in 1931 by an engineering draughtsman called Harry Beck. It was instantly popular and has remained so ever since, respected as a design classic and held in affection by generations of Londoners. It is both the aesthetic quality of this design and its symbolic clarity that has made it so timeless. This is applied art: it has no associative or expressive qualities, nor is it representational in a literal sense. It has achieved its goal by ignoring any literal portrayal of distance and direction (after all, once underground, these things are indiscernible and irrelevant). It works because it is visually pleasing (the aesthetic surface) and is effective in its communication of information. In creating an 'image-language' from simple shapes and colours, the designer's primary goal was a functional one – getting travellers from Mornington Crescent to Tooting Broadway or wherever. But it does that job by paying attention to the aesthetic elements – the interplay of shapes and colours – to create a satisfying whole.

those which are essentially analysing structure) is something also close to the heart of many Christians: looking at art in relation to worldview.

We have talked already about the necessity of understanding the worldview of the artist. This, of course, is never entirely objective. We can only ever see someone else's worldview through the spectacles of our own. Many of these newer approaches, however, make no pretence of objectivity. They are specifically concerned with analysing art from the perspective of a particular set of beliefs.

In 1986 a collection of essays was published under the title of *The New Art History*. Its editors summarised how important this new worldview approach had become:

> When an article analyses the images of women in painting rather than the qualities of the brushwork, or when a gallery lecturer ignores the sheen of the Virgin Mary's robe for the Church's use of religious art in the Counter-Reformation, the new art history is casting its shadow . . .
>
> In discrediting the old art history, words like connoisseurship, quality, style and genius have become taboo, utterable by the new art historians only with scorn and mirth . . . The presence of a new art history is signalled by a different set of words – ideology, patriarchy, class, methodology, and other terms which betray their origins in the social sciences.[7]

Initially it was the Marxists who most vigorously fulfilled the task of twentieth-century worldview watchdog, until the abrupt crumbling of communism meant there was suddenly no bite behind the bark. Coming right behind them were the PC vigilantes, determined to outlaw chauvinism, racism, sexism and classism wherever they reared their heads. Hard on their heels and much in evidence in the art colleges were a group we might dub the PMC brigade – not so much Political as Post-Modern Correctness. Ironically, whilst rejecting all value or belief systems which claimed universal validity, their ideology is often as dogmatic as any they attack.

The first person to address the issue of worldview in the Christian world was the late Hans Rookmaaker with his book *Modern Art and the Death of a Culture*. Published in 1970 and a rare example of Christians being ahead of the times, it examined the various secular worldviews underlying modern art from a specifically Christian perspective. Together with Francis Schaeffer, Calvin Seerveld and Nicholas Wolterstorff, Rookmaaker set about making a whole generation of Christians aware of the importance of art. For many it was an eye opener. Artist Peter Smith remembers how 'a real change came for many of us . . . This was the first time I encountered what I recognised as biblical Christianity saying something useful about the arts.'[8]

The Christian world owes these pioneers a great debt. They forced it to confront the culture that surrounded it, and look at it closely with intelligence, appreciation and understanding. They reminded us, in Seerveld's words, how essential it is that Christians know 'what time it is on the streets'.[9]

What they did *not* intend, however, is that Christians should evaluate art solely on the basis of whether or not it conveys a Christian message

When art critic Clement Greenberg looked at a Rouault painting in 1945, he was concerned almost entirely with the aesthetic surface:

> Rouault takes few real chances. He methodically exploits complementary colours and keeps the ostensible, strength-signifying rawness of his pigment well in hand under the formula of heavy black and umber lines. Interventions of black and brown (as well as grey), as most painters know, offer a safe way of guaranteeing the harmony of other colours. Rouault's real insecurity is further betrayed by his habitually dead-centered and symmetrical design.'[10]

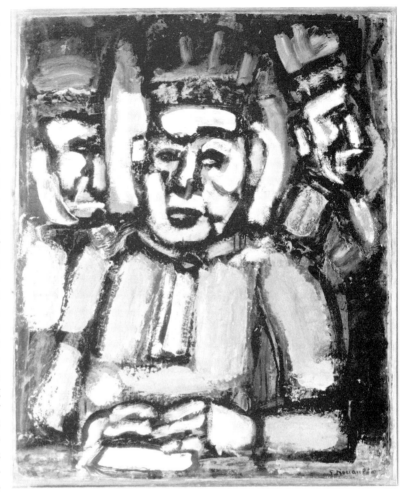

40. Georges Rouault, *The Three Judges* (c. 1936), oil on board laid on canvas support, 78.4 × 64.8 cm (London, Tate Gallery)

When Christian art historian Hans Rookmaaker looked at Rouault in the 1970s, what he saw was subject-matter, symbolism and spiritual values:

> Rouault is a contemporary of the fauves and cubists but he is different. His prostitutes are not amoral beings, symbolising the end of morality as such; they are symbols for prostitution, for cheap love for sale, for the depravity of this time. His judges are akin to those of Daumier: they stand for the corrupt courts of his time. He prophesies against the times in which he lives.[11]

Both Greenberg and Rookmaaker were primarily interested in only one aspect of the art work: Greenberg in the application and distribution of the paint on the flat surface, Rookmaaker in the meaning of the pictorial representation. In a fully integrated approach to art, both aspects need to be considered together.

or worldview. Sadly, for some believers – already over-conscious of themselves as a beleaguered minority entrusted with a vital message – this worldview aspect has dominated all others as they have approached the world of art. It is interesting, for instance, that Franky Schaeffer, son of Francis, complained that Christians always looked for the message in his films and paintings and were highly critical when they failed to find what they thought should be there.

Whilst the worldview aspect is highly important, too much attention to it can miss the point and reduce art to an ideological tract. The late Peter Fuller wrote, 'Even at my most relativist, I always avoided this dissolution of art into ideology. The reason was simple: I would stare into that hole, and faces like that of Vermeer's unknown woman would be gazing back at me. As a result, I have come to oppose vigorously the ideological reductions of art.'[13]

Our appreciation of a work of art should not depend on whether it happens to share our worldview. Rather, art is about a shared experience of what it means to be human.

Wholistic appreciation

It should be clear by now. A truly integrated evaluation considers art from as many aspects and angles as possible. It looks at *form*, *content* and *worldview* and savours the potential strengths and weaknesses of all of them.

An artwork can have skilled and compelling form, be visually and aurally stunning, and yet have an emptiness at its heart. Peter Greenaway's film *Prospero's Books* serves as a good example. In contrast, it can have content that has the Viewers and Listeners Association reaching for its green ink; be graphically homo-erotic, have a liberal smattering of f-words and a negative portrayal of the church, as in Jimmy McGovern's *Priest*, and yet be brilliantly written, sensitively filmed, and carry a more compelling message of Christian love than a thousand sermons.

Conversely, it can be well-made, entertaining, devoid of shock-value and apparently innocuous and yet carry a meaning that is at best misleading and at worst positively evil. *Four Weddings and a Funeral* is good clean romantic fun, until you sit down and analyse it. Is a relationship between a man who cannot cope with legal and public commitment and a woman who, on her own admission, has had 33 sexual liaisons and split up with her first husband after ten months really going to be such a good bet?

Then again, it can carry an impeccable Christian worldview, be pure and wholesome in content and yet be utterly predictable, forgettable and downright naff in its form. (In fact so much so, that although we, the authors, can each think of several examples, none of them has ever become big enough in the Christian world, let alone the wider secular market, to use as a commonly known example. We rest our case!)

But when art works at its glorious best, form, content and worldview are so well fitted to each other that you cannot see the join. As the painter Peter Smith says:

> When the language is used for its aesthetic value the form and content are bound together. It can be used in a way in which, for example, not only is the content nasty or joyful in some way, but the formal properties of the

---

As *Art* reaches its final scene the white painting with white lines comes close to destroying the friendship of Marc, Serge and Yvan:[14]

YVAN   To think we've reached these extremes . . . Apocalypse because of a white square . . .

SERGE   It is not white.

YVAN   A piece of white shit! . . .

He's seized by uncontrollable laughter.

> That's what it is, a piece of white shit! . . . Let's face it, mate . . . What you've bought is insane! . . .

Marc laughs, caught up by Yvan's extravagance. Serge leaves the room. He returns immediately with the Antrios.

SERGE   Do you have one of your famous felt tips? . . .

Serge takes the felt tip from Yvan and gives it to Marc.

SERGE   (to Marc) Go on.

Silence

> Go on!

Marc approaches the painting.
He looks at Serge.
Then he takes the top off the felt-tip.

YVAN   You're not going to do it! . . .

Marc leans towards the painting. Under Yvan's horrified gaze, he draws the felt tip along one of the diagonal scars. Serge remains impassive. Then carefully on this slope, Marc draws a little skier with a woolly hat.
When he's finished, he straightens up and contemplates his work.
Serge remains adamantine.
Yvan is as if turned to stone.
Silence.

language are equally disturbing or exhilarating . . . The form is as important and value-laden as any content.[16]

When form and content fuse in this way they create a *context* in which ideas are carried as natural allies, rather than protruding as awkward extras or what Murray Watts calls 'blunt instruments to club the . . . mind into submission'.[17]

There is a word to describe this healthy fusion of component layers: *integrity.* Is the form a true expression of the meaning? Is the meaning an added extra or does it arise as an integral part of the content? Is the content deliberately shocking or timidly bland, or is it an honest portrayal of life as sensed and felt by the artist?

Your average gallery- or cinema-goer would claim to know very little about the component layers that make up their favourite art form. In terms of background training and knowledge they are probably right. But, in fact, they know far more than they realise. Although they could never articulate it, they instinctively know integrity when they see it. Equally they sense when something is not right – when art strikes a pose, moralises or borrows a fashionable form that does not fit. The world is hungry for integrity and is not as easily fooled as some might suppose.

The apostle Paul told the novice followers of the Christian Way to think about 'whatever is true, whatever is noble, whatever is right, whatever is pure, whatever is lovely, whatever is admirable . . . excellent or praiseworthy . . .'[18] As a yardstick for integrity in form, content and worldview, we could do far worse.

By the close of the play *Art*,[19] the three friends have managed to wash the felt-tip drawing from the white painting. As it is restored, so they begin to restore their friendship. Marc 'sees' the painting in a different way:

Gradually the light begins to narrow down on the Antrios. Marc approaches the painting.

MARC   Under the white clouds, the snow is falling.
        You can't see the white clouds, or the snow.
        Or the cold, or the white glow of the earth.
        A solitary man glides downhill on his skis.
        The snow is falling.
        It falls until the man disappears back into the landscape.
        My friend Serge, who's one of my oldest friends, has bought a painting.
        It's a canvas about five feet by four.
        It represents a man who moves across a space and disappears.

Part 5

Rooted, Respectful and Real:
Some ways forward for Christians in the arts

16

Art and New Technology

More questions than answers

There is no doubt that we are living through one of the greatest periods
of change humankind has yet experienced. The computer revolution is
just as dramatic as the printing press was in its day; the accompanying
shift in philosophy just as marked as that from the Middle Ages to the
Reformation and Renaissance.

Yet 1984 has come and gone and Big Brother is not yet watching us.
2001 is unlikely to see us venturing through black holes. The brave new
world has turned out to be not such an alarming place after all.

Prediction is a dangerous game and looking idiotic is pretty much
part of the job-description for a prophet. For the nature of all major
technological advance is that it both changes and fails to change what it
supersedes. Old art forms have an amazing way of adapting and hanging on. New technologies show a remarkable tendency to be absorbed
into existing culture with far less impact than predicted.

Even so, the future *will* be a very different shape from the present. If
we want to be among those who form culture in the twenty-first century,
we need to look to the future and attempt to discern its outline. Glorious
opportunity or dangerous licence? The new technology will clearly give
both, but which way will the balance tip? One thing we can safely fore-
cast is that an awful lot of the old barriers are going to be broken down.

*Our world has
changed for better or
for worse. It is for us
to find truth and
beauty for today,
constantly
re-applying the truth
of God's word to our
own time and our
contemporary
situation.*
Hans Rookmaaker[1]

Between image and reality

The movies had monsters before *Jurassic Park*; they had talking toys
before *Toy Story*. What they did not have were human heads that could
swivel 360 degrees, human faces that could change seamlessly from
Asian to WASP before our eyes and actors whose legs could be cut off
halfway through a film. They couldn't make Tom Hanks chat to JFK or
show Lyndon Johnson his buttocks. When your characters can become
anything or do anything before your eyes, the dynamics of the story
begin to change.

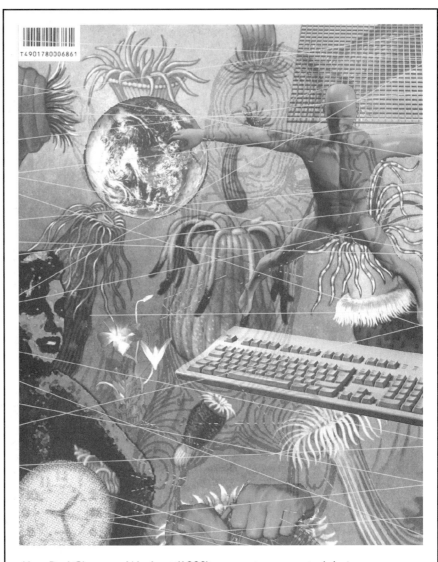

41.   Paul Clowney, *Weaknet* (1998), computer-generated design

Graphic designer and computer animator Paul Clowney has thought a great deal about the issues thrown up by Virtual Reality. He predicts that

> VR will not be viewed so much as a model of the world (still within the world), but as a separate reality outside the tangible . . . Idealists see the potential for a completely new sort of religious experience. In this electro- gnostic model you can literally define yourself and still be linked with kindred spirits around the world. Hence VR technology has enormous appeal to many New Age exponents who see the next stage of human evolution as a bionic change where humans can start to intelligently recreate the species . . . The definition of what constitutes identity is changing and will alter dramatically if fantasies and character projections become a dominant form of social intercourse.[2]

But it is when the audience themselves walk into the story, when they can become anything or do anything, that the dynamics really start exploding. What the artist conceived has become a creature with a life of its own. You can already buy computer packages that enable you to create your own episodes of your favourite story, from *Bart Simpson* to *Bladerunner*. The technology is still primitive, however, compared to its possibilities. 'Imagine pulling on your data suit,' says Paul Clowney, 'to enter a world where you can not only create a *Dungeons and Dragons* monster, but actually *become* the monster, complete with dialogue, sound and synthesised pain. You will emerge from your lair to meet someone else's *alter ego*, and jockey to implement your view of the world.'

How real will Virtual Reality be? Certainly, as Clowney predicts, 'It will be so real as to confuse what reality actually means.'[3]

Across national boundaries

The first collaborative on-line novel has already been written, with opening and closing paragraphs by John Updike, and other would-be authors from all over the world contributing the paragraphs in between. Organised by Amazon.com, the world's largest on-line booksellers, the competition to produce the novel was a huge attraction, with a daily average of 16,000 people entering the 45-day rolling competition.

Already, British dons are arguing nightly with American professors and Korean students as to the precise order in which C.S. Lewis's Narnia stories should be read. Occasionally, a Seattle Sunday School teacher or a German schoolboy will interrupt them to ask if they have any suggestions for a series of lessons or information for a project. The internet already has 30,000 registered newsgroups discussing different topics across the continents.

As the old geographical divides are bridged, so a new gulf is formed. Those who are on-line become stronger and more empowered; the 'off-line' poor become even more alienated. And power shifts into new hands. We have long known that *information is power*: have we grasped the extent to which *image is power*? Do we truly understand how much power is wielded both by those who create images and those who control access to them?

Between artist and audience

It was relatively easy for the law to define who went into a cinema, relatively easy to put the porn magazines on the top shelf of the newsagents and the sex and violence after the nine o'clock watershed. When the magazines, films and programmes come down the line and straight into your home it is a very different matter. Debate about the extent to which censorship is right has shifted to the extent to which it is even possible. Who legislates when international boundaries no longer exist? Does new technology mean control will have to be more draconian or will it be swept away altogether?

In the absence of any other mechanism, responsibility lies in the hands of the audience, specifically the finger on the 'Off' button. But what happens when the audience are only children?

And what of the artist? If no filter stands between the work and the vulnerable or perverted minds that might receive it, what responsibility does it place on the originator? What difference does it make when the work may be seen or heard not once, but over and over again? No artist can be responsible for anyone and everyone who might happen to see their handiwork. Neither can they wash their hands totally of the consequences. There is much thinking to be done, by politicians, parents, programmers, *and* artists. We need to try and grasp the philosophical, psychological and ethical questions looming through the mist, even if at present the answers remain hazy.

Across arts media

When is a rock album not a rock album? When it is also an art exhibition, computer game and dissertation on human relationships rolled into one. Just one example of many musicians and artists fascinated by the potential of multi-media is Peter Gabriel. In his 1996 CD-Rom *Eve* he collaborated with such artists as Helen Chadwick in Britain, Yayoi Kusama from Tokyo and Danish landscape installation artist Nils-Udo and even scientists such as geneticist Steve Jones. He has been quoted as describing his mix of songs, statement, video footage, and contemporary art as 'a sort of playpen'. Quite how one plays in this new environment, and who will do it once the novelty wears off, remains to be seen.

And what happens to the artist when one desk-top machine can create, integrate and then duplicate almost all of the arts? Specialisation or multi-skilling? More collaboration or more isolation? A more egalitarian art world or an even more privileged few?

Between museum and home

When he wants to unwind from his day job as Chairman and Chief Executive of Microsoft, Bill Gates amuses himself by designing his ideal home. Each person entering the house wears an electronic pin. The pin

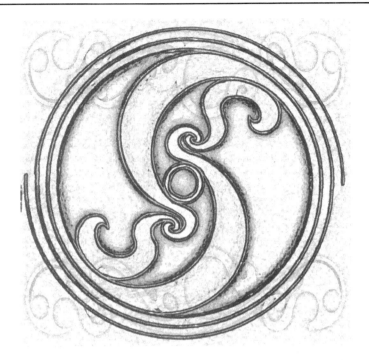

42.   Martin Crampin, *Matholwch*, detail of installation *Math, Son of Mathonwy* (1996), digital image

A graduate in the new discipline of Interactive Arts, Martin Crampin sees it as 'an environment for ideas and a space for thinking. Interactive art allows the audience to negotiate its own path through a variety of material and in doing so generate a more personal response and a deeper understanding. Exploring ideas in a more lateral way also demonstrates an interconnectedness, as parts are understood in the context of the whole.'

This non-linear approach is not a new one, according to Martin, who used combined Celtic design and Welsh myth and folk lore in his installation. 'Ancient and medieval writings do not always rely on a chronological narrative, but on the cumulative effect of material; history, literature, religion and mythology are not clearly defined, but part of an interrelated whole. It's interesting to explore how very ancient myths became incorporated with material that was up-to-date for its time; how influences came in from classical, Germanic and Mediterranean culture, drawn together and amalgamated over a span of a thousand years.'

Also interacting in his work is old and new technology. 'I prefer to start designs in pen or pencil – what I still think of as "real" media. Computers can do amazing things with images that are scanned into them, but for originating images they still can't quite match up to someone who can actually use a pastel or a pen.'[4]

tells the house where each person is and the house in turn offers them their already-programmed-in choices.

> The house will remember everything it learns about your preferences. If in the past you've asked to see paintings by Henri Matisse or photographs by Chris Johns of the *National Geographic*, you may find other works of theirs displayed on the walls of the rooms you enter. If you listened to Mozart horn concertos the last time you visited, you might find them on again when you come back.[6]

One of Gates' companies has already created a digital archive of more than a million images, available to commercial users and home browsers alike. He plans to use images from this agency on the walls of his own home and anticipates that in the future others will do the same. Gates does not think that instant access to works of art will mean the end of museums. 'There's nothing like seeing the real work.'

It may not be the end of museums, but will it be the death of the imagination? Paul Clowney likens computer technology to an amplifier, 'with a far wider dynamic range than anything people have ever had'.[7] The problem with this amplifier is sheer volume – images, sounds and information bombarding us on every side. The human spirit needs quiet contemplation in order to grow: is it in danger of being drowned out? How can artists ensure they add to the sum of human wisdom and not just to the cacophony?

Human experience can only yield wisdom when coupled with reflection. High-pressure, dense image streams are not very conducive to reflection.
Paul Clowney[5]

When the novelty wears off

At the moment reactions to new technology are rather in the manner of Dr Johnson's to a woman preaching: 'like a dog walking on its hinder legs'. We are scarcely interested in whether it is done well, it is the fact that it is done at all that amazes us.[8]

Rather like the response to women preachers, at present the IT revolution has both its devotees and its reactionaries with something of a gulf between the two. Hopefully, before this book goes out of print both innovations will have become more accepted, and we will understand more clearly their impact. We will also see that no matter what technology does, some things never change.

As the first computer-modelled animation, *Toy Story* marked a technological advance. But it is not that which made it a success with kids and adults alike. What made it work was that its creators understood the traditional craft of story-telling. They knew how to create empathetic characters and bring in moments of tension and surprise. It also worked because it dealt in real 'human' emotions. Everyone could laugh at Buzz Lightyear's delusions of grandeur and feel for poor old Woody's abandonment. It dealt in values like bravery and loyalty and moments of tough choice.

It is the quality of the content that matters, not the gender of the speaker. Similarly it is the human imaginativity that formed the artwork that will excite us, not the technical execution. It is still ideas and emotions striking an allusive chord with our own experience which will move us, whatever the medium of delivery. And however sophisticated the spin with which some products are marketed, there is something about a work with real integrity at its heart which has a remarkable tendency to shine out amid the surrounding dross.

Skills change. Walking behind the plough gave way to driving the tractor, paste-up has given way to desk-top, splicing tape to digital editing. Some drudgeries disappear. Others take their place. Techniques come and go, but the challenge of mastering them does not. Artistic disciplines shift and mutate, but the disciplined hard work of the artist remains.

17

Art as Honest Labour

One of the exhibits by Gavin Turk at the 'Sensation' exhibition at the Royal Academy was a blue plaque, identical to those hung by English Heritage on the former homes of distinguished people. It said simply 'Gavin Turk worked here 1993–95'. But did he? The plaque was created by Turk for his M.A. show at the Royal College of Art. It was the only piece in his exhibition space, some say the only piece he created all year, and rumour has it that he got a technician to make it.

Was it a witty comment on the nature of art, setting out, as the exhibition notes claimed, to 'question the Modernist notion of authorship and authenticity'? Or was it just a con? The RCA refused to pass him, but Saatchi bought the piece.

Opinions may continue to differ on whether Turk's plaque deserves the name of art. One thing is certain, as we move on now to look at making art as a responsible job of work, Gavin Turk is *not* who we have in mind as a role model! Perhaps we need to return to ancient times and good old Bezalel, the artist in charge of the Israelites' exuberant worship tent, to find a better one.

Rooted

Then the Lord said to Moses, 'See I have chosen Bezalel . . . and I have filled him with the Spirit of God, with skill, ability and knowledge in all kinds of crafts – to make artistic designs for work in gold, silver and bronze, to cut and set stones, to work in wood, and to engage in all kinds of craftsmanship.'
Exodus 31:1–3

Bezalel was obviously inspired, he clearly had natural talent, but he also had a thorough knowledge of his craft. Somewhere before this prize project came along, Bezalel had served a long and hard apprenticeship. And it could hardly have been in the desert. The chances are it was in the service of a very different worldview. How many Egyptian temples and palaces had Bezalel worked on before he came to this?

Franky Schaeffer believes it is an apprenticeship anyone serious about their art will need to undertake today:

We have to pay our dues . . . before we have the artistic freedom to choose the subjects we wish to express . . . Few seem to understand this. They expect quick dramatic results from what is necessarily a slow, very imperfect process . . .

We must at times create movies, television shows, books, art, music, theatre and dance that does not mirror our worldview, while working not to be tainted in our inner being by the unbelief around us. We must not lie to ourselves about what we are doing, but compromise bravely, keeping our eyes on our eventual goals. We must admit we need to walk before we can run.[1]

The element of learning a craft is self-evident in most of the contemporary arts – one cannot do architecture, film-making, photography, poetry, dance, theatre or music without it. The one exception to the rule, however, is in the world of 'fine art' and particularly in the training – or lack of it – offered by many art colleges.

Here one comes hard up against a completely different ethos. Because anything goes, no one can say what is right or wrong in art any more. Therefore we find ourselves in the bizarre situation that few can give the student an evaluation of what they are doing, since there are no real skills to teach. Because the old ways of doing things are generally being rejected, there is little point in studying art history. One might perhaps learn a little of the art of this century, but a college that offers, as part of its hands-on art courses, anything about the rich legacy of art before the Impressionists is a rarity indeed. Many art colleges have become primarily a space to work in and an environment to spark off ideas. Both of these, of course, are valuable, but it does mean that students who want to learn about their art heritage, or delve more deeply into the traditional crafts of painting, drawing or sculpting, may need to look outside their college to do so. They may also run the risk of being ridiculed as completely outmoded – although for the Christian, going against the flow may already be a way of life.

This is not to say that those who take time to study their traditional roots should then choose to work in a traditional manner. What is inescapable, however, is that any follower of Jesus is called to be humble and willing to be taught. The arrogance that says it has nothing to learn is far from being Christian. It is also likely to produce bad art, or at least art that will not last or be loved (an aspect of contemporary art that Gavin Turk's plaque was perhaps ironically acknowledging).

True originality, claims T.S. Eliot, comes from someone who has steeped themselves in the tradition of their art. It is a proper 'historical sense', he suggests, 'which makes a writer most acutely conscious of his place in time, of his own contemporaneity'.[2]

Since Eliot was one of the most innovative poets of his generation, it is advice to be taken seriously. Being rooted in a craft, a tradition and a thorough knowledge need not be a restriction. Rather it may prove the stock from which something totally new can flower.

Good art can only be realised when a creative individual encounters a living tradition with deep tendrils in communal life.

Peter Fuller[3]

We shall often find that not only the best, but the most individual parts of his [the poet's] work may be those in which the dead poets, his ancestors, assert their immortality most vigorously.

T.S. Eliot[4]

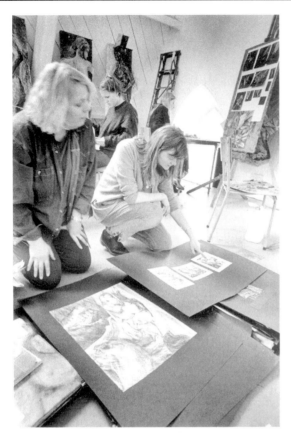

43.   Leith School of Art (photo: courtesy of Leith School of Art)

'Imagine if you can, an art school where art is actually *taught* – vigorously, intelligently, with passion – where tutors are constantly present encouraging and challenging their students, where students work hard, feel part of a community and realise their artistic potential.' When Rebecca Nanson, herself a practising artist and lecturer, went to report on a small independent art college housed in an old Norwegian Church in the dockside area of Edinburgh, she was excited about what she found. 'At Leith School of Art it *is* happening and has been for nearly ten years.'

The school's founders Mark and Lottie Cheverton (both tragically killed in a car crash in 1991) believed that mainstream art teaching was failing. Leaving students to develop untainted by tradition created a situation where there was, in Nanson's words, 'no explicit teaching, tutors with no commitment or energy, and confused students vastly underachieving'. They had discovered that 'freedom without guidance is no freedom at all'.

So the Chevertons and current principal Phil Archer created an environment where 'the acquisition of skills runs in tandem with learning how to think and to interpret'; a place where drawing has a central role and art history is inextricably linked to studio practice.

One unusual aspect is the adoption each year of a new theme (for example, *Spirit Level*, a collection of poems by Seamus Heaney) for the Foundation course. Since it is as new to the tutors as to the students, the theme encourages them to research and create their own work around it. It gives each course a vitality, a uniqueness and an edge: 'No one knows what the outcome will be.'

In contrast, more mainstream colleges, where the same projects are trundled out year after year, can easily produce 'a tendency for lecturers to withdraw to pursue their own work and a pervasive atmosphere of teaching being a necessary evil'.

One of the Chevertons' other aims was: 'To create an environment that grows from a Christian worldview, in its organisation, relationship with students, quality and focus of work produced.' This does not mean that all the students are Christians. Indeed Phil Archer insists that 'Our aim is not to proselytise.' The aim is, however, to produce an environment where each student is cared for and encouraged to develop in every aspect of their personhood. As one former student wrote, 'It feels like a community.'

Respectful

It doesn't seem too much of a mental leap to imagine how Bezalel had learned to love and respect those materials with which he worked. For any believer steeped in an understanding of Creator God, this love and respect should surely be a natural characteristic. If we understand all matter as God-breathed, we will not see it as merely a vehicle for an idea, like the Conceptualists; or an inconvenient veil to be penetrated, like Kandinsky and his fellow Theosophists. We will understand, like Schopenhauer, that genius lies in seeing 'the general in the particular';[6] and learn, like Blake, to 'see the world in a grain of sand, and Heaven in a wild flower'.[7]

We will discover that it is not essential to escape from representation, nor to stick strictly to it, in order to touch anything deep. As Peter Fuller insisted, abstraction does not necessarily mean a move away from objective order but 'an attempt to rediscover it in a profounder way'.[8]

But as we begin to engage with our medium we will soon discover that imposing our ideas upon it is far less easy than we thought. We will discover, in Nicholas Wolterstorff's words, 'the fascinating, mysterious, frustrating, exhilarating experience of being led along in conversation with one's material',[9] an experience that will probably lead to an outcome we never anticipated. When it works at its best, it is, as one dancer described it, 'as if the dance has danced you'.[10]

As we discover how each medium imposes its own nature upon us, so we will learn a proper respect for it. And we will discover, as Stravinsky did, that the laws which each medium by its nature holds within it are not irritating restrictions. Rather, in the same way that the Christian discovers the seeming contradiction of perfect freedom within God's moral law, so the artist discovers within the natural laws of his or her medium a safe place to be free.

As we learn to respect our medium, so we will also discover respect for our subject-matter. When, in the previous section, we looked at the various approaches to art, we did so from the observer's point of view. As an observer we may well start by looking at the background worldview and the technique and move on to how it is applied to the subject-matter.

From the artist's point of view the progression is different. We may begin with an object, a pattern, a character, a situation that we want to explore. But if we begin simply with an attempt to communicate a worldview it will miscarry: it will be merely propaganda. We need not worry that we are failing to put our worldview across – it is as inescapable as the accent, tone and word-formation with which we speak. And it will be at its most genuine when it is just that – the *way* in which we speak rather than the content of the speech itself.

I would argue for . . . the rootedness of art in substance, in the human body, in stone, pigment, in the twanging of gut, the blowing of air on reeds.

Jeremy Begbie[11]

*It's easy . . . to think that the artist has in mind a clear image of what he or she wants and then, having acquired an assortment of skills, deftly imposes that image on the material. Most of the time, the truth is far other. The work of art emerges as a **dialogue** between the artist and material.*

Nicholas Wolterstorff[12]

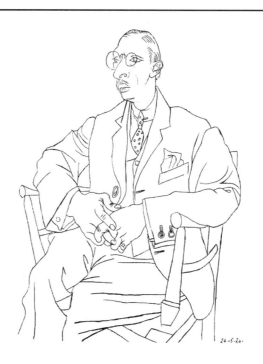

44.   Pablo Picasso, *Portrait of Stravinsky* (1920)

*I have the seven notes of the scale and its chromatic intervals at my disposal
. . . strong and weak accents are within my reach and . . . in all these I possess solid and concrete elements which offer me a field of experience just as
vast as the upsetting and dizzy infinitude that had just frightened me . . .
What delivers me from the anguish into which an unrestricted freedom
plunges me is the fact that I am always able to turn immediately to the
concrete things that are here in question.*

Igor Stravinsky[14]

[The business of the artist] *is not to escape from his material medium or bully it, but to serve it; but to serve it, he must love it. If he does so, he will realise that in its service is perfect freedom.*

Dorothy Sayers[13]

Every dramatist must learn to write stories that come from the characters and their situation, rather than starting with a theme or message
and imposing it on to those stories. 'The problem with Christians,' says
screenwriting teacher Bart Gavigan, 'is that they love theme more than
story.'[15] Story that is convincing and compelling comes from the characters' deepest inner motivations. The dramatist must learn, says Gavigan,
'to know his characters as God knows them,' and to love them, villains
included, in just the same way.

So then, respect takes time. It is only when we have the patience to
'listen' to what our medium and our subject-matter are saying to us,
rather than imposing our requirements on them, that we will begin to
create something authentic.

And could it be, perhaps, that we also need to learn respect for our own instinctive imagination? 'There is a deep and unique responsibility upon any artist to be faithful to that which rises within them,' says writer Mike Riddell. 'Unless one is committed to dragging that vision, wet and wild and pumping, from the creative womb, it is misleading to claim the title of "artist".'[16]

Being true to one's instincts may take courage, as Riddell himself discovered when he was asked to resign from his post at a Baptist Seminary after his superiors read his first novel. But an art that tries to fulfil other people's 'Christian' expectations may turn out to be no art at all.

Wrestling

There is a commonly held myth that the artist is a carefree person, producing great masterpieces in bursts of inspiration with no real effort. It must be said that this view is only held by those who have not tried it! All artists experience the gap between vision and reality. Only sustained, disciplined work will bridge it. If ever Edison's description of genius was valid, it is in the realm of art. Christians who think they have a direct inspirational line from God for their songs or poems should read Genesis 3 and think again. There are no short cuts. Art is very hard work.

Genius is one per cent inspiration and ninety-nine per cent perspiration.
Thomas Edison[20]

The writer Madeleine L'Engle describes going to hear Rudolph Serkin play a Beethoven sonata:

> We said to each other, 'That was a totally Spirit-filled performance. What did Rudolph Serkin have to do with it?' The answer was very simple: he practises the piano eight hours a day, every day. We have to practise our instruments. We don't sit and expect the Holy Spirit to come and do it for us. We have to be fit servants. Jesus talks about the servants being prepared, being ready for the coming of the Master. And so, whatever our art is we have to be prepared; we have to do our finger exercises.[17]

Thankfully, those moments of inspiration do come – that sudden spark for an idea or project you get when on a walk or in the bath, or that exhilarating feeling of an effortless performance – but we should be careful not to assume them synonymous with the work of the Holy Spirit. 'Bright ideas' do not always turn out to be Spirit-inspired, and the Holy Spirit is living in you, with or without bright ideas. Art often requires frustrating, exhausting and sustained effort. As Jeremy Begbie claims, 'It is just in this kind of toil that the Spirit is probably most active.'[18]

The irony, of course, is that the best end-results are those that have an air of deceptive ease. There is an oft-repeated story, quoted by Hans Rookmaaker,[19] of Hokusai, a great Japanese painter and engraver of

Inspiration in my experience does not so much float out of a clear sky as get washed up on the beach in a storm!
Graham Kendrick[21]

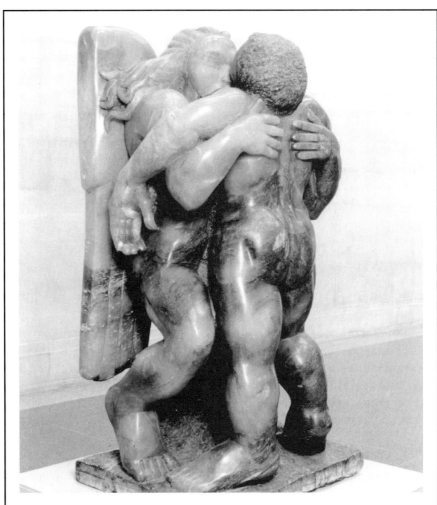

45.   Jacob Epstein, *Jacob Wrestling with the Angel* (1941), alabaster, 213 cm high (London, Tate Gallery)

Epstein's powerful sculpture is about a great deal more than a strange biblical incident.[22] It is about the experience many of us have of spiritual wrestling through a long, dark night. Whether it is with God, the devil, or our own errant emotions, whether with friend or enemy, we are often not too sure. Whether we label it 'prayer' or 'thinking things through' the experience is the same, and God is no less involved in either. We only know we cannot give up, however painful it may be. We may perhaps discover that the greatest 'blessing' only comes with our own brokenness.

But on another level, Epstein is speaking of the relationship every artist has with their material – part friend, part enemy, locked in an intimate relationship with it until the 'blessing' that it holds within itself has been fully revealed.

the nineteenth century. Once a great nobleman asked Hokusai for a painting of a rooster. He agreed, telling him to come back in a week. After a week the nobleman sent his servant to collect it, but Hokusai begged for a postponement. The servant came back two weeks later, then two months, then half a year: still the painting was not ready. After three years the nobleman was so furious that he came to see Hokusai for himself. Hokusai quickly took his brush and with a few elegant strokes drew the most perfect painting of a rooster. That made the nobleman even more angry.

'Why did you keep me waiting for years,' he asked, 'if you can do it in so short a time?'

'You don't understand,' said Hokusai. 'Come with me.'

He took the nobleman into his studio. There all over the walls were endless drawings of roosters, the product of three years' work.

Out of that came the mastery.

A line will take us hours maybe
Yet if it does not seem a moment's thought
Our stitching and unstitching has been nought.
W.B. Yeats[23]

18

Art as a Proper Job

Much as most artists would prefer to spend their lives closeted with canvas, keyboard or camera, leaving someone else to worry about putting food on the table or getting their work out to a waiting public, life is not like that. Artists have to live, not only in intimate relationship with their art, but with the nitty-gritty of the real world. They need a market for their work and money to live on. They need to be pragmatic, persevering and possible to live with.

Related

It may seem glaringly obvious to point out that everything we do as artists is related to those people we both love and hate – our audience. However, one hears so many artists blaming their lack of success on a philistine, undiscriminating public, that it is worth stating the obvious.

Anyone who has decided to follow Jesus cannot ignore his radical call to servanthood. Anyone who believes in God as Creator must take seriously a responsibility for tending and tilling our cultural earth. In other words, for the believer an 'art for art's sake' philosophy simply will not do. We cannot aggressively demand our right to practise our art, regardless of whether or not it connects with the world around.

Peter Fuller certainly was guilty of a little tongue-in-cheek exaggeration when he claimed that fine artists were irrelevant. One could easily say the same of philosophers or theologians. The point is not that society does not need philosophers, theologians or fine artists, but that it needs them to engage with the real issues that society itself is grappling with and to do it in a way which society has at least a chance of understanding! It needs them to relate to the real world.

Relating to an audience, however, is emphatically not the same as simply giving it what it wants. What it wants may well be nothing but guns and car crashes, sex and shopping, or prurient delving into other people's lives. Alternatively, what it wants may be a bland diet of 'nice' stories, neat endings, and art that comforts, reinforces prejudices and never, ever, stretches the brain. Christians, of course, are notoriously

It is only a mild exaggeration to say that no one wants Fine Artists except Fine Artists, and that neither they nor anyone else have the slightest idea of what they should be doing or for whom they should be doing it.
Peter Fuller[1]

quicker to condemn the first option, especially the sex. The latter seems so *harmless*. Paintings by the likes of Margaret Tarrant and Warner Sallman still hang on many a Sunday School wall, having convinced a whole generation that Jesus was a blond blue-eyed wimp in Persil-white, spending his time with middle-class children, deer and rabbits!

So here we are with another difficult path to tread. Without scorning our audience, without setting ourselves up as arbiter of their tastes and morals, without either pandering to them or milking them for all they are worth, we are to love them, respect them and give them the best gifts we have to offer. That begins, of course, by listening to what they actually want. Baptist minister and TV presenter Steve Chalke relates that when he first got involved in television, a seasoned reporter asked him what he thought of politicians in the media. Chalke replied that politicians never answer the question. 'Exactly', said the reporter, 'and evangelicals are worse than politicians.' 'And that's how we come across a great deal of the time,' says Chalke. 'The media are suspicious of evangelicals not because they're anti-Christian, but because they're looking for people who will listen and engage in real debate.'[2]

> *Evangelicals are very good at talking: we've got something to say and we go at it hammer and tongs. The problem is that we're not very good at listening.*
>
> Steve Chalke[3]

Realistic

A few facts and figures:

- Every two years the US art college system produces as many people as lived in the whole of Florence during the Renaissance.[4]
- Of 4,000 artists and writers surveyed in the USA in 1990, only 20 per cent earned their major income from their art or writing. Of the 83 per cent who earned anything at all, only half earned enough to cover their expenses.[5]
- In 1996, 14,000 British actors and other theatre workers were registered unemployed. In 1995 in a survey of its members, Equity, the British actors union, discovered that 25 per cent of its members had not worked at all in the previous year. Another 27 per cent had worked less than 10 weeks per year, a further 29 per cent had worked 30 weeks or less. To these statistics must be added the vast, but unknown, number of would-be performers who have not even managed to earn their Equity card.[6]

Going into the arts to find fame and fortune is a very bad bet indeed.

There is very little point grumbling that the world owes us a living. It is not necessarily going to give us one. As Christians we had better follow the example of St Paul, who made tents[7] so that he could support himself while pursuing what it was he passionately wanted to do – in his case preaching the gospel. The wise person setting out on a career in the arts will find themselves a 'tent-making' skill, and be prepared to use it.

> *Artists spend more time worrying about money than about art. At least I know I do. Money is the artistic problem – money to live on, money to buy artistic freedom, money to buy time to be creative.*
>
> Franky Schaeffer[8]

Working in the real world

What are the practical ways in which we can make sure we are plugged in to the real world? The following are adapted from some suggestions by Paul Clowney.[10]

Seek commissions
Working with a client and evolving a piece of work together can produce a much more satisfying result than soldiering on alone. Usually it is an enjoyable experience for the artist, knowing his or her talents are appreciated, and for the client, getting something unique and tailormade. Even at worst, when the process itself is fraught with difficulties, it is a far greater learning experience than working alone. And even under frustrating and limited circumstances, the resulting work may be as powerful, if not more so, than that produced in total freedom. Michelangelo took on the Sistine Chapel extremely reluctantly – he would much rather have been sculpting.

There is one other precious advantage in working to commissions – it avoids most artists' fatal tendency to procrastinate. As that wise observer Anonymous commented: 'The ultimate inspiration is the deadline.'

Be willing to compromise
Don't be too precious about your 'artistic integrity'. Be prepared to give a little. 'There is a lot of ground,' comments Clowney, 'between the Tate Gallery and horses' heads on black velvet!' In other words, most of art exists in the wide territory between high art and kitsch. We need not be afraid that falling below one will automatically make us end up in the other.

Be a conciliator
Try to explain your work, the process that led to it, and the principles behind it. Be prepared to act as a mediator. It may be a struggle to avoid jargon and find the right words for something that is essentially non-verbal, but if it provides a way in to art appreciation for those who think it is beyond them, it is well worth the effort.

Listen to criticism
Make sure you really hear what people – experts and non-experts alike – have to say about your work. Listen carefully for what they do *not* say, especially your friends. Distil criticism to its essence, look for common denominators and make sure you incorporate valid changes. Be prepared to have a good laugh at yourself.

Work in the community
Make sure you are willing to step outside the artistic élite for at least some of the time and create art among ordinary people. Put your painting on

When an artist is in the strict sense working, he of course takes into account the existing tastes, interests and capacity of his audience. These no less than the language, the marble, the paint, are part of his raw material; to be used, tamed, sublimated, not ignored or defied. Haughty indifference to them is not genius, it is laziness and incompetence.
C.S. Lewis[9]

the walls of subways and wine bars as well as galleries. Take your music and drama to the market place as well as the opera house, to schools as well as concert halls, to streets as well as theatres.

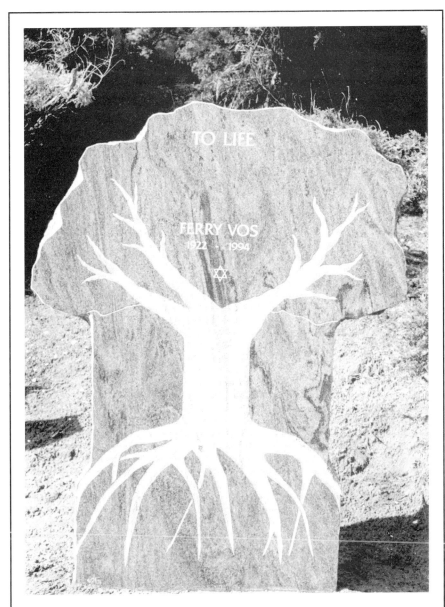

46.   Britt Wikström, *To Life* (1995), granite memorial, 1.5 metres high

Commissions come in all shapes and sizes and gravestones may not be every artist's idea of a fun assignment. In Britt Wikström's hands, however, they become moving affirmations of life; art that is truly related to the human need to mourn, remember and celebrate.

*Artists suffer
constant rejection
and this can lead to
unhealthy
self-analysis and
inward-looking
selfishness. When
allowed to flourish
this poisonous
mixture produces
towering, self-centred
egos . . . In history,
perhaps only military
commanders,
surgeons and
preachers have
rivalled artists in
their egos.*
  Franky Schaeffer[11]

Having found a means of financial support, the determined artist would do well to set about finding spiritual and emotional support – friends who will encourage and give you the odd kick up the backside, friends who will pray through success and failure, friends who will gently tell the truth when it is needed, who will prick any bubbles of pomposity and stop you believing your own publicity.

Such friends are not easy to find, but are worth seeking out. They are worth far more than gold, 'oil on Aaron's beard'[12] or whatever simile of wealth you care to think of. It is helpful if some, at least, are fellow Christian artists. There is a huge amount to be gained by seeking those on the same journey as yourself and travelling alongside them. And the local church, for all its possible failings, is a good source of loyal friends – unsophisticated maybe, aesthetically-challenged maybe, but the salt of the earth who will give you their seasoning through good and bad times alike.

For in the unlikely event that you do find success, you will surely need them. Success will always bring with it its own dangers and temptations. (This could, of course, be why God in his wisdom allows so many artists to remain in their garrets.) Art at its best reaches deep into its audience, touching emotion as well as intellect. That means it is very powerful, and as everyone knows except the person who has it, power corrupts. Applause and acclaim can all too easily lead to vanity and self-satisfaction, superficiality and complacency, not stretching or taking risks, not making hard choices, not living up to God's (rather than others') expectations. At worst, they can turn genuine creativity into cynical manipulation.

In the play *Amadeus* by Peter Shaffer,[13] Salieri, a musician who has gained fame and fortune and yet knows his own mediocrity, rails against God. He is struggling with something that many believers find hard – that God seems to give his most sublime gifts to those who deserve them least.

SALIERI   Dimly the music sounded from the salon above. Dimly the stars shone on the empty street. I was suddenly frightened. It seemed to me that I had heard a voice of God – and that it issued from a creature whose own voice I had also heard – and it was the voice of an obscene child!

 . . . I have worked and worked the talent you allowed me. You know how hard I've worked! – solely that in the end, in the practice of the art which alone makes the world comprehensible to me, I might hear Your Voice! And now I do hear it – and it says only one name: MOZART! . . . Spiteful, sniggering conceited, infantile Mozart! – who has never worked one minute to help another man! – shit-talking Mozart with his botty-smacking wife! – **him** you have chosen to be your sole conduct! . . .

There is nothing wrong with seeking success. Everyone wants to be good at what they do. Everyone wants to be loved. Everyone wants to communicate and touch the heart of someone else. But the world of the arts has a crazy value system and anyone seeking success would do well to realise it. Can Tom Cruise or Harrison Ford really be a thousand times better actors than those working on the New York fringe? The difference in salaries would seem to suggest it. What makes Andy Warhol's copy of a Campbell's soup-tin worth so much more than a graphic designer's new soup-tin label?

Sometimes it seems it is all down to the name game. If you want to sell your work, the important thing is to get people to remember who you are. How? Well, shock is always a good tactic. If it is not going to be shocking then it had better be 'in-yer-face'. Back to Gavin Turk again, the wily self-publicist.

The irony of this century has been that the more determinedly anti-art art becomes the more it just keeps on selling. But only with a name. When Duchamp first submitted his notorious urinal to an exhibition in 1917, he did so under the pseudonym of R. Mutt. No takers. Only when it was known that it was submitted by the famous Marcel Duchamp was it actually accepted as a work of art and acclaimed.[14]

And who made the artwork anyway? We might suggest, only slightly tongue-in-cheek, that as the world of fine art turns more and more to technicians to actually produce the artefact, would it not be a good idea for galleries to credit everyone involved? Rather in the way in which a film lists everyone from director down to key grip and accountant, perhaps it would be more honest for a Damien Hirst to credit farmer, taxidermist, display case manufacturer *et al.*

It seems the world of the arts has two ways of rewarding artists – vast sums for a few who happen to get noticed and peanuts for the rest. We had better not believe that our true value is indicated by the price our work commands, or we will end up egomaniacs or monkeys.

Responsible

In *Amadeus*, Salieri struggles with a contradiction we all recognise – sublime art produced by crass people. It sometimes seems that the genius of the artist's work is in direct proportion to the dysfunctionality of his/her life. If this is so, it poses a dilemma for Christian artists. Must we submit to addiction, severed ears or broken relationships to bring our talent to the full? Does it follow that indulging in sin will make us better artists? If Tolstoy's theory is correct, is it inevitable that we can perfect our art only at the expense of our lives? Thankfully, there is no evidence for this proposition. Self-controlled, well-integrated folk have produced masterpieces too.

The poet skims off the best of life and puts it in his work. That is why his work is beautiful and his life bad.

Leo Tolstoy[15]

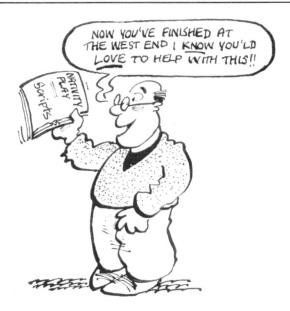

47.   Taffy Davies (1995)

A small aside here on the subject of Christian freebies. Sooner or later, and probably sooner, any Christian artist will be asked to do something 'for the Lord's work' for free, or at least on the cheap. *Just* design a poster, direct the nativity play, sing for the evangelistic event, give some architectural advice, edit the odd book. As an extra to a regular wage it is not so bad, but for freelancers it poses a real problem. What to do? There are no rules, but here are a few suggestions:

- Tell them you are willing to help in ways other than your own profession, but that for anything professional you wish to be paid the going rate.
- Offer a cut-price 'Christian' rate, but make sure your invoice shows the full price with a discount, so that they realise what your time and skills are really worth.
- Decide to give some time instead of money. One suggested way is to follow the Old Testament practice of 'tithing' (giving a tenth to God), a principle that can be used for time or money or a mix of both.
- Take on the job as a 'loss leader'. Using your gifts in a Christian context can be an excellent way to try them out, refine them and simply get them seen or heard.
- Do it as a love gift to God. If so, do it willingly and joyfully, never as a duty or because you can't say no.
- If you *are* irretrievably feeble when it comes to saying no, make a practice of saying you'll go away and pray about it.
- Do pray about it. God may have some opinions on the matter.

However, it sometimes seems that the balance is tipped the other way, and as Christians we must grapple with this. It is certainly true that pouring vast amounts of energy into our work, whatever it be, cannot be done without cost to other areas of our lives. Jesus told some stories to illustrate the importance of counting the cost before embarking on a grand project.[16] He did not say that the grand project (in this case giving up everything to follow him) should not be embarked on, only that it should be done with eyes wide open.

No work of art is more important than the artist's own life.
Francis Schaeffer[19]

There are choices to be made, but they need not be choices that harm ourselves or others. A contemporary of Michelangelo's remarked that 'Those who knew only his work knew the lesser part – his life was greater.'[17] And that means he must have led a pretty impressive life!

There will be times when, like Shaffer's Salieri, we are tempted to cry 'It's not fair.' Why do they get all the breaks? Why does it seem so easy for them? But comparisons are not only odorous but, as Shaffer demonstrates, ultimately destructive. However successful we get, there will always be someone ahead of us. Jesus' parable of the talents[18] is relevant here, although at first glance that too tempts us to complain of unfairness. Why was it the one who began with fewest talents who got condemned? Perhaps because Jesus understood how most of us perceive ourselves as one-talenters struggling behind the two-talenters and five-talenters who always find it so easy. Comparison is not the point. The point, says Jesus, is what *you* did with *your* talent. Leave the others to me.

As to why the bad guys seem to get all the good breaks – a question asked from time immemorial – that is one to be answered in heaven. For now, let us just observe that genius seems to be no respecter of persons, and, as we have observed before, all art, however inspiring, is made by fallen people in a fallen world.

Ruthless and risk-taking

One little postscript in our rundown of the demands of art as a proper job: the artist must be prepared to be brave. Get ready to paper your loo with rejection slips, watch the other gallery exhibits getting red dots, go to the hundredth audition where they tell you you are too tall/blonde/dark/thin, watch your twentieth film proposal get no further than 'development'. Smile bravely when your friends tell you they '*quite* enjoyed' your book or play, that your installation was 'mmm, interesting', and when the critics, with no such compunction, tell the world it was rubbish.

For here is a simple truth: *in order to do something well, you must first be willing to do it badly.*

The problem is that it is your baby out there that they are insulting or battering. It is something that came from the very depths of you, that

> Doesn't this translation of verses from Psalm 73 sound uncannily familiar and contemporary when thinking about the current art scene?
>
> *God is truly good . . .*
> *to those who have pure hearts.*
> *But I had almost stopped believing this truth,*
> *I had almost lost my faith*
> *because I was jealous of proud people.*
> *I saw wicked people doing well . . .*
> *They are looking for profits.*
> *They do not control their selfish desires.*
> *They make fun of others and speak evil.*
> *Proudly they speak of hurting others.*
> *They boast to the sky.*
> *Their mouths gossip on the earth.*
> *So their people turn to them*
> *and give them whatever they want . . .*
>
> Psalm 73:1–3,7–10[21]

There has to come a time in rehearsal when you have to 'murder your darlings' . . . You may treasure and nurture this bit of cleverness, but for the sake of the show it has to go. The show is more important than the individual contribution. You have to be tough on yourself . . . And when you murder your darlings, there is no time for weeping or the grand manner.

Trevor Nunn[20]

took long gestation and hard labour. No matter. You have to be prepared, in Trevor Nunn's phrase, to 'murder your darlings'. And do it many times over. Being an artist is a long haul.

The painter William Kurelek had a long painful journey before he found faith and success as an artist. He suffered from depression and mental illness and eked out a living making picture frames, before in his thirties becoming a Roman Catholic and, shortly after, having his first exhibition. When his paintings finally started selling, his managing agent raised the prices steeply. So Kurelek started doing smaller paintings to keep the prices down so that ordinary wage-earners could still buy them. One week after he died in 1977, the prices on Kurelek's work jumped 600 per cent. They can now be seen in the Museum of Modern Art in New York, the Smithsonian Institute and the National Gallery of Canada.

It is not an unusual story in the annals of art history. Van Gogh is the classic that springs to mind. He only sold one painting in his lifetime, but now collectors pay millions for just one of his works.

Kurelek perhaps found in his lifetime a measure of his true value that eluded the tortured van Gogh. But our worth can never be measured by the commercial price placed on us, or even by our own self-estimation. True value perhaps will only be understood when we hear from God his 'Well done, good and faithful servant.'

What you are doing now is just one part of a life's calling, just one more gruelling and exhilarating step in the pursuit of excellence. 'Those who succeed,' says one best-selling novelist, 'are those who go beyond what is comfortable.' He adds that it is important to see beyond the success or failure of *this* book, *this* project, to see yourself as a writer or artist for whom this is just one step further. Whether it turns out to be either of those two impostors triumph or disaster, it is part of a wider picture. If God has called you, the journey will not be in vain.

One does not discover new lands without consenting to lose sight of the shore for a very long time.

André Gide[23]

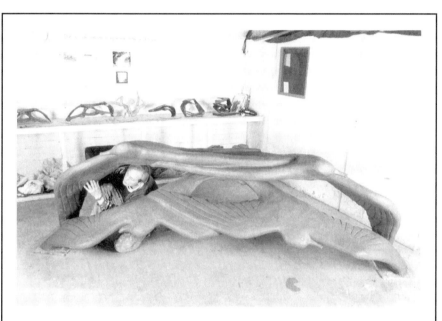

48.   Richard Miller working on sculpture for Glasgow City Council (1997) (photo: Mike Brunton)

Richard Miller is pleased that children are allowed to scramble over his sculptures. He enjoys creating work for a community setting, despite the fact that this can be a long and arduous process. When fulfilling commissions for public work, a whole host of new considerations come in – cost, strength, stability, the minutiae of health and safety regulations, the long wait for funding to come through. On such a time-consuming and stop–start process Miller has been grateful for the prayers of supportive friends. 'There was a time when I felt like giving up,' he comments, 'but God heard those prayers and it was only then that I started growing full swing.'[22]

19

Art as a Twenty-First Century Calling

Standing in the gap

We simply cannot afford another century in which the tastes of the public and the tastes of its aesthetic commentators are as divergent as they have been during the years of modernism.
Waldemar
Januszczak[1]

Art critic Waldemar Januszczak, commenting on the wide gap between the art to which the public relates (the Pre-Raphaelites and Salvador Dali, judging by Tate Gallery postcard sales) and that lauded by the fine art élite, observes: 'If there is one cultural development that absolutely must take place in the art years ahead, it is the bridging of such gaps.'[2]

Is this a role that responsible Christians could fill, that of standing in the gap? It is a crazy notion, admittedly. After all, Christians are more known for being behind the cultural times than ahead of them. But maybe it is not quite as crazy as it seems. Unlike the art establishment, dominated by scepticism and nihilism, we want to create art with meaning – and, on the whole, art that Jo Public can understand. At its worst, this tendency produces art that is execrable, at its best, work that has a gentle and enduring power. It is sometimes our weakness, but it could also be our strength.

Clinging to tradition?

It is short-sighted, not to say stupid, in the correct desire to be relevant as Christian artist in an unchristian age, to pick up the secular fashion of the immediate generation before us and immerse oneself in that as your tradition. That's why Christian artists so often seem to be a generation late.
Calvin Seerveld[3]

We have to acknowledge it: across the range of art forms – music, poetry, media, visual arts – there are very few Christian ground-breakers. Is it just that Christians are irrevocably old-fashioned? Certainly, as we have noted before, the refusal of the evangelical wing of the church to engage with the arts has left it struggling with an artistic ethos that is several generations behind.

There undoubtedly *is* a new generation of Christians desperate to move on and be part of the contemporary arts scene, but as Calvin Seerveld points out, this very desire to be 'relevant' can be the artist's downfall. In the urgent quest to communicate with lost humanity, the Christian picks on 'the secular fashion of the immediate generation before';[4] in other words, one that is still popular, but relatively safe. Having alighted on that form, it is all too easy to stick with it, rather than experiment. Hence the tendency of Christians always to be at least a generation behind the times.

Seerveld believes that before the church can make a really dynamic contribution to the arts, it has to have its own 'cultural infra-structure'. There is a catching-up process involved which cannot be circumvented or avoided:

> It takes a long time for an art-knowledgeable faith community to become a living tradition, a mulching ground that generates deeper-going artistry, which will have a certain undefensive slant and staying power.
>
> It probably takes more than one generation of artists, art critics, art public, art patrons, art theorists, art publicists, working together in communal perspective to develop the normal body for supporting the numerous second-rate artists one needs to get a few genial ones.[5]

It is a noticeable phenomenon that, of the best-known Christians in the visual arts, relatively few are working in contemporary media such as installations and video art. Many have stuck with painting, and of those a surprisingly high proportion are producing art that is representational. The interesting thing about this trend is that it is closer to a century, rather than a generation, behind the times. However, it is also curious to note that for many artists it is a deliberate choice to return to a more figurative style after working in more abstract and avant-garde ways.

Ironically, in *this* trend they are running ahead of the times. The contemporary art world's determination to strip away every vestige of old ideas is a trend that is running out of time and ultimately has nowhere to go. Critics have commented on a new breeze blowing, what Brandon Taylor refers to as a 'Post-Conceptual radicalism – an unexpected return to overt reference, iconography and symbolism . . . work for which "narrative" may be the key formal term'.[6]

A fierce debate is raging. There are still plenty who believe that 'Only a miracle could prevent [painting] from coming to an end.'[7] For others, 'a return to "narrative" and "painterly expression" could only mean a retreat from serious critical engagement with art'.[8] Whether they are right or not, only time will tell. Only the most foolhardy would attempt to predict where fine art will be a century from now. One thing is sure – it will be an exciting century.

It is surely unthinkable that the representation of human experiences, in other words, people and their emotions, landscapes and still lives could be forever excluded from painting.
Norman Rosenthal[9]

Telling our stories

One more thing is sure. The world wants stories, not one big one, but many small ones. Stories in which we recognise our own lives, narratives rooted in personal experience and a real, earthy, gritty world; anecdotes

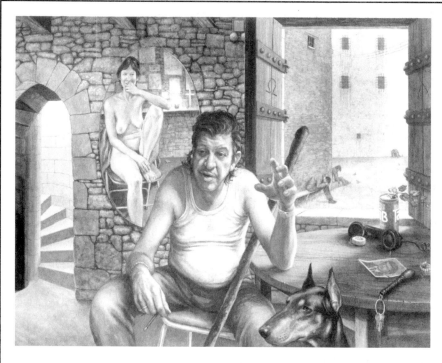

49. Fred Folsom, Danny Robson, or *Saint Danny of Tacoma Park* (1982), oil on panel, 91.5 × 122 cm (Collection of George Thompson)

Fred Folsom is a contemporary American painter who unashamedly uses 'narrative' and 'painterly expression'. There are some who would say he is little more than a clever illustrator, a Norman Rockwell in reverse, chronicling the dark underbelly rather than the small-town homeliness of American society. But a closer inspection of his work reveals that all is not as simple as it seems.

In this picture, symbols and references proliferate, from the stick, key-ring and dog that hint at Danny's macho character, to a proliferation of religious symbolism. The enigmatic naked woman (Folsom's paintings almost always contain a nude) is seen in an oval mirror which echoes the mandorla or full-body halo that surrounded medieval Virgins.

And what is this place? It looks like a medieval castle. (For those who know, it bears some resemblance to St Elizabeth's Institute for the criminally insane where Danny was once an inmate.) One enters Danny's 'cell' from the prison of despair; the brightly-lit staircase indicates that there just might be a way out.

Yes, there is a story behind this. 'Big Danny' was a mercenary, boxer and gangster, before being imprisoned for a double murder. It was in hospital that he experienced a revelation that made him a changed man. He spent the next 23 years working as a 'no-frills therapist' with drug addicts and alcoholics.

His story echoes Folsom's own. A dyslexic child of highly literate parents, Folsom dropped out into a world of drunkenness and debauchery until experiencing a Christian conversion. Folsom has described his paintings, which draw on the seedy world of his prodigal days, as 'Rorschach tests' – demanding you look at the ugliness of humanity and examine your reactions. *Danny Robson* celebrates, in Folsom's words, the fact that 'The Body of Christ has some really bizarre representatives.'[10]

and metaphors and illustrations that illuminate small-t truth, rather than lectures that demand allegiance to capital-T Truth.

All of this should present no problem to Christians – followers of a man who spent most of his life telling stories and the rest of it dramatically acting out the message he came to get across. Jesus took the everyday world of his hearers and transformed it into something different. He told stories that surprised and jolted and lodged in the memory and changed perceptions. He used the simple – a man fishing, a woman searching for a coin – and the absurd – one blind man leading another, someone with a beam in his eye trying to take a splinter from someone else's. He drew from psychology – how people react at a dinner party – and horticulture – how vines need to be pruned. He told stories that seemed to be about comfort for the underdog: a prodigal son returning to his father, a beggar rewarded in the after-life while a rich man had to suffer; and gave them a twist in the tail. It was his hearers who were the resentful older brother, they were the ones who had been warned of judgement and never listened. Sometimes he explained his stories, often he did not. Sometimes their meanings were obvious, sometimes frankly baffling.

His life, too, was crammed with incidents that told the story a different way. Meetings with tarts and lepers and quislings and widows and little kids became flesh and blood images of encounter with Father God. Familiar objects like wine-goblets and loaves and donkeys and towels and bowls of water became symbols of a spiritual dynamic. He turned his audience into part of the story-telling, inviting a small boy with loaves and fishes up on stage as part of the act! He subverted traditional myth, enacting the triumphant Messianic entry in the knowledge that the ending would be all too different.

In many ways, Jesus is an amazing model for the Christian artist in a post-modern age. Like him our raw material is the everyday world around us. Like him we can take the familiar stories and images of our day and subvert them into something unexpected.

However, this does *not* mean the artist's job is retelling Jesus' parables or his life, not even trying to give them a new gloss by setting them in our own time. In fact, it is *not* even necessarily telling parables, full stop. Parables, as such, are the tool of teachers, not artists. They are stories told with the clear aim of communicating a specific message. Art, by contrast, is the articulation of our perceptions and experiences of our inner and outer world, irrespective of whether or not this conveys a specific 'message'. As animator Nick Park has discovered, 'If you have some truth you want to somehow put in, I've found it never works. You have to forget the agenda. Stories sort of work themselves out.'[11]

Our task is to tell the stories that arise from our own culture, our own experience. God's created world is a renewable resource. Donkeys and vines might have been great symbols in first-century Palestine;

*Change comes from
small initiatives
which imitated
become the fashion.
We cannot wait for
great visions from
great people, for they
are in short supply at
the end of history. It
is up to us to light
our own small fires
in the darkness.*
Charles Handy[12]

supermarket trolleys, airports and the Internet are more appropriate at the end of the twentieth – and no less spiritual. If we believe God is at work in his world in every generation, then his fingerprints will be as evident in the twenty-first century as in the first chapter of Genesis.

At the end of the day, people cannot live without a grand story. (Post-modernism, in making the claim that there are no meta-narratives, is, of course, a meta-narrative in its own right!) In telling the stories of our world, we are not denying the existence of a Christian 'grand story'. Rather we are breaking through the barriers that have been raised against it. We are funding the imagination, opening up the possibility of wonder, not so much providing answers as reminding the world of questions it has forgotten to ask. We are sowing seeds, confident that human minds are still fertile soil and that God will never fail to provide water and sun.

Swimming against the tide

Jesus Christ has given us an example in one other aspect of Christian living – that of swimming against the tide. And over the centuries his followers have had plenty of practice. Christians know how to be a minority.

It is an experience that is both a strength and a weakness. At worst it leads to a ghetto mentality and a stubborn determination to ignore fashion on principle. At best it creates a courageous individuality and a refusal to be browbeaten into the latest artistic political correctness.

There are many ways in which Christians can and must swim against the contemporary art tide, and a few of them are worth picking out.

*Knee-jerk Irony: The
tendency to make
flippant ironic
comments as a
reflexive matter of
course in everyday
conversation.*

*Derision Pre-
emption: A lifestyle
tactic: the refusal to
go out on any sort of
emotional limb so as
to avoid mockery
from peers. Derision
Pre-emption is the
main goal of
Knee-jerk Irony.*
Douglas Coupland[13]

Rejecting knee-jerk irony
Irony is the *lingua franca* of the post-modern age. For Generation X, Brit-art, Brit-pop and the rest, irony is almost the only way to communicate. As a tactic to make a point it is a valid language for Christians, and a skill we should learn as an effective communication tool. After all, it is hard not to picture an ironic smile hovering on Jesus' lips as some of his deadpan comments had their barbed effect: 'If any one of you is without sin, let him be the first to throw a stone at her';[14] 'Give to Caesar what is Caesar's';[15] and in answer to Pilate's leading question, 'It is as you say.'[16]

But as 'a reflexive matter of course', it has no place in either the art or the conversation of a believer. Why? Because irony communicates detachment and lack of involvement. It implies ambiguity and a refusal to commit.

None of these qualities characterised Jesus. He knew when to be ironic, but he also knew when to be passionate and straightforward and affirming and real. His followers should aim for nothing less.

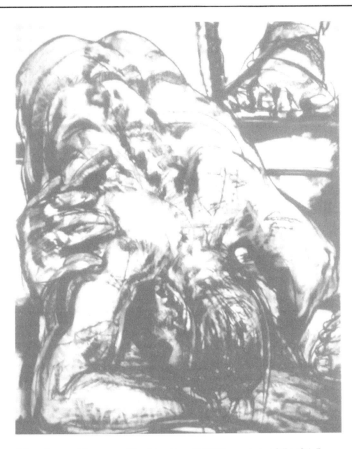

50.   Bruce Herman, *The Mocking* (1992), pastel, 127 × 96.5 cm

A recent letter from a museum director who had seen Herman's *Via Dolorosa* series (of which this is part) admired the formal qualities of the paintings, their brushwork and 'gutsy expressionism', but he also said he found it hard to believe that anyone beside Sunday School didacts would attempt 'meant' religious imagery. The unspoken implication was that an ironic use of religious iconography was intellectually defensible, but that sincerely intended religious painting was not.

Herman took the director's comments as back-handed praise, concluding that there is too much at stake in this life not to mean what you are saying. He sees the late twentieth century as a transitional period, a 'time between times, wherein those who stand in a particular tradition may meet with a great deal of resistance; hence the call for "silence, cunning and exile". But I've never been particularly silent or cunning – though I may be an exile.

'I blunder like a bull in a china shop of recent art history, ignoring the taboos and continuing to paint what seems in the secular world to be the new forbidden fruit: "meant" Christian imagery.'[17]

The art world may label us naive – as it has Craigie Aitchison, the Scottish painter whose work has been described as 'characterised by a gentle innocence which displays none of the self-conscious irony of much contemporary art'.[19] It may wonder whether we are genuine, as it did with Bruce Herman.

It takes courage to lower the ironic mask and offer honesty and vulnerability. But, as Diana, Princess of Wales demonstrated, they are qualities that have a compelling attraction in a cynical world. Society may be puzzled, embarrassed or infuriated by us, but it will also be forced to give its grudging admiration. Rather as it did with Jesus, in fact.

In place of irony offer vulnerability.
Mark Greene[18]

Refusing pretension and power

From John Hegley to Sarah Lucas, Jarvis Cocker to Quentin Tarantino, one thing for which we can applaud the artists of our generation is their determination to fight against pretension. Unfortunately, just as quickly as artists strip it away, publishers, curators, critics, managers and dealers re-instate it. The arts establishment is as pompous and pretentious as it ever was, perhaps far more so. For all those who stand out against it, there are many others who learn to play the game. And is it imagination, or are some of those who make the biggest show of refusing the conceits and conventions of a previous generation, all too happy to replace them with their own?

Jesus, far from being meek and mild, was a scourge to the establishment of his day. He expressed vitriolic anger at its control over ordinary people's lives, and used radical direct action against its commercial power base. But more often he simply pointed out its absurdities. He poked gentle fun at his society's value systems, told his stories and drew his verbal pictures and left his hearers to draw their own conclusions.

Far from being a self-publicist, he frequently told the recipients of his amazing gifts not to tell anyone[20] and slipped away just when he had the chance to have fans and critics alike eating out of his hand.[21] He avoided adulation – the one notable exception, the 'Triumphal Entry' to Jerusalem[22] was, in practice, a 'March to the Scaffold' (and perhaps a conscious use of dramatic irony).

Jesus' choices in the face of both applause and criticism were forged long before, in the loneliness of the wilderness.[23] By the time he found himself in a public role, he was already secure in his private choice – to serve God only. The artist would do well to do the same.

Taking responsibility for our actions

Post-modernism has taught that everyone brings their own 'reading' and meaning to a work of art and every intepretation is valid. Therefore, the logic runs, every artistic expression must be valid. It is a short step from there to conclude that the artist is absolved from any responsibility for how people respond to his or her work.

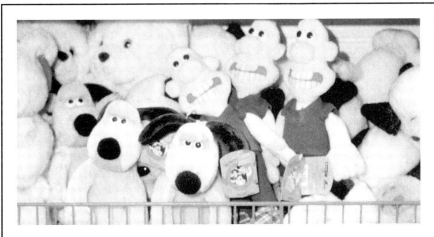

51.   *Everybody's favourites: Wallace and Gromit* (photo: Hilary Brand)

No one could describe Nick Park as pretentious. Despite three Oscars, four Baftas and a CBE, interviewers agree in describing him as 'unassuming' and 'diffident'.

Nor could they accuse his creations, Wallace and Gromit, of any pretensions to high art or deep philosophical statements.

'I worried about that for a long time,' says Park, 'because I thought what I'm merely interested in is giving people a good laugh, and doing things that are entertaining. But now I've come to believe that this can be pleasing to God . . . When you're at art school, there's always such a pressure to be radical and make statements with your art. If you link that to being a Christian as well, then it gets really exaggerated . . . I've had to calm down and learn.'[24]

The strange thing is that refusing to be drawn into grand statements or capital-A Art has produced work that, if the phenomenal popularity of Wallace and Gromit, Shaun the Sheep and Feathers McGraw the Penguin are anything to measure by, goes far beyond 'mere' entertainment. It would be interesting (but beyond the scope of these pages) to study the allusions these Plasticine characters awake. Is it nostalgia for some lost cosy domesticity, fond recognition of Gromit's exasperated loyalty or Wallace's eccentric enthusiasms? Or is it that Park so loves his characters and their world that his affection spills through and on to the screen? (It is said that Wallace is modelled on his father, who once built a wooden caravan and wallpapered the inside, much like the space rocket in *A Grand Day Out*.)

Certainly there is a love of the art form apparent in every shining detail. When you realise that the 23 minutes of *A Grand Day Out*, took six, virtually single-handed, years to complete and involved 33,120 separate shots, you begin to understand just how essential love was to the enterprise.

It is an attractive philosophy. It means no subject-matter is out of bounds. It allows the artist to have fun playing with connections, throwing ideas and subjects together to see what sparks they produce, without having to think about why or what the response will be.

Certainly, we cannot predict all the wide diversity of associations, memories and experiences that the viewer or listener will bring to our work. Someone who is a drag-racing enthusiast will bring very different associations to a film like *Crash*, from someone whose loved one was killed in a motorway pile-up.

Neither can we be bound by every sensitivity and moralistic whim, till our work is as bland as mayonnaise on white toast. Jesus was far from bland, and not at all averse to the use of shock tactics to make his point. He quite deliberately touched lepers,[26] flouted religious law by healing on the Sabbath,[27] refused to give priority to his family[28] and created havoc in the Temple.[29] And if, as the Bible teaches, the crucifixion was all part of God's plan, it was a pretty horrific event to put at the heart of a new religion. No bowing to sensitivities there.

But that does not mean that, like Cronenberg, we can toss all responsibility aside. In fact, as progress in technology disseminates art to an ever wider audience and makes censorship and control ever more difficult, they are even more our responsibility. It could be said that the harder it is to identify your audience, the greater the responsibility for what you give them.

God has commissioned us to be stewards of his cultural earth, responsible to him to do the best for his creation, human or otherwise. That means there will be times when it is right to hold back for fear of breaking the bruised reed of struggling conscience. There will be others when some brutal pruning of complacency and self-interest is needed! Discerning between the two will never be easy, but we cannot assume that anyone else will do it for us.

Affirming ultimate values

The arts world has had its fill of nihilism. The Christian world is sick to death of dogma, sentimentality and trivia. The world at large is satiated with sex and shopping.

To a society just as turbulent and dissatisfied, Jesus gave no easy answers. What he did offer was love of both God and neighbour, and hope of needs met and lives remade. He preached gratitude for good gifts and action against injustice. He affirmed that the world was a marvellous place and that God has never and will never give up on it.

Like Jesus, the Christian artist is called to an affirmation of basic and lasting values. Like Jesus, we will demonstrate more than we will speak. Like Jesus our authority will come from costly truthfulness and the crucible of hard choices.

At the time you're being an artist, you're not a citizen. You have, in fact, no social responsibility whatsoever.
David Cronenberg[25]

To me, the purpose of the arts is to introduce people to life in all its breadth and complexity and thereby to find oneself, others, the world and God more fully.
Gary Collins[30]

Nailing our colours to the mast

Many of us would hate to be called a 'Christian artist' or be referred to as making 'Christian art'. Apart from sounding rather pretentious, it is hardly a major selling-point to galleries or commissioning editors! But there is something which justifies these scandalous labels, even for those not doing overtly religious art. As we have already seen, worldviews pervade our life and actions in all that we do. Of course, it *is* possible to wear two different worldview 'spectacles' – one in church and one in the studio – and a surprising number of Christians seem unconcerned at doing so. But if we do our art with any integrity, our Christian worldview will unconsciously and inescapably enter our work. We are, whether we like the label or not, 'Christian artists'.

Nick Park again: 'At art school, I felt guilty for a long time that I was getting excited about ideas that were nothing to do with God, but I never got any ideas about God that were any good. I feel I've just got to do things which mean something to me and which come from the heart. I have to listen to myself. But I do regard my films as Christian.'[31]

There is one other reason why it is not such a bad thing to accept the label of 'Christian artist'. To do so is to acknowledge that we are not lone islands, entire unto ourselves, but part of something much larger: a community of the disciples of Jesus Christ reaching around the globe, back over two millennia and forward into generations to come. And there is much to be gained by actively gathering together with others not ashamed to wear the label; forming ourselves into like-minded creative communities; working, laughing and praying together, letting the sparks fly and the rough edges rub against each other until we are honed sharp and strong to meet the world.

Dancing to a different drum

Could it really be that God wants to take the feeble and fragmented body of Christians in the arts and use it to change society? Since taking weakness and transforming it into strength is one of the great themes running through the Bible, we at least have a few helpful precedents. The Old Testament is crammed with rebels and no-hopers whom God took by the scruff of the neck and made into prophets and leaders. The great edifice of the Christian church was begun by a team of twelve which no Human Resources consultant in their right mind would consider.

Who would have thought that, from that shaky beginning, within three hundred years Christianity would have become the world's strongest religion? It would have been as laughable a proposition in 34 AD, as is the proposition now that Christians should take a lead in the world of art.

A faith project in Christian artistry will never be healthy among us until there is a living sense of Christian community, and the misplaced emphasis on the 'individual' has been corrected. God has set things up so that cultural endeavour is always a communal enterprise, done by trained men and women in concert, gripped by a spirit that is larger than each one individually and that pulls them together as they do their formative work.
Calvin Seerveld[32]

In some ways the future need not concern us. If we are fully using our gifts as God's stewards, then the wider picture is his problem, not ours. If we are truly doing the work we are called to do – be it the most 'avant' of avant-garde or the most unreconstructed traditionalism, the most 'in-yer-face' shock-art or the lightest of light entertainment – then the world's verdict is of no importance.

However, if we remain entrenched in the Christian ghetto, trailing cautiously a generation behind, or repeating 'safe' or saleable formulae, then we need beware. It is the cultural equivalent of 'burying our talent',[33] something for which Jesus had the harshest possible words.

And if there are *no* Christ-believing artistic ground-breakers, then as a Christian community we are *not* truly doing what God calls us to do. As God's image-bearers, we are called to *form* culture, not simply follow on behind.

Launching into the deep

Now here is my secret:
I tell it to you with an openness of heart that I doubt that I shall ever achieve again, so I pray that you are in a quiet room as you hear these words. My secret is that I need God – that I am sick and can no longer make it alone. I need God to help me give, because I no longer seem capable of giving; to help me be kind, as I no longer seem capable of kindness; to help me love as I seem beyond being able to love.[35]

These words were written by the person who defined a generation. Douglas Coupland, author of *Generation X*, has also written of *Life after God*, about the world of privileged suburban children who once used to 'float at night in swimming pools the temperature of blood'[36] and now found themselves in 'McJobs', cushioned, restless and adrift.

Another writer, Dominic Crossan, has likened the post-modern world to a darkened sea:

There is no lighthouse keeper. There is no lighthouse. There is no dry land. There are only people living on rafts made from their own imaginations.[37]

It has become socially acceptable, as we hover between millennia, to admit to spiritual longing. There is no expectation of that longing being met. The church does little to change things, positioning itself on dry land with a loud hailer, occasionally launching rescue missions, but rarely venturing far enough out to actually save anyone.

There is a need for a new kind of Christian mission, one that is willing to travel far out on a fragile craft, one that consents to be vulnerable and

I want to suggest to you that the day of the artists has come. That there are things about symbols and the genuine indirectness of art with integrity that can speak into a lost and stuck imagination . . . We are awakening the imagination of people who have become cynical about the old 'grand stories' that have done so much harm. We are sowing the possibility that there might be one which could actually set them free.
Graham Cray[34]

fallible, one that understands what it feels like to be adrift, but is still able to describe from experience what it is like to have the rock beneath your feet.

This, then, is the journey of the Christian artist.

References

Preface
1 Bragg, Melvyn quoted in *Third Way* (June 1997)
2 Veith, Gene *State of the Arts* (Wheaton, Ill., Crossway 1991)
3 Seerveld, Calvin *Rainbows for a Fallen World* (Toronto, Tuppence Press 1980)

Introduction
1 Ryken, Leland *The Liberated Imagination* (Wheaton, Ill., Harold Shaw 1989)
2 Rookmaaker, Hans *Modern Art and the Death of a Culture* (Leicester, IVP 1970; 2nd edn (1973) re-issued Leicester Apollos 1994)
3 Ryken, Leland op. cit.
4 Januszczak, Waldemar 'Making Sense of the Century', *Sunday Times* (11 May 1997)

1 Art in a Post-Modern Age
1 Taken from review by Whitford, Frank 'The Provinces Square up to the City', *Sunday Times* (10 August 1997)
2 Reputed to be Damien Hirst's definition of a work of art, in Sewell, Brian 'New Contemporaries and the Whitechapel Open', *Alphabet of Villains* (London, Bloomsbury 1995)
3 McLuhan, Marshall quoted in Appignanesi, R. and Garratt, C. *Postmodernism for Beginners* (Cambridge, Icon 1985)
4 Longley, Clifford, introduction to Sacks, J. *Faith in the Future* (London, Darton, Longman & Todd 1995)
5 Lyotard, Jean-François *The Postmodern Condition* (Manchester University Press 1984)
6 Cupitt, Don *Creation out of Nothing* (London, SCM 1990)
7 Fuller, Peter *Theoria: Art and the Absence of Grace* (London, Chatto & Windus 1988)
8 Hill, Sally *Weekend Guardian* (31 May 1997)
9 Eno, Brian in programme to U2's *Zooropa* tour, 1993
10 Bauman, Zygmunt *Life in Fragments* (Oxford, Blackwell 1995)

11 Cray, Graham, 'Goodbye to the Grand Story', taped lecture at Arts Centre Group, London 1996

12 Jeffries, Stuart 'British Art is High on its own Vulgarity', *Guardian* (19 April 1997)

13 Amis, Martin quoted by McGregor, Jock *Madonna: Icon of Postmodernity*, L'Abri Lectures Series, No. 9 (Greatham, Hants, L'Abri Fellowship n.d.)

14 McGregor, Jock op. cit.

15 Lyotard, Jean-François op. cit.

16 Baudrillard, Jean quoted by Appignanesi and Garratt op. cit.

17 Williamson, Judith 'This Life: A Glimpse of the Void', *Weekend Guardian* (13 September 1997)

18 Sewell, Brian op. cit.

19 Hume, Gary quoted by Burton, J. 'Dumbed-down Brit-art', *Express* (17 January 1997)

20 Steen, Ronald quoted by Fuglie, Gordon 'Postmodern Mystic' in *Image* 17 (1997)

21 Derrida, Jacques quoted by Appignanesi and Garratt op. cit.

22 Eco, Umberto, *Reflections on 'The Name of the Rose'* (London, Secker & Warburg 1985)

23 Cray, Graham op. cit.

24 Bellow, Saul *Mosby's Memoirs* (London, Weidenfield & Nicolson 1969)

2 Art and the Quest for the Spiritual

1 Henderson, Stewart 'Paintings', from *A Giant's Scrapbook* (London, Hodder & Stoughton 1989)

2 Rae, Barbara in letters page, *Independent on Sunday* (November 1996)

3 Exodus 35

4 Quoted from Porter, David 'The Self-Regarding Image' in Dean, T. and Porter, D. (eds.) *Art in Question* (Basingstoke, Marshall Pickering 1987)

5 Wordsworth, William 'Lines Composed a Few Miles Above Tintern Abbey' (1798)

6 Wordsworth, William 'The Tables Turned' (1798)

7 Coleridge, Samuel Taylor 'Kubla Khan' (1816)

8 Leonardo da Vinci, quoted in Clark, Kenneth *Leonardo da Vinci* (1939; rev. Harmondsworth, Middx, Penguin 1967)

9 Quoted by Küng, Hans *Mozart, Traces of Transcendence* (Munich, SCM 1991)

10 Smith, Peter 'Making Paintings' in Dean, and Porter op. cit.

11 Rookmaaker, Hans *Modern Art and the Death of a Culture* (Leicester, IVP 1970; 2nd edn (1973) re-issued Leicester, Apollos 1994)

12 Puccini, Giacomo quoted in Cameron, J. *The Artist's Way* (London, Souvenir Press 1992)

13 Marc, Franz as translated by Wolf-Dieter Dube *The Expressionists* (London, Thames & Hudson 1972) quoted by Begbie, J. op. cit.

14 Van Gogh, Vincent 'Letter no. 133', in *The Complete Letters of Vincent van Gogh* (Connecticut, New York Graphic Society 1958) quoted in Chipp, H.B. (ed.) *Theories of Modern Art* (Los Angeles, University of California Press 1968)

15 Hughes, Robert *Shock of the New* (London, Thames & Hudson 1980, new edn 1991)

16 Munch, Edvard quoted by Hughes, R. op. cit.

17 Tillich, Paul *Systematic Theology* quoted by Begbie. J. *Voicing Creation's Praise* (Edinburgh, T. & T. Clark 1991)

18 Kandinsky, Wassily quoted by Hughes, R. op. cit.

19 Beckmann, Max quoted by Hughes, R. op. cit.

20 Kandinsky, Wassily *Concerning the Spiritual in Art*, trans. M. Sadleir (London, Constable 1914; re-issued New York, Dover 1997)

21 Kandinsky, Wassily quoted by Hughes, R. op. cit.

22 Klee, Paul quoted by Hughes, R. op. cit.

23 Rothko, Mark quoted by Hughes, R. op. cit.

24 Newman, Barnett 'The Sublime is Now', excerpt from 'The Ides of art, six opinions on what is sublime in art', *Tiger's Eye* (1948) quoted in Chipp, H.B. op. cit.

25 Hughes, Robert op. cit.

26 Rookmaaker, Hans op. cit.

3 Art and a Suspicious Church

1 Quotes from members and guests of Arts Centre Group in conversation with Hilary Brand

2 Sayers, Dorothy, 'Towards a Christian Aesthetic', in Jellema, R. (ed.) *Christian Letters to a Post-Christian World* (Grand Rapids, Eerdmans 1969) as quoted in Wolterstorff, N. *Art in Action* (Grand Rapids, Mich., Eerdmans 1980; re-issued Carlisle, Solway 1997)

3 Plass, Adrian in *Artyfact*, newsletter of Arts Centre Group, Eastbourne, (Winter 1995)

4 Kidner, Derek *The Christian and the Arts* (London, IVP 1959)

5 Trotsky, Leon quoted in Seerveld, C. *Bearing Fresh Olive Leaves* (unpublished manuscript)

6 Church Fathers quoted by Wilson, J. *One of the Richest Gifts* (Edinburgh, Handsel Press, 1981)

7 Watts, Murray *Christianity and the Theatre* (Edinburgh, Handsel Press 1986)

8 Pope Gregory the Great quoted by Wilson, J. op. cit.

9 Machiavelli quoted by McNair, P. 'Seeds of Renewal' in Dowley, T. (ed.) *The History of Christianity* (Oxford, Lion 1977)

10 Luther, Martin quoted in Blume, F. *Protestant Church Music* (London 1975) quoted by Wilson-Dickson, A. *The Story of Christian Music* (Oxford, Lion 1992)

11 Karlstadt, Andreas quoted in Rupp, G. *Patterns of Reformation* (London, Epworth 1969)

12 Luther, Martin quoted in Bainton, R.H. *Here I Stand* (Nashville, Abingdon Press 1950) quoted by Wilson, J. op. cit.

13 Karlstadt, Andreas quoted in Rupp, G. op. cit.

14 Karlstadt, Andreas quoted in Rupp, G. op. cit.

15 Calvin, John *Golden Booklet of the True Christian Life* (Grand Rapids, Mich., Baker 1975)

16 Calvin, John quoted by Wilson, J. op. cit.

17 Calvin, John *Commentary on Genesis* (Edinburgh, Banner of Truth 1965) quoted by Wilson, J. op. cit.

18 Calvin, John *Institutes* quoted by Wilson, J. op. cit.

19 Calvin, John quoted by Wilson J. op. cit.

20 Calvin, John *Institutes* quoted by Wilson, J. op. cit.

21 Watts, Murray op. cit.

22 Ordinance of Parliament 1644 quoted by Long, K.R. *The Music of the English Church* quoted by Wilson-Dickson, A. op. cit.

23 Thomas, R.S. 'The Minister' (1955), from *Selected Poems 1946–1968* (Newcastle, Bloodaxe 1986)

24 Turner, Steve 'History Lesson' from *Nice and Nasty* (London, Marshall, Morgan & Scott and Manchester, Razor Books 1980)

25 James, William quoted by Edgar, W. *Taking Note of Music* (London, SPCK 1986) quoted by Begbie, J. *Voicing Creation's Praise* (Edinburgh, T. & T. Clark 1991)

26 Keillor, Garrison in Brown, D. 'A conversation with Garrison Keillor', *Image* 9 (1995)

27 Seerveld, Calvin *Rainbows for a Fallen World* (Toronto, Tuppence Press 1980)

4 Art and the Bible

1 Kidner, Derek *The Christian and the Arts* (London, IVP 1959) quoting Ecclesiastes 1:14

2 Kidner, Derek op. cit.

3 Matthew 5:3–10

4 Schaeffer, Franky *Sham Pearls for Real Swine* (Tennessee, Wolgemuth & Hyatt 1990)

5 Romans 12:2

6 2 Corinthians 10:5

7 Seerveld, Calvin *Rainbows for a Fallen World* (Toronto, Tuppence Press 1980)

5 Art and a Playful God

1 Seerveld, Calvin *Rainbows for a Fallen World* (Toronto, Tuppence Press 1980)

2 Genesis 1:1–31

3 Einstein, Albert quoted by Madeleine L'Engle in *Image* 4 (1993)

4 Seerveld, Calvin op. cit.

5 Seerveld, Calvin op. cit.

6 Seerveld, Calvin op. cit.

7 Colossians 1:16

8 Einstein, Albert quoted by Dan Wakefield in *Expect a Miracle – the miraculous things that happen to ordinary people* (San Francisco, Harper 1995) extracted in *Image* 9 (1995)

9 Seerveld, Calvin op. cit.

10 Acts 17:27,28

11 Matthew 6:26–30, 10:29–31

12 Genesis 1:26

13 Burgard, Michel quoted in *Image* 8 (Winter 1994–5)

14 Seerveld, Calvin op. cit.

15 Wolterstorff, Nicholas *Art in Action* (Grand Rapids, Mich., Eerdmans 1980; re-issued Carlisle, Solway 1997)

16 Genesis 1:28

17 Wolterstorff, Nicholas op. cit.

18 Genesis 2:15

19 Wolterstorff, Nicholas op. cit.

20 Wolterstorff, Nicholas op. cit.

21 Genesis 2:19,20

22 Genesis 2:23

23 Genesis 1:26

24 Seerveld, Calvin op. cit.

6 Art and a Fallen World

1 Kafka, Franz in Friedman, M. (ed.) *The Words of Existentialism* (Chicago, University of Chicago Press 1973) quoted by Wilson, J. *One of the Richest Gifts* (Edinburgh, Handsel Press 1981)

2 Genesis 3:8

3 Storkey, Alan, taped lecture (Tisbury, Wilts, Arts in Mission 1997)

4 Genesis 3:17

5 Romans 8:22

6 Riches, Colin interview in *Telling Images* (London, Arts Centre Group 1996)

7 Wolters, Albert M. *Creation Regained* (Grand Rapids, Mich., Eerdmans 1985)

8 2 Corinthians 11:14

9 Seerveld, Calvin *Rainbows for a Fallen World* (Toronto, Tuppence Press 1980)

10 Wilson, J. op. cit.
11 Romans 1:25
12 Wilson, J. op. cit.
13 Halliday, Nigel, review of 'Sensation' in *Third Way* (October 1997)
14 Psalm 8:5; Hebrews 2:7
15 Lewis, C.S. *The Weight of Glory* (New York, Macmillan 1965)
16 Philippians 4:8
17 Schaeffer, Francis 'Art Norms', taped lecture at L'Abri Fellowship, Greatham, Hants
18 Schaeffer, Francis op. cit.
19 Begbie, J. *Voicing Creation's Praise* (Edinburgh, T. & T. Clark 1991)
20 Einstein, Albert (literally: 'At any rate, I am convinced that he does not play dice') letter to Max Born (1926), *Oxford Dictionary of Quotations* (Oxford University Press, 4th edn 1992)
21 Hughes, Gerard *God of Surprises* (London, Darton Longman & Todd 1985)
22 Romans 7:19
23 Peck, M. Scott *Further Along the Road Less Travelled* (London, Simon & Schuster 1993)

7 Art and the Possibility of Redemption

1 Etchells, Ruth 'God and our Books' in Dean, T. and Porter, D. (eds.) *Art in Question* (Basingstoke, Marshall Pickering 1987)
2 Begbie, J. 'The act of creation', *Voicing Creation's Praise* (Edinburgh, T. & T. Clark 1991)
3 Begbie, Jeremy op. cit.
4 Revelation 21:5 (emphasis added)
5 Wolters, Albert M. *Creation Regained* (Grand Rapids, Mich., Eerdmans 1985)
6 2 Corinthians 5:18
7 Mather, William, taped lecture (Tisbury, Wilts, Arts in Mission 1997)
8 Wolters, Albert M. op. cit.
9 2 Corinthians 4:6,7
10 Pope, Nicholas, talk at Tate Gallery, London 1996 (from author's notes)
11 Gidney, Chris, interview in Brand, H. (ed.) *Telling Images* (London, Arts Centre Group 1996)
12 Matthew 5:13–16
13 Seerveld, Calvin *Rainbows for a Fallen World* (Toronto, Tuppence Press, 1980)
14 Robbins, Tim (Writer/Director) *Dead Man Walking* (Produced: Working Title/Havoc, distributed: Polygram, 1995)
15 Gavigan, Bart 'Principles of Screenwriting', taped lecture (Chobham, Surrey, Spark Productions, no date)

8 Art and an Integrated Worldview
1 Matthew 20:16 (also Mark 10:31; Luke 13:30)
2 Matthew 16:25 (also Mark 8:35; Luke 9:24)

9 Art as a Valid Christian Activity
1 Plato, *Phaedo* trans. Church, P.J. (New York, Bobbs Merrill 1951) quoted by Walsh, B.J. and Middleton, J.R. *The Transforming Vision* (Downers Grove Ill., InterVarsity Press 1984)
2 1 John 2:15,16
3 Augustine quoted by Maurer, A.A. *Medieval Philosophy* (New York, Random House 1962) quoted by Walsh and Middleton op. cit.
4 Wolterstorff, N. *Art in Action* (Grand Rapids, Mich., Eerdmans 1980; re-issued Carlisle, Solway 1997)
5 Tolstoy, Leo quoted in Troyat, H. *Tolstoy* (New York, Dell 1969) quoted by Fox, M. *On Becoming a Musical, Mystical Bear* (New York, Paulist Press 1972)
6 Vine, W.E. *Expository Dictionary of Bible Words* (London, Marshall Morgan Scott 1981)
7 John 10:10
8 Matthew 7:11
9 Matthew 25:14–30
10 Kuyper, Abraham quoted by Begbie, J. *Voicing Creation's Praise* (Edinburgh, T. & T. Clark, 1991)
11 Colossians 1:16,17
12 Matthew 28:18
13 Survey 'Making it God's Business', quoted by Mark Greene, *Third Way* (September 1997)
14 Peck, M. Scott *Further Along the Road Less Travelled* (London, Simon & Schuster 1993)
15 Schaeffer, Franky *Sham Pearls for Real Swine* (Tennessee, Wolgemuth & Hyatt 1990)
16 Bonhoeffer, Dietrich quoted in Rasmussen, L. *Dietrich Bonhoeffer: Reality and Resistance* (Nashville, Abingdon Press 1972) quoted by Begbie, J. op. cit.
17 Walsh and Middleton op. cit.
18 Kidner, Derek *The Christian and the Arts* (London, IVP 1959)
19 Seerveld, Calvin *Rainbows for a Fallen World* (Toronto, Tuppence Press 1980)
20 Survey quoted by Greene, Mark, taped lecture (Tisbury, Wilts, Arts in Mission 1997)
21 Auden W.H. quoted in Ellmann, R. and Feidelson, C. (eds.) *The Modern Tradition* (New York, OUP 1965) quoted by Begbie, J. op. cit.
22 Sewell, Brian *An Alphabet of Villains* (London, Bloomsbury 1995)

23 Owen, Stephen quoted in *Artyfact*, newsletter of Arts Centre Group, London (February 1997)

24 Watts, Murray in Dean, T. and Porter, D. (eds) *Art in Question* (Basingstoke, Marshall Pickering 1987)

25 Begbie, J. op. cit.

26 Gavigan, Bart 'Aristotle, Hollywood and the Craft of Story', taped lecture at Arts Centre Group, London 1996

27 1 Corinthians 1:27

28 2 Corinthians 12:9

29 Watts, Murray in Dean, T. and Porter, D. op. cit.

30 Kidner, Derek op. cit.

31 Eliot, T.S. quoted by Wilson, J. *One of the Richest Gifts* (Edinburgh, Handsel Press 1981)

32 O'Connor, Flannery *Mystery and Manners: Occasional Prose*, (ed.) Fitzgerald, S. and R. (London, Faber & Faber 1972) quoted by Begbie, J. op. cit.

33 Psalms 139:19,22; 109:10; 90:9; 88:14

34 Genesis 9:21

35 Deuteronomy 34:1–4

36 McKillop, Iain, unpublished interview by Hilary Brand

37 Smith, Peter in Dean, T. and Porter, D. op. cit.

38 Schaeffer, Francis *Art and the Bible* (London, Hodder & Stoughton 1973)

39 Clark, Timothy quoted in Taylor, B. *The Art of Today* (London, Everyman 1995)

40 Seerveld, Calvin op. cit.

41 Thoreau, Henry David *Walden* (1854): 'If a man does not keep pace with his companions, perhaps it is because he hears a different drummer. Let him step to the music which he hears, however measured or far away.' Quoted in *Oxford Dictionary of Quotations* (Oxford University Press, 4th edn 1992)

10 Art as a Means of Worship
1 Exodus 25:18–30

2 Exodus 25:31–36

3 Exodus 28:33,34

4 Exodus 32

5 Numbers 21

6 2 Kings 18:4

7 Veith, Gene *State of the Arts* (Wheaton, Ill., Crossway 1991)

8 Veith, Gene op. cit.

9 Malraux, André *Voices of Silence*, trans. S. Gilbert (St Albans, Paladin 1974) quoted by Wolterstorff, N. *Art in Action* (Grand Rapids, Mich., Eerdmans 1980; re-issued Carlisle, Solway 1997)

10 Postman, Neil *Amusing Ourselves to Death* (London, Methuen 1985)

11 'Gekko, Gordon' in the film *Wall Street* (Fox 1987)

12 2 Samuel 6:6,7

13 Hughes, Robert *Shock of the New* (London, Thames & Hudson 1980, new edn 1991)

14 Harvey, David *The Condition of Post-Modernity* (New York, Blackwell 1990)

15 John of Damascus quoted by David Fetcho 'The Light through everything' in *Image* 8 (1994)

16 Lewis, C.S. *An Experiment in Criticism* (Cambridge University Press 1961)

17 Kidner, Derek *The Christian and the Arts* (London, IVP 1959)

18 Watts, Isaac quoted in Wilson-Dickson, A. *The Story of Christian Music* (Oxford, Lion 1992)

19 Lowly, Tim quoted in *Image* 7 (1994)

11 Art in its Rightful Place

1 Mellor, David quoted in *Guardian* (28 March 1995)

2 Huizenga, C. Nolan in Ryken, L. (ed.) *The Christian Imagination* (Grand Rapids, Mich., Baker 1981)

3 Seerveld, Calvin *Rainbows for a Fallen World* (Toronto, Tuppence Press, 1980)

4 Begbie, J. *Voicing Creation's Praise* (Edinburgh, T. & T. Clark 1991)

5 Aquinas, Thomas *Summa Theologica I* quoted by Wolterstorff, N. *Art in Action* (Grand Rapids, Mich., Eerdmans 1980; re-issued Carlisle, Solway 1997)

6 John 6:1–5, 25–40

7 Russell, Bertrand *Philosophical Essays* (London, Longmans Green 1910)

8 Harries, Richard 'Beauty and the Priest', *Samson's Wig* (September 1995)

9 Haworth, Bryn 'Good Job' on *Sunny Side of the Street* (Island Records 1975, Signalgrade Music Ltd)

10 Isaiah 53:2,3

11 Schaeffer, Francis 'Art Norms', taped lecture at L'Abri Fellowship, Greatham, Hants

12 Schaeffer, Francis op. cit.

13 Ecclesiastes 2:4–11

14 Clemo, Jack 'The Excavator' from *The Clay Verge* (London, Chatto & Windus 1951) reprinted in *Selected Poems* (Newcastle, Bloodaxe 1988)

15 Ezekiel 27:36

16 Ephesians 6:12

17 Klee, Paul 'Creative Credo' (1920) in Chipp, H.B. (ed.) *Theories of Modern Art* (Los Angeles, University of California Press 1968)

18 Picasso, Pablo quoted in Chipp, H.B. op. cit.

19 Stravinsky, Igor *Poetics of Music in the Form of Six Lessons*, trans. A. Knodel and I. Dahl (Cambridge, Mass., Harvard University Press 1947)

20 Greenberg, Clement 'The New Sculpture' in *The Collected Essays and Criticism*, vol. 1 (Chicago, University Press 1968) quoted by Begbie, J. op. cit.

21 Sarbiewski quoted by Tatarkiewicz, W. *A History of Six Ideas* (The Hague, Martinus Nijhoff 1980)

22 Speaker at congress 'Art in Today's Society' 1967 quoted by Tatarkiewicz op. cit.

23 Tatarkiewicz, W. op. cit.

24 Rookmaaker, Hans *Art Needs No Justification* (Leicester, IVP 1978)

25 Seerveld, Calvin op. cit.

12 Art and a Way of Seeing

1 Gulistan of Moslih Eddin Saadi in *Best Loved Poems of the American People* (Doubleday 1936) quoted by Wilson, J. *One of the Richest Gifts* (Edinburgh, Handsel Press 1981)

2 Edwards, Betty *Drawing on the Right Side of the Brain* (London, Souvenir Press 1981)

3 Seerveld, Calvin *Rainbows for a Fallen World* (Toronto, Tuppence Press 1980)

4 Seerveld, Calvin op. cit.

5 Seerveld, Calvin ('I am convinced') op. cit.

6 Ecclestone, Ben, unpublished interview by Hilary Brand

7 Picasso, Pablo quoted in Cameron, J. *The Artist's Way* (London, Souvenir Press 1992)

8 Lewis, C.S. *Letters of C.S. Lewis* (New York, Harcourt Brace Jovanovich 1966)

9 Picasso, Pablo 'Statement' (1923) quoted in Chipp, H.B. (ed.) *Theories of Modern Art* (Los Angeles, University of California Press 1968)

10 Bettelheim, Bruno *The Uses of Enchantment* (London, Thames & Hudson 1976; re-issued Penguin 1991)

11 Watts, Murray in Dean, T. and Porter, D. (eds.) *Art in Question* (Basingstoke, Marshall Pickering 1987)

12 Watts, Murray quoted by Stone, Norman in Brand, H. (ed.) *Telling Images* (London, Arts Centre Group 1996)

13 O'Connor, Flannery *Mystery and Manners: Occasional Prose*, (ed.) Fitzgerald, S. and R. (London, Faber & Faber 1972)

14 Sacks, Oliver *The Man who Mistook his Wife for a Hat* (London, Picador 1986)

15 Kundera, Milan quoted by Seerveld, Calvin *Bearing Fresh Olive Leaves* (unpublished manuscript)

16 Seerveld, Calvin *Rainbows for a Fallen World*

17 Bennett, Alan *Writing Home* (London, Faber & Faber 1994)

18 Okri, Ben 'Beyond Words' in *Birds of Heaven* (London, Orion Books 1996)

19 Nouwen, Henri *The Way of the Heart* (London, Daybreak 1981)

20 Ephesians 3:19

21 Taylor, John V. *The Go-Between God* (London, SCM 1972)

13 Art and Blurred Boundaries

1 Sewell, Brian *An Alphabet of Villains* (London, Bloomsbury 1995)

2 Rosenthal, Norman quoted by Sewell, B. op. cit.

3 Rookmaaker, Hans *Art Needs No Justification* (Leicester, IVP 1978)

4 Quoted by Taylor, B. *The Art of Today* (London, Everyman 1995)

5 This concept is borrowed from Benton, Tim and Scharf, Aaron *Introduction to Art* (Bletchley, Open University 1971)

6 Wittgenstein, Ludwig *Philosophical Investigations* (Oxford, Basil Blackwell 1953) quoted by Benton, T. and Scharf, A. op. cit.

7 Woolf, Virginia quoted by Wolterstorff, N. *Art in Action* (Grand Rapids, Mich., Eerdmans 1980; re-issued Carlisle, Solway 1997)

8 Catalogue of minimal art exhibition quoted by Fuller, P. *Aesthetics after Modernism* (London, Writers and Readers 1983) quoted by Begbie, J. *Voicing Creation's Praise* (Edinburgh, T. & T. Clark 1991)

9 McLeish, Archibald quoted in Wolterstorff, N. op. cit.

10 Valéry, Paul quoted in Wolterstorff, N. op. cit.

11 Chadwick, Helen quoted in 'Profile', *Sunday Times* (13 April 1997)

12 Genesis 2:9

13 Baldessari, John quoted in *The 20th-Century Art Book* (London, Phaidon 1996)

14 Warhol, Andy quoted by Wrenn, Mike *Andy Warhol, In his Own Words* (London, Omnibus Press 1991)

15 Toroni, Niele quoted by Taylor, B. op. cit.

16 Bacon, Francis quoted in Chipp, H.B. (ed.) *Theories of Modern Art* (Los Angeles, University of California Press 1968)

17 Ibid.

18 Ferren, John quoted in Wolterstorff, N. op. cit.

19 Clark, Timothy quoted in Taylor, B. op. cit.

20 Ibid.

21 Cronenberg, David quoted by Appleyard, B. 'Crash Course in the Sick Art of the Salon of the Sixties', *Sunday Times* (23 March 1997)

22 Brennan, John quoted by Edgar, W. 'The Message of Rock Music' in Dean, T and Porter, D. (eds.) *Art in Question* op. cit.

23 Searle, Adrian 'Searching for the Spiritual and Sexy', *Guardian* (1 January 1998)

24 Ryken, Leland *The Liberated Imagination* (Wheaton, Ill., Harold Shaw 1989)

25 Rookmaaker, Hans op. cit.

26 Wolterstorff, N. op. cit.

27 Tatarkiewicz, W. *A History of Six Ideas* (The Hague, Martinus Nijhoff 1980)

28 Seerveld, Calvin *Rainbows For a Fallen world* (Toronto, Tuppence Press 1980) (nb. the relevant chapter is omitted in the Greenbelt edition, reinstated in Solway reprint)

14 Art and How it Works

1 Heidegger, Martin *The Origin of the Work of Art* quoted in Appignanesi, R. and Garratt, C. *Postmodernism for Beginners* (Cambridge, Icon 1995)

2 Seerveld, Calvin *Bearing Fresh Olive Leaves* (unpublished manuscript)

3 Begbie, J. *Voicing Creation's Praise* (Edinburgh, T & T Clark 1991)

4 Park, Nick interviewed by Barrett, P. in 'Let there be light entertainment', in *Third Way* (November 1994)

5 Seerveld, Calvin *Rainbows for a Fallen World* (Toronto, Tuppence Press 1980)

6 Smith, Peter 'Making Paintings' in Dean, T. and Porter, D. (eds.) *Art in Question* (Basingstoke, Marshall Pickering 1987)

7 Polanyi, Michael and Prosch, Harry *Meaning* (Chicago, University of Chicago Press 1975) quoted by Begbie, J. op. cit.

8 Nyman, Michael Sleeve notes for CD *The Piano* (Virgin Records 1993)

9 Smith, Peter op. cit.

10 Edgar, William 'The Message of Rock Music' in Dean, T. and Porter, D. op. cit.

11 Halliday, Nigel Review of 'Sensation' in *Third Way* (October 1997)

12 McKillop, Iain, unpublished interview with Hilary Brand

13 Ibid.

14 Greer, Germaine in *Late Review* (BBC2 1997), quoted in advertising for Braque exhibition, Royal Academy 1997.

15 Adams, Tim 'Curve Oeuvre', *Observer* (1 June 1997)

16 Schaeffer, Francis 'Art Norms', taped lecture at L'Abri Fellowship, Greatham, Hants

17 Lewis, C.S. *Letters to Malcolm: Chiefly on Prayer* (London, Geoffrey Bles 1964)

18 Seerveld, Calvin *Rainbows for a Fallen World*

19 De Klijn, Henny unpublished notes

15 Art and Interpretation

1 Reza, Yasmina *Art* trans. Christopher Hampton (London, Faber & Faber 1996)

2 Revelation 3:20

3 Shapiro, Meyer 'The Still Life as a Personal Object – A Note on Heidegger and van Gogh' in *Theory and Philosophy of Art: Style, Artist and Society – Selected Papers vol. IV* (New York 1994) quoted by Adams, Laurie Schneider *The Methodologies of Art: an Introduction* (New York, Harper Collins 1996)

4 Hughes, Robert *Shock of the New* (London, Thames & Hudson 1980; rev. edn 1991)

5 Wilde, Oscar *The Picture of Dorian Gray* (1891)

6 Denis, Maurice 'Definition of Neo-traditionalism' (1890) quoted in Chipp, H.B. *Theories of Modern Art* (Los Angeles University of California Press 1968)

7 Rees, A.L. and Borzello, F. (eds.) *The New Art History* (London, Camden Press 1986)

8 Smith, Peter in Preface to Seerveld, Calvin *Bearing Fresh Olive Leaves* (unpublished manuscript)

9 Seerveld, Calvin *Philosophical Aesthetics at home with the Lord: an untimely valedictory* (Toronto, Institute for Christian Studies 1996)

10 Greenberg, Clement *Art and Culture* (1945; re-issued Boston, Beacon Press 1961)

11 Rookmaaker, Hans *Modern Art and the Death of a Culture* (Leicester, IVP 1970; 2nd edn (1973) re-issued Leicester, Apollos 1994)

12 Schaeffer, Franky *Sham Pearls for Real Swine* (Tennessee, Wolgemuth & Hyatt 1990)

13 Fuller, Peter *Beyond the Crisis in Art* (London, Writers and Readers 1980)

14 Reza, Yasmina Art op. cit.

15 Smith, Peter 'Making Paintings' in Dean, T. and Porter, D. (eds.) *Art in Question* (Basingstoke, Marshall Pickering 1987)

16 Smith, Peter op. cit.

17 Watts, Murray in Dean, T. and Porter, D. op. cit.

18 Philippians 4:8

19 Reza, Yasmina Art op. cit.

16 Art and New Technology

1 Rookmaaker, Hans *Modern Art and the Death of a Culture* (Leicester, IVP 1970; 2nd edn (1973) re-issued Leicester, Apollos 1994)

2 Clowney, Paul 'Virtual Reality', *Third Way* (May 1993)

3 Clowney, Paul op. cit.

4 Crampin, Martin unpublished interview with Hilary Brand
5 Clowney, Paul op. cit.
6 Gates, Bill *The Road Ahead* (London, Viking 1995)
7 Clowney, Paul op. cit.
8 Boswell, James *The Life of Samuel Johnson* (1791)

17 Art as Honest Labour

1 Schaeffer, Franky *Sham Pearls for Real Swine* (Tennessee, Wolgemuth & Hyatt 1990)
2 Eliot, T.S. 'Tradition and Individual Talent', *Selected Essays* (London, Faber & Faber 1932) quoted by Begbie, J. *Voicing Creation's Praise* (Edinburgh, T. & T. Clark 1991)
3 Fuller, Peter *Aesthetics after Modernism* (London, Writers and Readers 1983)
4 Eliot, T.S. op. cit.
5 Nanson, Rebecca 'The Leith School of Art', *Articulate* (1998)
6 Schopenhauer quoted by Appleyard, B. in 'Lighting up our lives', *The Sunday Times* (22 June 1997)
7 Blake, William *Auguries of Innocence* (1803)
8 Fuller, Peter *Theoria: Art and the Absence of Grace* (London, Chatto & Windus 1988) quoted by Begbie, J. op. cit.
9 Wolterstorff, N. *Art in Action* (Grand Rapids, Mich., Eerdmans 1980; re-issued Carlisle, Solway 1997)
10 Wood, Patrick interviewed in Brand, H. (ed.) *Telling Images* (London, Arts Centre Group 1996)
11 Begbie, J. op. cit.
12 Wolterstorff, N. op. cit.
13 Sayers, Dorothy *The Mind of the Maker* (London, Methuen 1941) quoted by Begbie, J. op. cit.
14 Stravinsky, Igor *Poetics of Music in the Form of Six Lessons* trans. A. Knodel and Dahl, I. (Cambridge, Mass., Harvard University Press 1947) quoted by Begbie, J. op. cit.
15 Gavigan, Bart 'Principles of Screenwriting', taped lecture (Chobham, Surrey, Spark Productions, no date)
16 Riddell, Mike 'Art for Art's Sake', *Artyfact*, newsletter of Arts Centre Group, London (March 1998)
17 L'Engle, Madeleine in *Image* 4 (1993)
18 Begbie, J. op. cit.
19 Rookmaaker, Hans *Art Needs No Justification* (Leicester, IVP 1978)
20 Edison, Thomas quoted in *Harper's Monthly Magazine* (September 1932)
21 Kendrick, Graham *Worship* (Eastbourne, Kingsway 1984)
22 Genesis 32:22–31
23 Yeats, W.B. 'Adam's Curse' (1904)

18 Art as a Proper Job

1 Fuller, Peter *Beyond the Crisis in Art* (London, Writers and Readers 1980) quoted by Begbie, J. *Voicing Creation's Praise* (Edinburgh, T. & T. Clark 1991)

2 Chalke, Steve quoted by Wall, P. 'Our Man on the Comfy Sofa', *Third Way* (December 1996)

3 Chalke, Steve op. cit.

4 Quoted by Hughes, Robert *Shock of the New* (London, Thames & Hudson 1980; rev. edn 1991)

5 Survey from *Art in America* (February 1990) quoted by Schaeffer, Franky *Sham Pearls for Real Swine* (Tennessee, Wolgemuth & Hyatt 1990)

6 Figures from British Actors Equity Association

7 Acts 18:3

8 Schaeffer, Franky op. cit.

9 Lewis, C.S. *The World's Last Night and Other Essays* (New York, Harcourt Brace Jovanovich 1960)

10 Clowney, Paul 'Art and Social Responsibility', taped lecture at L'Abri Fellowship, Greatham, Hants n.d.

11 Schaeffer, Franky op. cit.

12 Psalm 133

13 Shaffer, Peter *Amadeus* (London, Penguin 1980)

14 Mink, Janis *Marcel Duchamp 1887–1968: Art As Anti-Art* (Köln, Taschen 1995)

15 Tolstoy, Leo quoted by Fox, M. *On Becoming a Musical, Mystical Bear* (New York, Paulist Press 1972)

16 Luke 14:28–32

17 Quoted by Collett-White, Thomas 'Michelangelo – Poet and Painter', taped lecture at Arts Centre Group, London, 1997

18 Matthew 25:14–30

19 Schaeffer, Francis *Art and the Bible* (London, Hodder & Stoughton 1973)

20 Nunn, Trevor in *Daily Mail* (7 January 1986)

21 Psalm 73 *International Children's Bible, New Century Version* (Anglicised edition) (Milton Keynes, Nelson Word 1991)

22 Miller, Richard, unpublished interview by Hilary Brand

23 Gide, André quoted in Cameron, J. *The Artist's Way* (London, Souvenir Press 1992)

19 Art as a Twenty-First Century Calling

1 Januszczak, Waldemar 'Just a Pervert with a Pointed Moustache', *Sunday Times Culture* (14 September 1997)

2 Januszczak, Waldemar op. cit.

3 Seerveld, Calvin *Bearing Fresh Olive Leaves* (unpublished manuscript)

4 Seerveld, Calvin op. cit.

5 Seerveld, Calvin op. cit.

6 Taylor, B. *The Art of Today* (London, Everyman 1995)

7 Taylor, B. op. cit.

8 Crimp, Douglas quoted by Taylor, B. op. cit.

9 Rosenthal, Norman in *A New Spirit in Painting* exh. cat. (London, Royal Academy 1981)

10 Folsom, Fred from profile by Wolfe, G. in *Image* 1 (December 1992)

11 Park, Nick, interviewed by Barrett, P. 'Let There be Light Entertainment', *Third Way* (November 1994)

12 Handy, Charles *The Empty Raincoat: Making Sense of the Future* (London, Hutchinson 1994)

13 Coupland, Douglas *Generation X* (London, Abacus 1992)

14 John 8:7

15 Matthew 22:21

16 Matthew 27:11

17 Herman, Bruce quoted by Hanlon, Patricia 'Bruce Herman, a profile', *Image* 7 (1994)

18 Greene, Mark taped lecture (Tisbury, Wilts, Arts in Mission 1997)

19 *The 20th-Century Art Book* (London, Phaidon 1996)

20 Matthew 8:4; 9:30; Mark 5:43

21 Matthew 14:19–23; 16:1–4; Mark 1:32–38

22 Mark 11:1–11

23 Matthew 4:4–11

24 Brighton, David 'A Close Shave with Nick Park', *Articulate* (1998)

25 Cronenberg, David from interview quoted on David Cronenberg's website

26 Luke 5:13

27 Mark 3:1–6

28 Mark 3:31–5

29 Matthew 21:12–17

30 Collins, Gary unpublished interview by Hilary Brand

31 Park, Nick in interview with Barrett, P. op. cit.

32 Seerveld, Calvin *Rainbows for a fallen world* (Toronto, Tuppence Press 1980)

33 Matthew 25:14–30

34 Cray, Graham 'Goodbye to the Grand Story', taped lecture at Arts Centre Group, London 1996

35 Coupland, Douglas *Life after God* (London, Simon & Schuster 1994)

36 Coupland, Douglas op. cit.

37 Crossan, Dominic *The Dark Internal* quoted by Walsh, B.J. and Middleton, J.R. *Truth is stranger than it used to be* (London, SPCK 1995)

List of Illustrations

1. *The death of the modernist dream?* (1998) (photo: Hilary Brand)
2. Tracey Emin *Everyone I've Ever Slept With* (1995), appliqued tent, mattress and light 122 × 245 × 215 cm (detail) (photo: Stephen White)
3. Mike Gough *The Queen of My Heart* (1998), screen prints on paper
4. Laura Lasworth *St Thomas and Mr Eco* (1994), oil on panels, each panel 198 × 84 cm (courtesy of the collection of Ronald Steen)
5. J.M.W. Turner *Steamboat in a Snowstorm* (1842), oil on canvas, 91 × 122 cm (London, Tate Gallery)
6. George Grosz *The Gratitude of the Fatherland is Assured You* (1921). Book illustration from *Das Gesicht der herrschenden Klasse* (The Face of the Ruling Class) © DACS 1998
7. Bill Viola *The Messenger* (1996), video installation for Durham Cathedral, commissioned by the Chaplaincy to the Arts and Recreation in N.E. England (photo: Edward Woodman)
8. Lorenzo Ghiberti Detail from the doors of the Baptistry, Florence (1403–24), bronze (photo: Hilary Brand)
9. Unattributed *Destruction of images* (17th century), engraving (Mary Evans Picture Library)
10. *Babette's Feast* (Director: Gabriel Axel; 1987, Panorama/Nordik/Danish Film Institute)
11. Paul Hobbs *Attitudes* (1997), wood and acrylic, 193 × 193 cm
12. Ann Bridges *Brussels Sprouts* (1991), textiles, 63 × 45cm
13. Michel Burgard *Marsh 1: Witness* (1994), egg tempera, water gilding on birch, 81 × 61cm
14. Roger Wagner *Menorah* (1993), oil on canvas, 193 × 155 cm (collection of the artist)
15. Colin Riches *Like Dreams in Sleep* (1994), mixed media, 123 × 46 × 36 cm (photo: Geoff Pigott)
16. Louiz Kirkebjerg Nielsen *Connecting Paths* (1997), silkscreen print on paper, 56.5 × 42 cm
17. *Schindler's List* (Director: Steven Spielberg; 1993, Universal/Amblin)

43. Leith School of Art (photo: courtesy of Leith School of Art)
44. Pablo Picasso *Portrait of Stravinsky* (1920) © Succession Picasso/ DACS 1998
45. Jacob Epstein *Jacob Wrestling with the Angel* (1941), alabaster, 213 cm high (London, Tate Gallery) (by permission of the Epstein estate)
46. Britt Wikström *To Life* (1995), granite memorial, 1.5 metres high
47. Taffy Davies cartoon (1995), ink on paper
48. Richard Miller working on sculpture for Glasgow City Council (1997) (photo: Mike Brunton)
49. Fred Folsom *Danny Robson, or St Danny of Tacoma Park* (1982), oil on panel, 91.5 × 122 cm (Collection of George Thompson)
50. Bruce Herman *The Mocking* (1992), pastel, 127 × 96.5 cm
51. *Everybody's favourites: Wallace and Gromit* (photo: Hilary Brand)

Recommended Resources

For Further Reading

Jeremy Begbie: *Voicing Creation's Praise* (Edinburgh, T. & T. Clark 1991)

Tim Dean and David Porter (eds): *Art in Question* (Basingstoke, Marshall Pickering 1987)

William Edgar: *Taking Note of Music* (London, SPCK 1986)

Nigel Forde: *The Lantern and the Looking-Glass: Literature and Christian Belief* (London, SPCK 1997)

George S. Heyer: *Signs of the Times* (Edinburgh, Handsel Press 1980)

David Lyon: *Postmodernity* (Milton Keynes, Open University Press 1994)

Hans Rookmaaker: *Modern Art and the Death of a Culture* (Leicester, IVP 1970; 2nd edn (1973) re-issued Leicester, Apollos 1994)

Leland Ryken: *The Liberated Imagination* (Wheaton, Ill., Harold Shaw Publishers 1989)

Steve Scott: *Crying for a Vision* (Exeter, Stride 1991)

Calvin Seerveld: *Rainbows for a Fallen World* (Toronto, Tuppence Press 1980)

Calvin Seerveld: *Bearing Fresh Olive Leaves* (unpublished manuscript)

Jane Stuart Smith and Betty Carlson: *The Gift of Music: Great Composers and Their Influence* (1978; 3rd edn Wheaton, Ill., Crossway 1995)

Gene Veith: *State of the Arts* (Wheaton, Ill., Crossway 1991)

B.J. Walsh and J.R. Middleton: *The Transforming Vision* [on worldviews] Downers Grove, Ill., InterVarsity Press 1984)

B.J. Walsh and J.R. Middleton: *Truth is Stranger Than it Used to Be – Biblical Faith in a Postmodern Age* (London, SPCK 1995)

John Wilson: *One of the Richest Gifts* (Edinburgh, Handsel Press 1981)

Nicholas Wolterstorff: *Art in Action* (Grand Rapids, Mich., Eerdmans, 1980; re-issued Carlisle, Solway 1997)

Nicholas Wolterstorff: *Works and Worlds of Art* (Oxford, Clarendon 1980)

Image – A Journal of the Arts and Religion, ed. Gregory Wolfe, PO Box 3000, Denville, NJ 07834, quarterly (UK and European subscriptions: Paternoster Publishing, PO Box 300, Carlisle, UK CA3 0QS)

Useful Organisations

Arts Centre Group
59a Portobello Road, London W11 3DB
Tel: 0171 243 4550; fax: 0171 221 7689; e-mail: acg@dial.pipex.com
A national association of Christians professionally involved in the world of the arts, media and entertainment, the ACG aims to help members integrate their faith with their artistic activities and so become a transforming influence in the arts and media. The ACG has an annual journal, *Articulate*, with in-depth articles on the interface between faith and the arts, and a bi-monthly newsletter, *Artyfact*, containing news and features on Christian activity in arts and media. It is also setting up a resources library of books and tapes on Christianity and the arts.

Art and Christian Enquiry
4 Regents Park Road, London NW1 7TX
Studies and promotes the engagement of the visual arts with Church and theology.

Arts in Mission
4 Targetts Mead, Duck Street, Tisbury, Wilts SP3 6SR
Tel: 01747 870036
Promotes the use of arts in churches.

Christians in the Arts Networking
21 Harlow Street, PO Box 242, Arlington MA 02174-0003, USA
Tel: 617/646-1541; fax: 617/646-7725; e-mail: canhq@aol.com
Links Christian arts organisations around the world.

Greenbelt
The Greenhouse, Hillmarton Rd, London N7 9JE
Tel: 0171 700 1335
Annual Christian arts festival with seminars, music and other arts activities. Also occasional London events. Its catalogue of audio tapes (for sale) includes many seminars of interest to artists.

L'Abri
The Manor House, Greatham, Near Liss, Hants GU33 6HF
Tel: 01420 538436
Residential centre for study and debate on current Christian issues, including the arts. Also has a catalogue of tapes for sale or available on a cassette exchange scheme.

Leith School of Art
25 North Junction Street, Edinburgh EH6 6 HW
Offers Foundation Courses, evening and day classes, summer schools and special workshops.

Theology through the Arts
Ridley Hall, Cambridge CB3 9HG
Tel: 01223 741078; e-mail: fjb22@cam.ac.uk
Aims to discover and demonstrate ways in which the arts can contribute towards a renewal of Christian theology and an engagement between the church and contemporary culture, and to generate through the arts new methods of Christian education.

UCCF (Universities and Colleges Christian Fellowship)
38 De Montfort Street, Leicester LE1 7GP
Tel: 0116 255 1700; fax: 0116 255 5672; e-mail: email@uccf.org.uk
Works with students and college Christian Unions. Has one worker dedicated to art colleges. Offers a list of speakers including some on arts related subjects. Also offers an Arts Resource Pack including booklets (recommended): Derek Kidner, *The Christian and the Arts*; and Hans Rookmaaker, *Art Needs No Justification*.

Index

The art of God
and the religions of Art
David Thistlethwaite

Foreword by Richard Kenton Webb

"For anyone who cares about the visual arts in today's culture, this is essential reading. David Thistlethwaite combines the learning of years of reading and reflection with a passion for the practical and down-to-earth. It is gracious, engaging and rich in wisdom. I commend it warmly."
Jeremy Begbie, Director, Theology Through the Arts, Centre for Advanced Religious and Theological Studies, University of Cambridge

"Here is a book on art and religion that is mercifully free of Art-speak. Unlike any received notion of fundamentalists that one might have, the writer David Thistlethwaite is sophisticated, highly literate and intellectually able to fight his corner for his faith. Although, for the moment at least, I do not necessarily share all of the writer's beliefs, I welcome this book for the opportunity it allows to look critically at art through the eyes of a thoughtful Christian."
Michael Sandle, FRBS

The art of God traces the progressive loss in the West of contact with, or faith in, a real created order, and discusses the manifestations of this loss in fine art. Making detailed reference to specific artists and works, Thistlethwaite shows how the diversity of our responses to modern art, as well as that of previous centuries, raises inescapably the question of truth.

This readable and thought-provoking book breaks new ground as it links the pleasures of art to the dynamic character of God, and asks what happens to creativity and to artists when the appreciation of God is absent. It thus offers readers a fresh perspective from which to appreciate art.

David Thistlethwaite began work for this book as a research student at Cambridge, after four years in a leading Bond Street commercial art gallery. He has lectured on art to university and art students, and recently has co-ordinated study groups for Christians in the professions and academic life. He, his wife and two children live in Leicester.

ISBN 1-900507-78-1

solway

In Him We Move
Creative Dancing in Worship
Janet Randell

Foreword by Dame Margot Fonteyn

Dance is used as a means of expressing and experiencing some of the mysteries in life that are beyond verbal expression. *In Him We Move* provides an inspiring case for dance and movement to be restored in worship and celebration alongside singing and praying.

The author expresses the historical, theological and biblical inspiration behind modern dances used in worship, revealing how dance has often been associated with revival. Practical exercises for individuals, groups and whole congregations, including pew-bound worshippers and those in wheelchairs are set out along with a sample dance.

This thorough and unique treatment of an important but neglected topic restores a Christian balance to the art of dance at a time when outreach and worship are key features of the Christian church at the end of the millennium.

"I hope this book will be a source of inspiration in the coming years."
Dame Margot Fonteyn

"I guess that, for many of us, dance and movement in worship remain something outside our experience. It's OK at parties and clubs, but in church? Janet Randall's book gives a Christian perspective that is both practical and inspiring. It may open your eyes, as well as move your feet!"
Sir Cliff Richard

Janet Randell, Associate of the Imperial Society of Teachers of Dancing, choreographer, teacher, lecturer and writer, has a high reputation throughout the world as an internationally renowned free-lance choreographer among major dance companies. She is the founder of The Cedar Theatre Company.

ISBN 1-900507-83-8

solway

God through the Looking Glass
Glimpses from the Arts
William David Spencer and Aida Besancon Spencer

We know that poetry and music may be used to praise God in psalms and hymns, but what about sculpture, dance, literature, drama and the cinema? Do these areas have a place in Christian life?

"Art can tell us so much about ourselves and about God's working with us and in the unique worlds around us," say William and Aida Spencer. Our creativity mirrors God's grand creative act of forming this world. As we express ourselves through the arts, we can catch glimpses of God's nature.

This book gives an artistically and theologically sound method of integrating your faith into your view of and work in the arts. The authors first define art, then build a biblical framework for evaluating a work. Interspersed among the chapters are suggested exercises for exploring the art forms.

Contributors include William David Spencer, Aida Besancon Spencer, Bruce Whitney Herman, Norman M. Jones, Richard Pearce, Celeste Snowber Schroeder, Jasmin Sung and Gwenfair M. Walters.

ISBN 1-900507-85-4

solway

The Sound of the Harvest
Music's Mission in Church and Culture
J. Nathan Corbitt

"Nathan Corbitt is writing a blueprint for the use of music in our postmodern churches. His emphasis on how music functions as communication in worship is indispensable for all who teach or plan the place of music in worship."
Robert Webber, director, The Insitutue for Worship Studies

Martin Luther, noting music's role in worship, once commented that "he who sings prays twice." Serving as a vital complement to preaching and teaching – and in a sense, preaching and teaching through its own medium – music has helped to characterise Christian denominations and spread the gospel to the far corners of the globe.

Presenting an integrative blend of music, communications and missions theory, *The Sound of the Harvest* examines music's role in the church and culture today, and also presents a multicultural outlook on this art form.

"In this much needed book Corbitt challenges Christians in the West to re-examine the place of music in the life and mission of the church. Drawing on biblical studies and illustrations from around the world, Corbitt shows that music is central to vital Christian worship, teaching and ministry."
Paul G. Heibert, Chairman of the department of mission and evangelism, Trintiy Evangelical Divinity School

"The Sound of the Harvest is for any church leader, clergy or musician who recognises the relative poverty of current musical practice in most Protestant worship experiences today and who wants to tap into the God-given resource of music in more resonant ways."
C. Michael Hawn, professor of Church music, Perkins School of Theology, Southern Methodist University

J. Nathan Corbitt, professor of communications and music at Eastern College, spent eleven years working in Africa in cross-cultural communications and music.

ISBN 1-900507-88-9

solway